SIGHT AND SOUND
A Fiftieth Anniversary Selection

Sight and Sound

A Fiftieth Anniversary Selection

Edited and with an Introduction by
DAVID WILSON

faber and faber in association with BFI Publishing

First published in 1982
by Faber and Faber Limited
3 Queen Square London WC1N 3AU
in association with BFI Publishing
Filmset by Wilmaset, Birkenhead, Merseyside
Printed in Great Britain by
Ebenezer Baylis & Son Ltd
The Trinity Press, Worcester and London
All rights reserved

Library of Congress Cataloging in Publication Data

Main entry under title:

Sight and sound

1. Moving-picture plays—History and
criticism—Addresses, essays, lectures
2. Moving-pictures—Production and direction—
Addresses, essays, lectures. I. Wilson,
David, 1942-   II. Sight and sound
PN1995.S4936   1982   791.43'09   82-4524
ISBN 0-571-11943-3   AACR2

British Library Cataloguing in Publication Data

Sight and sound: a fiftieth anniversary selection
1. Moving-pictures—History and criticism
I. Wilson, David 1942-
791.43'75   PN1993.5.A1

ISBN 0-571-11943-3

Contents

8　　　　　　　　　　*Contents*

Illustrations

Acknowledgments

Grateful acknowledgment is made to *Sight and Sound* and the British Film Institute for permission to reprint material from the magazine, and to the writers whose contributions are reprinted here. The article 'Pabst and Lulu' is also reprinted in Louise Brooks, *Lulu in Hollywood*, published by Alfred A. Knopf, Inc. in the United States and by Hamish Hamilton Ltd. in Britain (© Louise Brooks 1982), and acknowledgment is made for permission to reprint here. Acknowledgment is also made to *The Atlantic Monthly* and to Mrs Helga Greene for permission to reprint the article 'Oscar Night in Hollywood' by Raymond Chandler. My thanks to Frank Pike for encouraging and nurturing this project; to Tom Milne for communicating his sheer enthusiasm for the cinema; and especially to Penelope Houston, editor of *Sight and Sound*, who would have compiled this anthology herself if she had not been too preoccupied with the next issue. Acknowledgment is also made to the distributors of the films illustrated here, and to the Stills Library of the British Film Institute. Finally, my thanks to Gilly Hodson; and to Mr Pooter, Lupin and Daisy Mutlar for keeping me company through many days and nights in the forest of words.

Introduction

Fifty years ago, when the cinema was still young and talking pictures a recent and by no means universally welcomed innovation, you could have counted the number of serious publications on film on the fingers of one hand. Films were for the masses, if not an opium then a harmless (to some minds a harmful) diversion; to take them seriously was an intellectual aberration. Even as late as 1944, Auden could write to the editors of the *Nation* this backhanded compliment to the film reviews of James Agee: 'I do not care for movies very much and I rarely see them; further, I am suspicious of criticism as the literary genre which, more than any other, recruits epigones, pedants without insight, intellectuals without love.' A decade earlier, Bloomsbury had been embarrassed by its slumming in the dark.

In this unfriendly climate *Sight and Sound* was born, in 1932. In tune with the Reithian–Griersonian ethic of a mass medium as a mass educator, the magazine was launched as 'A Quarterly Review of Modern Aids to Learning published under the auspices of the British Institute of Adult Education'. Messages of welcome came from such luminaries as Professor Julian Huxley and the Archbishop of York; and there was a firm division, enshrined in the list of contents, between 'Entertainment' and 'Educational' films. This first issue included an article, by the Secretary to the Commission on Educational and Cultural Films, on 'The Cinema and the Empire', a theme which was to persist well into the 1940s. But the times were ripe for some pioneering on the home front. The magazine was already contemplating the prospects of television as armchair educator. And a column by C. A. Lejeune, somewhat nervously entitled 'Films You Ought to See', recommended such films as *Westfront 1918*, *Kameradschaft* and *A Nous la Liberté*. European films, that is: Hollywood was still beyond the pale, or at least not quite 'educationally' respectable. If a good word could be said for California's Babylon, it was mainly a technical compliment. Of Lubitsch's *Trouble in Paradise*, for instance, the magazine airily commented: 'It is a delight to listen to this film; the sound is like satin, probably the best bit of recording yet put out.'

In these early days *Sight and Sound* took its title literally. An interview with René Clair sat with no editorial discomfort next to reports on lantern slides, Workers' Educational screenings in Devon, a review of gramophone recordings of English dialects. The tension between film as an audio-visual aid to learning and film as entertainment or even as an art form could accommodate this rebuke in C. A. Lejeune's column in 1933: 'America should have realised five years ago, when talking pictures began to be popular, that about 80 per cent of the English-speaking world speaks "straight" English, and only 20 per cent speaks American.' Meanwhile, rival magazines like *Close-Up* and *Cinema Quarterly* were proclaiming the film as an art form and celebrating the birth of the British documentary movement. For its part, *Sight and Sound* could celebrate the foundation in 1933 of the British Film Institute, for which it had campaigned from its first issue. Within the year the Institute was the magazine's publisher.

For at least the next decade *Sight and Sound* occupied an uneasy position between house magazine and independent journal. It attracted writers like Rudolf Arnheim, Alistair Cooke, Elizabeth Bowen, Robert Herring and Graham Greene (whose best film writing, however, appeared in his columns in the *Spectator* and *Night and Day*), and from the documentary school Paul Rotha and John Grierson, who loosed an occasional polemic. Some of this writing ruffled official feathers. But it must be said that most of what appeared in the magazine during this decade is, in retrospect, of more interest to the social historian than to the student of film history. In particular a certain anti-Americanism can be detected, by no means uncharacteristic of British writing both in the complacent Baldwinian twilight of the pre-war years and in the inward-looking 1940s, but in *Sight and Sound* it was revealed in the implicit assumption that the American films which were the staple diet of the British film-going public were at best an awkward appendage to the proper business of disseminating serious 'film appreciation'.

It would be misleading to imply that *Sight and Sound* during these years wholly ignored Hollywood cinema. But it is the case that, at least until the late 1940s, the names of John Ford, Rouben Mamoulian, Frank Capra, George Cukor, Howard Hawks and Josef von Sternberg did not often appear in its pages. In this, the magazine was merely reflecting the prevailing critical climate. The products of the studios (and not just, be it said, of the Hollywood studios) were simply that: mass-produced entertainment for the masses. The time when popular culture could be the subject of critical analysis was yet to come. It was then at least as important, it seems, to devote space to what now seem peripheral matters, such as the historical accuracy of costume films; as late as 1947 the magazine published an article by a fellow of the Gemmological Association on 'Jewellery and the Period Film'. The same issue includes, without editorial comment, a demented attack by Eisenstein on Hollywood film-makers, vituperated as 'Purveyors of Spiritual Poison'. The insularity which marked British critical writing of the period—and not just on films—belongs, of course, to an era when the Empire meant rather more than the name of a cinema in Leicester Square. With hindsight, it is not so remarkable that in the year Chamberlain was consulting a map to discover the whereabouts of Czechoslovakia *Sight and Sound* could unblushingly publish a survey of the Japanese cinema under the title 'Honourable Movie-Makers', or that a recurring theme should be the problems involved in showing films to the native populations of imperial outposts.

This was a time when words like 'highbrow' and 'lowbrow' were much bandied about, when John Grierson, introducing a characteristically rhetorical piece on propaganda, could write that he had 'no great interest in films as such'. Graham Greene, surveying the films of 1937, whimsically positioned himself atop a metropolitan pedestal and delivered Olympian judgment on what mere mortals were queueing to see in the cinemas below. We too easily forget, of course, how difficult it was then to establish a perspective on film history: there was no National Film Theatre to present retrospectives of a director's work, and the proposition that film could be studied as an academic discipline would have been inconceivable. But all was not complacency. It is worth quoting from an article published in *Sight and Sound* in 1939 entitled (prophetically) 'The Importance of Being Angry':

> We are living in an age of wrath. . . . Let, then, the cinema interpret the anger and the restlessness of that society which gave it birth; let it dramatise, with all of its inherent forces of eloquence, the living scene in which it finds itself. . . . In our time the film, more than any other form of expression, has the dramatic power to stimulate, to educate and to conquer the imagination of the people. There is so much to say! Is there no one articulate?

Later, that was to become *Sight and Sound*'s critical credo. Meanwhile the enforced economies of the war years reduced the magazine in size and ambition. The issues published during the war were concerned with the war. Alarms were sounded about the effectiveness of Nazi film propaganda and (interestingly) about the relative inefficiency of the British cinema's call to arms: a plea from New York, by the managing editor of the *March of Time*, complained that America was not impressed by little England's domestic morale boosters. The magazine ventured occasional forays into the aesthetics of cinema, and a number of critics waxed blandly about their roles and responsibilities. In these little homilies there was at least a dawning awareness that there might be more than one way of looking at films.

If *Sight and Sound* had lacked a clear editorial voice before and during the war, the brave new world of the people's peace required a statement of principle. In the years following the war two currents flowed, uncertainly but in approximately the same direction, across the magazine's pages.

There was a hesitant but growing recognition of the cinema as a director's medium: the discernment of a personal signature, real trees amid the illusionist forest. *Sight and Sound* began to publish special supplements on the work of directors like Lang, Griffith and Stroheim; and in a 1948 article on Stroheim can be seen a crude formulation of what was later to be refined into the *auteur* theory. At the same time, and by no means only because of the emergence of neo-realism in Italy, there began to emerge a preoccupation with realism as the cinema's dominant—and proper—mode of expression.

This trend, along with a more welcoming approach to the popular art of Hollywood, coincided with the appearance of the magazine *Sequence*, launched by Oxford students and later published from London. And in no time the editors of what *Sight and Sound* had nervously welcomed as a 'new and fresh and lively' journal had moved house. One of them, Gavin Lambert, took over *Sight and Sound*'s editorial chair at the end of 1949; another, Penelope Houston, joined him as assistant editor. There was so much to say, so many cupboards to be cleared and bright new furniture to be installed, that for a year the magazine appeared as a monthly. The impetus behind these changes came from the British Film Institute's new Director, Denis Forman, who was determined that the magazine—hitherto directed mainly at the Institute's membership—should address a wider audience, to be reached via bookstalls as well as by individual subscription. Circulation rocketed; and soon afterwards a burgeoning interest in cinema was reflected in the establishment of a National Film Theatre.

Gavin Lambert's editorship changed the face of *Sight and Sound*. A series called 'Revaluations' plugged a few past gaps, but in truth it was not so much a matter of rediscovery as of long overdue celebration of an art now half a century old. But the main interest was, naturally, to celebrate new cinema. Or to deprecate it. A review of the Ealing police drama *The Blue Lamp*, considered in more conservative quarters a masterpiece of British realism, attacked the film for its cosy complacency about working-class life and compared it unfavourably with the vigorous American realism of *The Naked City*. A round-table discussion on British cinema echoed some of the same concern.

But the magazine was not simply, or even primarily, iconoclastic. The keyword of the time (a time when, after the post-war Socialist experiment, Britain was embarking on thirteen years of Tory rule) was 'humanity'. The renaissance of Italian cinema, in the neo-realism of Zavattini, De Sica and Rossellini, was held up as a mirror (*Bicycle Thieves* easily topped a 1952 *Sight and Sound* critics' poll of the Ten Best films ever made). Renoir was discovered. Hollywood, while not escaping stricture, was seen as tough, sharp-edged, alive to the way people actually lived and to the cultural myths which comforted their living. Ken Tynan wrote inimitable panegyrics to Cagney, Fields, Garbo. Lindsay Anderson affirmed the 'poetry' of John Ford. Humphrey Jennings was hymned as the poet of British cinema. It was a time of openness, of generosity, of making connections, a good (and perhaps an easier) time to be writing about the cinema. The *Sequence* generation—Lambert, Houston, Anderson, Karel Reisz, Tony Richardson—knew what they wanted of cinema and were not afraid to say so: a literary, and literate, generation who enjoyed the cinema and relished its capacity to astonish. It would itself have been astonished by a later generation's adulation of the pulp cinema of Sam Fuller. Noting the presence of *Pick-up on South Street* at the Venice Film Festival in 1953, Lambert called it 'indecent'.

This was a generation of critics who required, of the best of cinema, a moral commitment. And 'commitment' was to be the next rallying cry. In 1954, reviewing a selection of French criticism, Lindsay Anderson had written: 'The adulation of directors like Howard Hawks, Preminger, Hitchcock, even Robert Wise, seriously vitiates much of the writing in *Cahiers.*' The next year he attacked the last sequence of Kazan's *On the Waterfront* for its 'demagogic dishonesty of argument'. A year later, in the wake of the Free Cinema movement of which he was the guiding spirit, he wrote 'Stand up! Stand up!' in response both to a letter from a reader (John Russell Taylor, later a regular contributor as well as film critic of *The Times*) and to a cinema exhibition organised by the *Observer* newspaper. The context, it is worth recalling, was also the year of Suez and of Osborne's *Look Back in Anger*, the first stirrings of revolt against complacent, conservative, class-bound Britain.

By now Gavin Lambert had left to work in Hollywood and Penelope Houston was *Sight and Sound*'s editor, a position she still holds. Along with commitment the magazine championed the personal voice: the anguish of Bergman, the Forsterian modesty of Satyajit Ray, the hitherto unremarked cinema of Japan. But the critical issue had been raised and would not lie down. Celebrating its 25th anniversary in 1958, *Sight and Sound* published a revealing retrospective discussion on criticism between Basil Wright and Paul Rotha (representing the documentary tradition), Penelope Houston and Lindsay Anderson, in the course of which Wright identified the need for 'an anarchic paper, run by a group of probably rather scruffy young men . . . who will let off squibs and roman candles and rockets in all directions and generally stir up the whole thing'. Anderson seemed to agree: 'The criticism we desperately need should be enthusiastic, violent and responsible, all at the same time.' He could not have foreseen where the violence would come from. Two years later, while *Sight and Sound* was enthusing about Resnais, Antonioni, the French new wave and the American new spontaneity, a younger generation of Oxford opinionists was rocking the boat.

Sight and Sound was under siege, though no one seemed able to define precisely the critical ground being fought over. It was loosely—very loosely—about form (the scruffy young men, actually aesthetes to a man, of *Oxford Opinion* and later *Movie*) versus content (*Sight and Sound*), then as now a non-starter as a critical argument. Penelope Houston's response, 'The Critical Question', is reprinted here. In the same issue Richard Roud attempted to explain, for the benefit of bemused readers of *Sight and Sound*, the mysteries of *Cahiers du Cinéma*, with its pantheon of directors and its seraphic sensitivity to 'the thousand beauties of Nicholas Ray's *Party Girl*'. At this distance it is difficult to see what the argument was about, and curious to observe how both sides retreated behind barricades of their own making. But it was not, as was implied in the heat of the moment, about a definitive choice between the cinema of Nicholas Ray and that of Satyajit Ray, between Hollywood and humanism. In any case, as the editors of *Oxford Opinion* implied in a letter replying to Penelope Houston's article, there were internal dissensions within both camps.

The lines of demarcation blurred as the critical dust settled. Writers from *Cahiers* (Godard, Chabrol, Truffaut) and from *Sight and Sound* (Anderson, Reisz, Richardson) had already gone on to make films. As the 1960s progressed, and the cinema's internationalism was taken for granted, commitment was a forgotten word and nobody talked of form and content as though they were divisible. *Sight and Sound* has often been accused, sometimes within its own pages, of having no critical position. What this has meant in practice, for at least the last two decades, is that the magazine has been open to a variety of views. Indeed, as a magazine sponsored by a national Film Institute committed to disseminating knowledge about world cinema, it had a critical duty (and desire) to take a broad perspective. If *Sight and Sound* has resisted identification with any particular critical theory, its critical attitude was indicated in a comment by Penelope Houston in 1961. What film criticism should be trying to elucidate, she said, is 'the exact communication, in a moment of screen time, of mood or place or relationship or tension'.

An open view was needed in the 1960s to take in the cinema's expanding horizons. The 1962 London Film Festival, for instance, included films by Renoir, Bertolucci, Satyajit Ray, Ozu, Buñuel, Polanski, Kurosawa, Wajda, Bresson and Godard. *Sight and Sound*, making a broad church rather than a narrow cult of the cinema, could respond to all of them. Different writers, of course, had different enthusiasms: the magazine has never insisted on an editorial imprimatur. The case—for Godard, *cinéma-vérité*, Ozu or Antonioni—had merely to be well argued. A *politique des auteurs* was by no means inadmissible evidence, as long as it was not recited in a monotone. The virtue of this open view, which has exasperated critics of the magazine who would like to see it wear a critical straitjacket, is precisely that it has been able to accommodate without discomfort a range of writers and a range of opinions.

By 1970 the horizons had changed again. The tenth muse had now entered the grove of academe, as university courses in 'film studies' proliferated, first in the United States, then in Britain and elsewhere. We now talked not of the cinema but of 'film culture', an unfortunate phrase but one we shall have to live with. Film theory, launched without ballast, was tossed and turned on currents brought in from other academic disciplines: structuralism, semiotics, psychoanalytical theory. Some of this was assimilated by *Sight and Sound*, too much or too little according to which quarter of the now bloody critical battlefield the attack was coming from. But there was no radical change of direction. A magazine about the cinema in all its aspects, informational as well as critical and with an international circulation by now of some 30,000, could not (nor wanted to) turn itself into a journal of film theory without losing most of its readers; although from 1971 a larger format and more pages meant that there was room for longer and more analytical articles.

The other major change of the 1970s was the cinema's conversion from pleasure dome and art house to a Tower of Babel. Cinema now speaks in a hundred languages, most of which do not speak to one another. There is minimal cinema and structural cinema, feminist cinema and oppositional cinema, Hollywood and the movie brats, television and the new technology. During the last decade *Sight and Sound*'s contents have reflected this fragmentation of the cinema and its audiences. It is not easy to identify particular preoccupations, though a continuing interest in certain areas can be detected, such as a concern with political cinema and, more recently, with the emergence of a new generation of American directors. Television, a recurring interest since the magazine's early days, has received regular attention since 1974 (in the early 1960s *Sight and Sound* had a sister magazine, *Contrast*, entirely devoted to television). There has also been space for historical articles based on original research, and for close analysis of such subjects as existential motifs in the *film noir*, the use of slow motion in the Riefenstahl and Kurosawa Olympics films, the point-of-view shot in Mizoguchi.

All of which, it seems to me, reflects not so much an esotericism in *Sight and Sound*'s contents as a recognition of the many ways of looking at the cinema. In the fifty years since the magazine was launched (and it is by many years the oldest serious film magazine in continuous publication) the cinema has changed beyond recognition. *Sight and Sound* has charted those changes, predicted many of them, commented on all of them. This anthology celebrates the magazine's reflections on some moments of screen time.

A word about selection. I have sifted, read and re-read many millions of words, and my original short list of contents would have filled a book ten times this long. I have tried to represent *Sight and Sound*'s variety of interests and range of contributors over fifty years. But there are inevitably some aspects of the magazine which, for one reason or another, have had to be omitted. There are no items from the magazine's diary column or from its regular news and information section; some articles, particularly in recent years, excluded themselves by sheer length; and I have not included any of the magazine's many surveys of the film industry, its recurring crises and its eternal optimism. There are certain key articles which it would have been odd not to include (I regret the exclusion of one key article, at the express wish of its author)—and very many more which I have had to leave out.

DAVID WILSON

Introduction to a New Art

JOHN GRIERSON

The best way to start theorising about sound is to start off, as we used to do in silent theory, by considering first principles. Here we said, beginning at the beginning, is an oblong patch of white, a *tabula rasa*. Here is a camera. What can we put on the *tabula rasa*, what art can we develop within the limits of the screen? By examination of our instruments, by examination of the camera and the cutting bench, it soon became evident that we were not limited to the example of the stage. The perspectives of a new world and a new silent art opened out before us.

If only to formulate the method more clearly I shall run over some of these old arguments. The camera clearly can do much more than reproduce an action staged before it. It is a creative instrument, if properly directed, and not just a reproductive instrument.

It is light. It can get about in the world. Your screen accordingly is no longer the proscenium of a staged theatrical action. It can be a window on reality.

By the addition of close-up you give your camera power of intimacy. By the addition of one lens or another, you have a telephoto command of detail and intimacy. You have a microscopic power over reality.

By bringing in the element of angle you add new view points, which if properly used, can add to the dramatic, that is to say, to the creative power of your description. Put your camera high, you get one power, put it low you get another.

These were elementary powers which immediately indicated a direction for the silent film. When we considered the possibilities of the cutting bench, the possibilities of montage, still further powers opened up before us.

We could create rhythms and tempos, crescendos and diminuendos of energy to help our exposition.

We could bring detail together in mass formation. We could cross-section a street or a factory or a city.

We could work in images to add atmosphere to our action, or poetry to our description.

We could, by the juxtaposition of shots, explode ideas in the heads of our audience. We could arrange the juxtaposition of our detail for particular dramatic effect.

Out of such *a priori* considerations was created a theory which gradually took cinema from the example of the stage into a world of its own.

Films like *Potemkin*, even the Wild West films, had very little to do with stage example. They represented a new art which depended for its effects on powers peculiar to itself.

With sound film we must go through the same process. It is obviously not enough to seize on its power of reproducing synchronistically the spoken words of actors. At first it was a sufficient novelty to hear our shadows speak and sing, and hear their ham and eggs sizzle in the frying pan, but if you look into the matter you will see that the microphone, like the camera, can do better things than merely reproduce, and that at the cutting bench and the re-recording bench, as many new possibilities open out before sound film as once opened out before the cutting bench of silence.

The microphone, too, can get about in the world. By doing so, it has the same power over reality as the camera had before it. It has the power to bring to the hands of the creative artist a thousand and one vernacular elements, and the million and one sounds which ordinarily attend the working of the world. Regarded simply as a collector of raw material, the microphone, like the camera before it, has still to be released from the bondage of the studios.

The raw material of course means nothing in itself. It is only as it is used that it becomes the material of art. The final question is how we are to use sound creatively rather than reproductively.

Here perhaps it is useful to remember the example set us by the BBC. This great organisation has been in possession of microphones for years. It has had an unparalleled freedom in the handling of sound effects, yet it is still content with an almost exclusive use of the microphone for reproductive purposes. It reproduces speech, it reproduces music, it brings the experts of one sound medium or another to our ears, but in the process it has added nothing. For it the microphone is simply a reproductive mechanism.

Its only contribution is in its dramatic department. There it attempts to build up effects drawn from a dozen different studios or a dozen different locations. Some Napoleon at centre presses a button to bring in studio A and the piece starts with some music. At the proper point he mixes in studio B and overlays some conversation. At another point a button brings in a wind mechanism or the sound of a door banging.

Now, sound film permits all this to be done with greater certainty, greater exactitude, and much greater subtlety and complexity. If your sounds are on film you can with a pair of scissors and a pot of paste join any single sound to any other. You can orchestrate bits and pieces of sound as you please. Call that horizontal orchestration. You can also, by re-recording, put any single sound on top of another sound. A simple case is music in the background and a voice in the foreground, but, for that matter, you can have a dozen sounds all with their different reference sounding together. Call that vertical orchestration. Add to these two possibilities the fact that the image is on one strip of film, and the sound on another strip of film. You can obviously put any sound or sounds you select, alongside any given picture. There you have the secret of the whole business.

I take it one is ready to admit the principle that we must make our sound help out the mute rather than reproduce it. Sometimes it is useful, of course, to hear what people are saying and see their lips move, but we may take it as a principal guide that wherever we can make the sound add to the general effect we should. Our rule should be to have the mute strip and the sound complementary to each other, helping each other along. That is what Pudovkin means when he talks about asynchronistic sound. He talks of the mute and the sound following each a separate rhythm, as instruments in an orchestra follow their separate parts to the end of creating together a larger result.

Sound can obviously bring a rich contribution to the manifold of the film—so rich a contribution in fact that the double art becomes a new art altogether. We have power of speech, power of music, power of natural sound, power of commentary, power of chorus, power even of manufacturing sound which has never been heard before. And these different elements can all be used to give atmosphere, to give drama, to give poetic reference to the subject in hand. And when you remember that you can cut sound as you cut film and that you can, by re-recording, orchestrate any or all of these elements together in exact timing with the mute, the possibilities become enormous.

Most of you will have noticed some of the new uses of sound which have been creeping into the studio pictures. There was a great critical noise, you remember, when Hitchcock repeated the word 'knife', 'knife' in one of his early films. It represented a use of sound that described the subjective side of a situation. This use has been developed greatly since then. In the Hitchcock example this word, which stood out from the mumble of conversation, was simply a word which was drumming in the mind of one of the actors. In *Hell's Heroes* words subjectively spoken were cut similarly with words objectively spoken. In *Strange Interlude* almost the entire issue of the film was the fact that the people said one thing to their neighbours and a different thing to themselves. On the stage, as I first saw this O'Neill technique developed, the actors had to use masks. They spoke with masks for the objective words and spoke without them for the subjective words, but the mechanics were of course clumsy. Here, in what you might call the world of monologue, sound film can do and do easily what is outside the power of the stage. It means of course that a new perspective can be brought to the personal drama, a perspective which if it is handled deeply might give the cinema some of the psychological power of the novel.

Another field in which sound technique is likely to develop greatly is in the use of chorus. I remember seeing in Paris before sound came the Russian film *The Village of Sin*, and when the harvest scene came on, a chorus of émigrés concealed behind the screen broke into a Russian harvest song. This was very effective at the time. When Creighton synchronised the ill-fated *One Family* he used the same device for a Canadian prairie sequence, and was very much before his time. All of you will have noticed too the use of chorus in both René Clair and Lubitsch: not just as simple background chorus but as something taken up by different characters at different points of the action. You have a René Clair chorus used to cross-section a tenement building. The first line is sung by a man shaving on the second floor, the second line by a fat lady doing her hair on the ground floor and so on. So, by a chorus, characters are brought together and a single mood permeates a whole location. The Lubitsch use of chorus is similar. The characters begin it in a railway train, but it is taken up by the engine driver, by the guard, by the wheels playing rhythmically on the rails—even by the peasants in the passing fields. So too with Disney. A musical sequence is beaten out by the most various fantastic elements in the mute—or more rarely, though more excitingly, it is counter-pointed by the mute.

But the permeation of the silent images with a musical mood represents only an elementary use of chorus possibilities. In *Three Cornered Moon*, you may remember, there was a quick cross-section of the American unemployed. The picture flashed from one desolate figure to another and the sound strip in complement picked up various bits of conversation revealing the lost hopes of the people on the bread queues. Call this the chorus of bits and pieces. With a sound strip into which you can cut any excerpt of sound you like, there is no limit to the cumulative selections of conversations you can build up. Conversational scraps from a street, from a factory, from any scene or situation, may very well help you to give colour and point to your description. You will find glimpses of this in two of the GPO films recently completed: in *6.30 Collection* and in *Weather Forecast*.

Then there is another kind of chorus altogether. You may call it the recitative chorus. The very crudest form of it is the commentary which you find ordinarily attached to interest films. Imagine, however, that your commentary is spoken by a poet, or imagine that you are back with Greek chorus and that your poet is no longer describing the fact of the matter but delivering a recital which adds dramatic or poetic colour to the action. There was an example of this in a Hollywood melodrama called

1. The image of sound: *Weather Forecast*

Beast of the City which began with a survey of the Chicago underworld, in which the camera trucked from one dark side-walk to another. The recital in this case was the monotonous rigmarole of the wireless messages going out from police headquarters. It went something like this: 'Calling Car 324 324 Calling Car 528 528 Calling Car 18 18' etc., etc.

There is nothing, however, to prevent our developing this recitative business further. In *6.30 Collection* you will see masses of letters parading on the moving belt of a large sorting office. The sound is simple, for we contented ourselves in this film with a straight documentary account of the noises that were there. We could very easily have made the letters read themselves out in snatches, or for that matter we could have hired a poet to make *vers libres* of their contents. Or we could have made the different senders come forward to say in snatches what their letters were seeking. I do not mean these would have been good methods in this particular instance, for they would probably have overloaded the occasion. My point is that the different choral possibilities are there to develop.

There is still another direction in which sound will develop very considerably, and that is in the direction of imagery. A great exponent of the silent film like Pudovkin could always be reckoned on to bring very beautiful images into his description. At the beginning of *End of St. Petersburg* there is a sequence describing the birth of a child and a small boy is sent off to pass the word to his father in the fields. As he runs, a single puffy cloud in the sky is cut into the sequence. In *Mother* the happiness of a woman is described in terms of waving trees and rushing water. In *Ecstase*, the Czechoslovakian film, and in the *Romance Sentimentale* of Eisenstein, the moods of the central figure were similarly described by the introduction of appropriate attendant images. Sounds, of course, have not the same precise significance as visuals. If you watch very carefully some of the effects in *Weather Forecast* you may notice how effective some seemingly irrational crossing of sound can be: the sound of an aeroplane attached to a shot of a high mast, for example. The point is that once you start detaching sounds from their origins you can use them as images of those origins. In the first place it allows you to carry more ideas together in the presentation of a single image. For example, the racketing of teleprinters in *Weather Forecast* is associated with a BBC broadcast. In *6.30 Collection* the sound of a departing train is associated with the sweepers in the sorting office when the work is over and the mail bags have gone. In *Cable Ship* the sound of the cable ship itself is associated with a trucking shot of the International Telephone Exchange.

Another curious fact emerges once you start detaching sounds from their origins, and it is this. Your aeroplane noise may become not the image of an aeroplane but the image of distance or of height. Your steamer whistle may become not the image of a steamer but of isolation or darkness.

I cannot tell you how far this imagery will go because I think we are only beginning for the first time to become dramatically and poetically conscious of sound. The whole power of sound imagery will only come as, in the practice of sound film, more and more sounds are detached and matured into the special significance which I believe is latent in them.

(An interesting example from *The Road to Life*. When the train arrives carrying the body of the dead hero, a large crowd awaits it. The crowd does not sigh. It is silent. The sigh of the crowd is carried by the last exhaust puff of the engine.)

But by discussing in this way chorus and imagery and monologue I only mean to give the broadest indication of the new possibilities. Practice has a habit of exploding all theories and generalisations, and you will get far more by watching this new sound medium at work than by reading

2. Recitative as sound: *Pett and Pott*

articles about it. *Deserter* is a far richer discourse on sound than any of Pudovkin's articles, and there is a more exciting discourse on sound in Cavalcanti's new film *Pett and Pott* and in Evelyn Spice's *Weather Forecast* than in anything I could possibly define.

The main thing is that sound must help to fulfil the mute, and mute must help to fulfil the sound. This is not silent film with sound added. It is a new art—the art of sound-film.

In *Pett and Pott* you will find the relation of sound and mute so close all the way through that you may very well regard the film as of historic importance in the development of sound film. For certainly no sound film before has depended so little on stage example. Notice how the music has been written to create the mood of the theme. Notice how the sound strip invades the silent strip and turns a woman's cry into an engine whistle. Notice that a recitative is used in the train scene instead of the usual sound of the wheels on the rail. Notice how a commentator—a voice of God in the last instance—may be used effectively even in a story film. Notice the effect of joining a drum and fife band with a domestic quarrel, and notice particularly the dramatic point that can be achieved by cutting from one sound sequence to another.

Sound film is at the same stage of development as the silent cinema before the war. It is glued to stage example, and however many the variations we see or hear, they do not represent any fundamental breakaway from the dialogue drama of the theatre. But that breakaway must come. The documentary film will do pioneer work for cinema if it emancipates the microphone from the studio and demonstrates at the cutting and re-recording benches how many more dramatic uses can be made of sound than the studios at present realise.

1934

Films of the Quarter

ALISTAIR COOKE

This is the time of the year when critics find themselves suffering from seasonal prostration, or second-wind cynicism. After six months' interne work in smoky cinemas, ministering to this sinking patient, dissecting that corpse, the smell of spring is no joke. It only tantalises you with the reminder that there is outside a real world (*pace* Hitler, Mussolini, the Naval Conference, and the Defence Programme) where sanity may come from a glimpse of crocuses, where the box-office formula for gaiety may be no more than a seat in Hyde Park and cost a million dollars less than any Hollywood knows. But it's still a world you will know nothing of for four more months. If the reader detects a gleam of malice in the turn of too many sentences, let him remember that a critic's spite is sharpened by the constant recollection that Hollywood had last year 3,002 hours of the sun its bad works keep him from.

There is some compensation in knowing that this has been the Funny Men's quarter. We have had them all—Chaplin, Lloyd, the Marx Brothers, Eddie Cantor, all except Fields who is, thank Heaven, now almost recovered from a grave and once hopeless illness. After as pretentious a build-up as the next war, the Chaplin film disappointed as much as that will if it is fought with bow and arrow. That disappointment would certainly be an enjoyable experience in itself, but before we get there most of us will be in hospital from anticipatory nerve diseases. By the time the critics finally got the film shown to them, at the most jittery press show on record, they were babbling so pitifully about 'satire', 'machine civilisation', and the other neural incantations, that when it was all over nobody knew what it was about. For most of them the notice they'd thought of writing a year ago was as good as any other. And now the general public, besides suffering from the general neurosis, has to climb through volumes of conflicting rubbish in order to see the film straight at all. Its innate fault, that of clumsy and uncertain continuity, is due I think to Mr Chaplin's courageous departure from pathos. For he knows no better continuity than the moments of fantasy generated by pathetic incidents. And here there are none. The idea to develop beyond the frustrated clown was a worthy one, but it demanded the repression of the instincts he works by. It had to be given an air of smoothness and efficiency by a production strangely foreign to the rambling Chaplin studio. And *Modern Times* has to be seen three times before one can first get used to, then discount, the symphonic luxury of the music and production. There is no discounting hurried and uneven direction (though Mr Joseph Breen, who deleted six sequences at the last moment, may have much to answer for). But untamed behind all the lavish scoring are a few vagrant Chaplin tunes, and untailored through all the over-dressed production is the pantomimist himself, energetically nose-thumbing his own incongruous prosperity, sharpening the old marvellous gestures with a new Latin flipness, his mercurial body scribbling through the piece like a caricaturist's pencil through an album of photographs.

A *Night at the Opera* had every virtue that *Modern Times* lacked. Beautifully and carefully built by George Kaufmann, pruned by a

3. *A Night at the Opera*

preliminary road-tour on which the perceptive Harpo kept a critical notebook, it came sprucely to Hollywood without the old cluttering of irrelevant whimsy, without having to snatch gags from the air to fill in ninety minutes. And of course in London, the absurd Marxian cult liked it not at all. Bloomsbury and Mayfair will never forgive Groucho for demonstrating, once for all in *A Night at the Opera*, that his middle name was never Salvador. 'Those who know their Marx Brothers,' they said, 'will recognise an inferior work.' In which case, the other 127,000,000 Americans must be wrong. The cultists here have always thought that their best gags had a unique quality of unattached whimsy. But the Marx Brothers are not unique. They are a thousand American comedians brought to the boil. And their dialogue always has a pointed application (Bloomsbury, unaware of the institution being parodied, takes refuge in calling it surrealism). As here most exquisitely in the contract scene, which would be better called the saloon scene (with an unconscious tenor as the brass-rail), in the parody automobile accident with two trunks (*Groucho*: 'Hit-and-run driver, eh?—just look what you've done to that fender!'). The operatic fill-ins are dull enough, but we had to take a rest somewhere and only Fields of the screen comics can spread his stuff carefully enough to dispense with the need for rest intervals. Chaplin's sentimental heroines are no less desperate bolsters against fatigue.

Whereas Mr Cantor sells his concession in fatigue directly to the box-office and the Goldwyn girls and the writers of torch-songs. In *Strike Me Pink*, it is hard to know which is comedy and which is recovery. Mr Cantor has trusted too much to that put-upon look in the first half of the film. And the best of the film is a couple of situations which did not need Mr Cantor's specific talent. One needed anybody and Edward Brophy, and the other needed only a trick photographer and an alive editor. Both situations received their due, and their reward in mad laughter. The Harold Lloyd film [*The Milky Way*] made one situation the whole film, asked for more acting than Lloyd has ever known, but threw Adolphe Menjou into brilliant bewildered relief.

The worst of the American films has been *Soak the Rich*, most 'colossal' *Mutiny on the Bounty*, and the best *Ah, Wilderness*. The much-championed rebellion of the Messrs Hecht and MacArthur becomes increasingly trivial and increasingly reactionary. The latest effort is a shabby, amateur little cynicism about radicalism on the campus. The authors' low trick is to offset vacuous socialites with morons (handpicked) to represent the socialists. By comparison, the said socialites appear about as civilised and amiable as life can be. Hollywood has a lot to fear, but not while it has Hecht and MacArthur on the sidelines.

Mutiny on the Bounty took two years to make, was originally fifteen times its projected length, was conceived as an epic and cost a fortune. And it still remains a good film. I'm afraid its only practical effect on the history of film may be to give to other studios the hint that sadism is now an indispensable box-office ingredient. But it could boast the temporary triumphs of a strong even tempo, a decisive performance from Charles Laughton, much artful glorifying of the ship by Arthur Edeson's camera, and several Captain Bligh Editions of *The Times*.

King Vidor has again confessed, in *So Red the Rose*, that his gifts are sprawling into lushness, yielding to the pure sentimentality his early observation of people (*vide The Crowd, Street Scene*) helped him to resist. He admittedly took his cue from Stark Young, who wrote the book. It seems hard enough nowadays for any American to think about that mythical old South without moaning a mammy song and reaching for a mint juleep. Certainly King Vidor, presented with a theme which must sometimes make a great movie, must have been too blinded by tears to see a fact, and he turned a deaf ear even to the right music. But New England, even after *Little Women*, has somehow managed not to turn into a Christmas card. It's still a place where people live (or used to) and it has always been eminently screenable. Clarence Brown, who is in the myth business himself (remember the Russia of *Anna Karenina*), has taken his spring vacation with Eugene O'Neill and in *Ah, Wilderness* they wander back with never a false step into a Connecticut of thirty years ago. It must be O'Neill's script and the tender authenticity of his dialogue that give it undeniable distinction. Yet in retrospect Brown is never mawkish, is more than ingenious in the graduation scene, is neat and economical with the big scene of the play, a dinner table conversation that might have grown woolly in the screen version. And the acting of, especially, Eric Linden and Lionel Barrymore save Wallace Beery from the woeful emphasis he receives from being in the film at all, or even from the shock *we* receive at finding him within bellowing distance of Connecticut.

The best of the Continental films have been *Sans Famille* and Sacha Guitry's *Bonne Chance*. (I suppose under this heading I should say the most entertaining, but I've never been able to work out what is the difference between entertaining films and good ones.) The first had to withstand some pretty confident scorn from the more sophisticated patrons of the Academy, who turned silly with laughter at the idea of a Frenchman playing an English policeman. Needless to say, the policemen were three times as good as our own film Frenchmen, stage Irishmen, and at least five times as plausible as English vaudeville tumblers trying to pretend they are something very remarkable back on Broadway. Decidedly unfunny, and a knock-out blow for any native director who has ever thought about probing the East End, was the French idea of a thieves' kitchen in those parts. It was brilliantly played, directed with a venom of detail and verisimilitude that I doubt very much any English director dare have the courage to reproduce. Guitry's film was a pretty surprise to anybody who shies at the mention of theatre

4. *Things to Come*

people in films. M Guitry can flick at gaiety with as sure a touch in cinema as he does on the stage. There were sequences (a conversation in the car, the working out of the budget on the restaurant table) which a man might think of whose profession is to look through a lens and never from an auditorium.

The British films this quarter are a proud and, on the whole, a creditable lot. After a good-looking, but dull, first appearance with *The Amateur Gentleman* and *Koenigsberg* (which were at least smoothly made), our cinema sounded an air-raid warning and *Things to Come* droned and thundered into our ken. There has been a lot of wrangling about this film. I have done my share and maintain that the acting would be creditable in Madame Tussaud's, the dialogue is pre-war (that little 1914 affair) and that the social psychology is crude materialism. But Vincent Korda and Georges Périnal between them have created at least a half-hour of a world that remains, as a patriotic poet said about an earlier world, 'a shining thing in the mind'. I don't know what that means, but that makes it all the more apt for *Things to Come*, which doesn't mean much that is profound but sounds tremendous and looks a million dollars—or more. Its faults are defections from the standards we film critics carry round with us waiting to fire off at the first adult film that comes our way. There have been not more than a dozen or so in twenty years, and it may be some compliment to *Things to Come* to say that it at least gets our hand on the trigger. A better film, whose ambition is comparatively microscopic, but not so unlike the other as you might think, is the Wright-Grierson documentary *Night Mail*. For the first time it makes documentary film as careful and thorough a document as the best written journalism, as, say, *Fortune's* current pieces on Families on Relief. I have seen documentary films that looked like headmaster's reports, and others that would have gone better on to cigarette cards. But in *Night Mail*, Grierson (I suppose) respects the intricacy of the job that is to be done and Wright by a fine swinging movement and dramatic editing receives the information in one hand and 'takes it away' into enchantment with the other, the camera hand. Not much below the first class of historical films, and the only British one I can recall that is sensible and decent in retrospect, is Berthold Viertel's *Rhodes of Africa*. For one thing, it makes our more sober English tempo of living and thinking a positive quality of the film instead of a drag on a hurrying plot; for another, it balances the sympathy between the opposite sides not as fairly as Time or Providence will, but at any rate as evenly as you could expect from a protagonist. All the performances have some sort of charm, and even bad editing cannot mar the sense of proportion which kept the South African outdoor scenes objectively in long shots.

There is no end to a quarter other than the films you've seen. But in the dying moments of this critic's quarter came *Desire*, in which Frank

5. *Desire*

Borzage's direction has been trimmed and polished by a Lubitsch in his best form since *Trouble in Paradise*. That is a strong sentence, and it was meant to be. After the tribe of knockabouts, gagmen, wisecrackers, the purveyors of 'smart' comedy, Mr Lubitsch's picture is like—I almost said—a breath of spring. It's not that, but it makes this indoor confinement less painful. For to the strong light, the trees and the mountains of southern California (here called Spain, so that the audience may admire aloud with fewer misgivings) is added a sure, beautifully written piece about the usual Lubitsch trifles, about crooks and fake countesses breathless before the dawn of romance. Somehow Mr Lubitsch's style has regained enough strength to make this stuff take on a vintage body long after the captains of industry and the kings of jazz depart.

1936

My Own Methods[1]

ALFRED HITCHCOCK

Many people think a film director does all his work in the studio, drilling the actors, making them do what he wants. That is not at all true of my own methods, and I can write only of my own methods. I like to have a film complete in my mind before I go on the floor. Sometimes the first idea one has of a film is of a vague pattern, a sort of haze with a certain shape. There is possibly a colourful opening developing into something more intimate; then, perhaps in the middle, a progression to a chase or some other adventure; and sometimes at the end the big shape of a climax, or maybe some twist or surprise. You see this hazy pattern, and then you have to find a narrative idea to suit it. Or a story may give you an idea first and you have to develop it into a pattern.

Imagine an example of a standard plot—let us say a conflict between love and duty. This idea was the origin of my first talkie, *Blackmail*. The hazy pattern one saw beforehand was duty—love—love versus duty—and finally either duty or love, one or the other. The whole middle section was built up on the theme of love versus duty, after duty and love had been introduced separately in turn. So I had first to put on the screen an episode expressing duty.

I showed the arrest of a criminal by Scotland Yard detectives, and tried to make it as concrete and detailed as I could. You even saw the detectives take the man to the lavatory to wash his hands—nothing exciting, just the routine of duty. Then the young detective says he's going out that evening with his girl, and the sequence ends, pointing on from duty to love. Then you start showing the relationship between the detective and his girl: they are middle-class people. The love theme doesn't run smoothly; there is a quarrel and the girl goes off by herself, just because the young man has kept her waiting a few minutes. So your story starts; the girl falls in with the villain—he tries to seduce her and she kills him. Now you've got your problem prepared. Next morning, as soon as the detective is put on to the murder case, you have your conflict—love versus duty. The audience know that he will be trying to track down his

---

[1]This revealing account of Hitchcock's methods is an abridged version of an article written by the director for the book *Footnotes to the Film*.

own girl, who has done the murder, so you sustain their interest: they wonder what will happen next.

The blackmailer was really a subsidiary theme. I wanted him to go through and expose the girl. That was my idea of how the story ought to end. I wanted the pursuit to be after the girl, not after the blackmailer. That would have brought the conflict on to a climax, with the young detective, ahead of the others, trying to push the girl out through a window to get her away, and the girl turning round and saying: 'You can't do that—I must give myself up.' Then the rest of the police arrive, misinterpret what he is doing, and say, 'Good man, you've got her,' not knowing the relationship between them. Now the reason for the opening comes to light. You repeat every shot used first to illustrate the duty theme, only now it is the girl who is the criminal. The young man is there ostensibly as a detective, but of course the audience know he is in love with the girl. The girl is locked up in her cell and the two detectives walk away, and the older one says, 'Going out with your girl tonight?' The younger one shakes his head. 'No. Not tonight.'

That was the ending I wanted for *Blackmail*, but I had to change it for commercial reasons. The girl couldn't be left to face her fate. And that shows you how the films suffer from their own power of appealing to millions. They could often be subtler than they are, but their own popularity won't let them.

But to get back to the early work on a film. With the help of my wife, who does the technical continuity, I plan out a script very carefully, hoping to follow it exactly, all the way through, when shooting starts. In . fact, this working on the script is the real making of the film, for me. When I've done it, the film is finished already in my mind. Usually, too, I don't find it necessary to do more than supervise the editing myself.

Settings, of course, come into the preliminary plan, and usually I have fairly clear ideas about them; I was an art student before I took up with films. Sometimes I even think of backgrounds first. *The Man Who Knew Too Much* started like that; I looked in my mind's eye at snowy Alps and dingy London alleys, and threw my characters into the middle of the contrast. Studio settings, however, are often a problem; one difficulty is that extreme effects—extremes of luxury or extremes of squalor—are much the easiest to register on the screen. If you try to reproduce the average sitting-room in Golders Green or Streatham it is apt to come out looking like nothing in particular, just nondescript. It is true that I have tried lately to get interiors giving a real lower-middle-class atmosphere—for instance, the Verlocs' living room in *Sabotage*—but there's always a certain risk in giving your audience humdrum truth.

However, in time the script and the sets are finished somehow and we are ready to start shooting. One great problem that occurs at once, and keeps on occurring, is to get the players to adapt themselves to film technique. Many of them, of course, come from the stage; they are not cinema-minded at all. So, quite naturally, they like to play long scenes straight ahead. But if I have to shoot a long scene continuously I always feel I am losing grip on it, from a cinematic point of view. The camera, I feel, is simply standing there, *hoping* to catch something with a visual point to it. I want to put my film together on the screen, not simply to photograph something that has been put together already in the form of a long piece of stage acting. This is what gives an effect of life to a picture—the feeling that when you see it on the screen you are watching something that has been conceived and brought to birth directly in visual terms.

You can see an example of what I mean in *Sabotage*. Just before Verloc is killed there is a scene made up entirely of short pieces of film, separately photographed. This scene has to show how Verloc comes to be killed—how the thought of killing him arises in Sylvia Sidney's mind and connects itself with the carving knife she uses when they sit down to dinner. But the sympathy of the audience has to be kept with Sylvia Sidney; it must be clear that Verloc's death, finally, is an accident. So, as she serves at the table, you see her unconsciously serving vegetables with the carving knife, as though her hand were keeping hold of the knife of its

6. 'The thought of killing him': Sylvia Sidney, Oscar Homolka in *Sabotage*

own accord. The camera cuts from her hand to her eyes and back to her hand; then back to her eyes as she suddenly becomes aware of the knife making its error. Then to a normal shot—the man unconcernedly eating; then back to the hand holding the knife. In an older style of acting Sylvia would have had to show the audience what was passing in her mind by exaggerated facial expression. But people today in real life often don't show their feelings in their faces: so the film treatment showed the audience her mind through her hand, through its unconscious grasp on the knife. Now the camera moves again to Verloc—back to the knife—back again to his face. You see him seeing the knife, realising its implication. The tension between the two is built up with the knife as its focus.

Now when the camera has immersed the audience so closely in a scene such as this, it can't instantly become objective again. It must broaden the movement of the scene without loosening the tension. Verloc gets up and walks round the table, coming so close to the camera that you feel, if you are sitting in the audience, almost as though you must move back to make room for him. Then the camera moves to Sylvia Sidney again, then returns to the subject—the knife.

So you gradually build up the psychological situation, piece by piece, using the camera to emphasise first one detail, then another. The point is to draw the audience right inside the situation instead of leaving them to watch it from outside, from a distance. And you can do this only by breaking the action up into details and cutting from one to the other, so that each detail is forced in turn on the attention of the audience and reveals its psychological meaning. If you played the whole scene straight through, and simply made a photographic record of it with the camera always in one position, you would lose your power over the audience. They would watch the scene without becoming really involved in it, and you would have no means of concentrating their attention on those particular visual details which make them feel what the characters are feeling.

One way of using the camera to give emphasis is the reaction shot. By the reaction shot I mean any close-up which illustrates an event by showing instantly the reaction to it of a person or a group. The door opens for someone to come in, and before showing who it is you cut to the expressions of the persons already in the room. Or, while one person is talking, you keep your camera on someone else who is listening. This over-running of one person's image with another person's voice is a method peculiar to the talkies; it is one of the devices which help the talkies to tell a story faster than a silent film could tell it, and faster than it could be told on the stage.

Or, again, you can use the camera to give emphasis whenever the attention of the audience has to be focused for a moment on a certain player. There is no need for him to raise his voice or move to the centre of the stage or do anything dramatic. A close-up will do it all for him—will give him, so to speak, the stage all to himself.

I must say that in recent years I have come to make much less use of obvious camera devices. I have become more commercially-minded; afraid that anything at all subtle may be missed. I have learnt from experience how easily small touches are overlooked.

The film always has to deal in exaggerations. Its methods reflect the simple contrasts of black and white photography. One advantage of colour is that it would give you more intermediate shades. I should never want to fill the screen with colour: it ought to be used economically—to put new words into the screen's visual language when there's a need for them. You could start a colour film with a boardroom scene: sombre panelling and furniture, the directors all in dark clothes and white collars. Then the chairman's wife comes in, wearing a red hat. She takes the attention of the audience at once, just because of that one note of colour.

A journalist once asked me about distorted sound—a device I tried in *Blackmail* when the word 'knife' hammers on the consciousness of the girl at breakfast on the morning after the murder. Again, I think this kind of effect may be justified. There have always been occasions when we have needed to show a phantasmagoria of the mind in terms of visual imagery. So we may want to show someone's mental state by letting him listen to some sound—let us say church bells—and making them clang with distorted insistence in his head. But on the whole nowadays I try to tell a story in the simplest possible way, so that I can feel sure it will hold the attention of any audience and won't puzzle them.

I know there are critics who ask why lately I have made only thrillers. Am I satisfied, they say, with putting on the screen the equivalent merely of popular novelettes? Part of the answer is that I am out to get the best stories I can which will suit the film medium, and I have usually found it necessary to take a hand in writing them myself. There is a shortage of good writing for the screen. In this country we can't usually afford to employ large writing staffs, so I have had to join in and become a writer myself. I choose crime stories because that is the kind of story I can write, or help to write, myself—the kind of story I can turn most easily into a successful film. It is the same with Charles Bennett, who has so often worked with me; he is essentially a writer of melodrama. I am ready to use other stories, but I can't find writers who will give them to me in a suitable form.

Sometimes I have been asked what films I should make if I were free to do exactly as I liked without having to think about the box-office. There are several examples I can give very easily. For one thing, I should like to make travel films with a personal element in them. Or I should like to do a verbatim of a celebrated trial. The Thompson-Bywaters case, for instance.

7. Hitchcock directing *Sabotage* (1936)

The cinema could reconstruct the whole story. Or there is the fire at sea possibility—that has never been tackled seriously on the screen. It might be too terrifying for some audiences, but it would make a great subject worthwhile.

British producers are often urged to make more films about characteristic phases of English life.

Why, they are asked, do we see so little of the English farmer or the English seaman? Or is there not plenty of good material in the great British industries—in mining or shipbuilding or steel? One difficulty here is that English audiences seem to take more interest in American life—I suppose because it has a novelty value. They are rather easily bored by everyday scenes in their own country. But I certainly should like to make a film of the Derby, only it might not be quite in the popular class. It would be hard to invent a Derby story that wasn't hackneyed, conventional. I would rather do it more as a documentary—a sort of pageant, an animated modern version of Frith's 'Derby Day'. I would show everything that goes on all round the course, but without a story.

Perhaps the average audience isn't ready for that, yet. Popular taste, all the same, does move; today you can put over scenes that would have been ruled out a few years ago. Particularly towards comedy, nowadays, there is a different attitude. You can get comedy out of your stars, and you used not to be allowed to do anything which might knock the glamour off them.

In 1926 I made a film called *Downhill*, from a play by Ivor Novello, who acted in the film himself, with Ian Hunter and Isabel Jeans. There was a sequence showing a quarrel between Hunter and Novello. It started as an ordinary fight; then they began throwing things at one another. They tried to pick up heavy pedestals to throw and the pedestals bowled them over. In other words I made it comic. I even put Hunter into a morning coat and striped trousers because I felt that a man never looks so ridiculous as when he is well dressed and fighting. This whole scene was cut out; they said I was guying Ivor Novello. It was ten years before its time.

I think public taste is turning to like comedy and drama more mixed up; and this is another move away from the conventions of the stage. In a play your divisions are much more rigid; you have a scene in one key—then curtain, and after an interval another scene starts. In a film you keep your whole action flowing; you can have comedy and drama running together and weave them in and out. Audiences are much readier now than they used to be for sudden changes of mood; and this means more freedom for a director. The art of directing for the commercial market is to know just how far you can go. In many ways I am freer now to do what I want to do than I was a few years ago. I hope in time to have more freedom still—if audiences will give it to me.

1937

Fiction and Fact

RUDOLF ARNHEIM

The cinema started with documentary films. The first films ever made had subjects as 'The arrival of a train' or 'Workmen leaving a factory', and although the first public show of Messrs Lumière's films included also the narrative film, we know that the famous 'Arroseur arrosé' fascinated the spectators not so much by its 'plot', i.e. by presenting a gardener teased by a malicious companion, but for the fact that the leaves of the trees were shown moving naturally in the wind—as they had never been able to do on the stage. In the following forty-five years, the gardener gained a complete victory over the moving leaves, as far as the film audiences are concerned; but if we wish to deal seriously with the cinema those leaves remain the essential fact as they had been in 1895.

Very soon, actors of the most unnatural kind obtained a leading part on the screen, but it is well to remember that even the slapstick comedies showed real houses, real streets and real trains. In the course of time, however, reproduction more and more displaced reality, and when huge Egyptian temples and Roman castles were constructed on the studio grounds the contribution of nature was limited to sunlight, sky and wind. Even these last elements proved not to be indispensable: the film companies locked themselves up in rooms without windows and when, in the *Cabinet of Dr Caligari*, the painter's brush transformed chairs, desks and even human faces into abstract ornaments nature seemed to be definitely exorcised.

The cinema had started as a simple mass-entertainment. But when it became self-conscious and claimed to be an art of its own kind it had to face strong theoretical objections. It was stated that works of art could not be produced with mechanical tools; but this objection had been made before against nearly every new art tool and it was comforting to know that Leonardo da Vinci had to defend painting against poetry with the following words: 'If you call it mechanical because the hands represent by their craft what the painters invent in their phantasy, even you, the writers, have to note down with your pen by hand-craft what you find in your mind.'

A much graver objection asserted that the mechanical reproduction of real things excluded the liberty of creation necessary for artistic work. *Dr*

Caligari gave no counter-evidence against this because the liberty of the art-director's phantasy belonged to the old art of the stage. To establish the cinema theoretically as a new art it was necessary to show that certain differences between reality and its reproduction on the screen allowed the artist to influence the aspect of real things in a deliberate way. The practical demonstration of this theory was given on the one hand by the Russian films, which enhanced the authenticity of the photographed facts to the utmost but succeeded nevertheless in giving them a very strong expression by developing the specific art of taking and editing the pictures; it was given on the other hand by the French avant-garde which by a clever use of the camera and montage melted the images of everyday things into surrealistic compositions.

The reign of cinematographic art seemed to be definitely secured but it was not. Theory and practice had demonstrated, it is true, that the cinema was not mere reproduction but nevertheless there remained, indubitably, a test of material reality which could not be overcome. The painful aspect of actors of flesh and bone sitting on abstract chairs in Dr Caligari's cabinet proved that the film could not reach the absolute sovereignty of abstract painting and in the avant-garde films even the most artful combination of real elements could not conceal the seams between the single things: they were joined together only by montage, that means by addition, and artistic creation is something more than addition. The more recent films of Charlie Chaplin, as *City Lights* and *Modern Times*, showed obviously a loss of that precious special atmosphere which had formerly procured an unreal background to unreal happenings and acting. It was not Chaplin's fault; he had perfectly maintained his style; but the improvement of the lighting technique and the higher sensibility and better tone rendering of modern emulsions had destroyed the crude black-and-white effects which had given the photographic picture the abstractness of a wood-cut. There was now a clear contradiction in seeing knockabouts moving in a perfectly real everyday-world. This inherent disunion between reality and fiction was less evident in films of a more normal type. But it concerned the cinema in general.

The unavoidable collaboration of reality had not only negative effects. On the contrary, after many years of film production it became very clear that the more lasting and profound impressions had not been given by the refined studio work. If the cinema wanted to stay the comparison with other activities of human culture it could not rely on the best part of those 'works of art' which were idolised within the frontiers of the film kingdom but faded away hopelessly when confronted with the simplest Mozart minuet or Rembrandt drawing. But it could rely on some of the Russian films, on the large production of documentary and scientific films and, to a certain extent, on the half-documentary cinema of the Flaherty, Dalsheim and Fanck type. This means that the cinema has given its best

8. Reality distorted: *The Cabinet of Dr Caligari*

where its work has been based on the natural expressiveness of the real fact. Being prevented by reality from reaching the very heights of free creation it has used reality to produce values which by no other means can be given. It has transformed a drawback into an advantage.

The prerogative of reality has been decisively strengthened by the development of the film technique, the whole effort of which has been dedicated completely to perfect more and more the faithfulness of imitation. We already mentioned the panchromatic emulsions and the improvement of lighting. But the turning point was given by the introduction of the spoken word. This represented an enormous progress in the recording of real facts but deprived the film art of two essential qualities: the disintegration of the continuity of space and time and the independence of the camera from the actor. Attempts to save the agility of the picture by limiting the use of the spoken word to small doses represented the sacrifice of the new means without preservation of the old one. As to colour, the richest means of pictorial expression, it also completed considerably the faithfulness of reproduction but confined the film to the rendering of local colour, i.e. fixed the optical character of every object whereas the monochromatic film allowed to give every object, by means of the lighting, nearly every desired shade from black to white. (As I cannot give here a full demonstration of these facts I have to refer—beyond my book on 'Film'—to my theory of the talking film which I exposed in a booklet 'New Laocoon' published in Italian in 1938 by the Rome Film School Centro Sperimentale and to an article on colour film previously published by *Sight and Sound*.)

The only conclusion from all these facts could be that the cinema was destined, by its own nature, for the complete and faithful reproduction of reality and that its development tended to this aim. Such a theory seemed rather daring and heretical but happened recently to be confirmed by the facts in a surprising way. It began when the newsreel, in search of a method which should allow it to give a more complete survey of the present-day events, added reconstructed scenes to the actual documents of reality. Personages of contemporary history were represented by actors, real events were remade in the studio.

Of course, such a method involves serious dangers. As it pretends to give the authentic truth fiction becomes falsification. Even if the utmost is done to prevent subjective interpretations—a thing which is almost beyond human power—the mere fact that fictive and authentic material is indistinguishably melted in a whole tends to spoil our sense of reality. If a thing pretends to be the whole truth and nothing but the truth it cannot be allowed to smuggle in stage performances.

The enormous success of this new type of newsreel had an immediate influence on the narrative film. Authenticity was a new attraction for a public surfeited with fiction of the most superficial and monotonous kind and now a method had been demonstrated how to mix the two elements. The film *Confessions of a Nazi Spy* was launched with the claim to be a faithful reproduction of facts. Actors assumed the parts of well-known personages of our time; newsreel material was sporadically inserted. Although a very efficient piece of propaganda, the film was apt to cause a feeling of uneasiness. Because whereas on the stage such a performance would clearly appear as a reconstruction, the very fact that it is given in photographic pictures—which are able to reproduce real events—creates an illusion of authenticity, which is inadmissible for a work of fiction.

It must be fully realised that—from the point of view of moral responsibility—a very delicate situation arises as soon as instead of using reality as an element of fiction we begin to use fiction as an element of reality. A very interesting example is given by the recent film *The Lion Has Wings* [1939, directed by Michael Powell, Brian Desmond Hurst and Adrian Brunel]. This film must be considered as a milestone in the history

9. Reality reconstructed: *The Lion Has Wings*

of the cinema because it represents an almost dramatic attempt to eliminate the element of fiction from the feature film. Although unique in its kind, it determines exactly the point which the development of the cinema has now reached. In comparison with the immediate strength of this type of film, all the other films of the usual kind appear suddenly pale and old-fashioned. They seem artificial without being art, whereas the RAF film shows how the mere sticking to the facts produces, I would say, automatically more dignity and a keener human interest.

Documentary and reconstructed material is mixed in this film, and the reconstructions give the effect of a foreign substance; not only because the documentary scenes are very strong but also because the meaning even of the reconstructed scenes lies so exclusively in the facts that no actor's art seems necessary to give them a psychological content. When the RAF central station is shown where the vigilance and presence of mind of a few men has to guarantee the security of a whole country it seems superfluous if not positively unpleasant to stress the pathetic fact by means of acting. It is true that a reconstruction in the studio gives better and clearer pictures and that to the man in the street an actor personating an airman seems more 'real' because more expressive than a real airman. But if the cinema has any mission at all then it is to demonstrate that the few pictures which show the real raiders of Kiel alighting from their 'planes are much more effective and worthy to be looked at than the expression of cheerful courage which any actor can easily give to his face.

The clash between documentary and fictive material is very obvious in one of the opening scenes when two women are listening in to the speech of the Prime Minister of September 3rd. The speech is taken from the authentic record whereas the women are performed by actresses. Although the performance is of good taste something appears very clearly to be wrong with the combination of the two things.

Of course we are not going to condemn fiction in itself. All art justifies by the fact that fiction can give a higher truth than reality. But as it is not art's task to reproduce reality art is out of place where reality shall be reproduced. The question is to know whether, in the future, the cinema will try to go on with fiction or to go over completely to authenticity.

The documentary cinema reduces narration to a minimum. It cannot substitute the narrative film as a mass-entertainment. But it appears that the cinema, in the present state of its technique, has only two ways to get rid of its hybridism. Either it becomes photographic theatre—and it is well to remember that television, which is probably destined to supersede the cinema, succeeds only with the most artificial efforts to introduce some simple cinematographic devices into its theatrical technique. Or it becomes reproduction of reality.

We do not want to prophesy. But it seems necessary to become conscious of the facts and to face the consequences.

1940

Charlie the Kid

S. M. EISENSTEIN

The Kid. The name of this most popular of Chaplin's films is fully worthy to stand side by side with his own name: It helps to reveal his character role just as the prefixes: 'The Conquerer', 'The Lion Heart', or the 'Terrible' themselves determine the inner aspects of William who conquered the Islands of Great Britain, of the legendary courageous Richard of the Crusades or the wise Moscovite Tsar Ivan Vasilievitch the Fourth.

Not Direction. Not Method. Not Tricks. Not the Comic Technique. None of these things move me. I do not wish to delve into these things.

In thinking about Chaplin, one wants above all to delve into that strange structure of thought which sees Phenomena in such a strange fashion and replies to it with images of equal strangeness. And within that struggle—to see that part which exists as a stage of perception of the outside world, before it becomes a conception of the world.

In short, we shall not concern ourselves with Chaplin's world outlook (Weltanschauung) but with his life-perception which gives birth to the inimitable and unrepeatable conceptions of the so-called Chaplin humour.

The fields of vision of a rabbit's eyes overlap behind the back of its head. He sees behind him. Condemned to run away, rather than to track down, he doesn't complain about that. But these fields of vision do not overlap each other in front. In front of a rabbit is a piece of space it does not see. And a rabbit running forward may bump into an opposing obstacle.

The rabbit sees the world in another fashion than we.

A different kind of vision produces accordingly a different kind of picture-image.

Not to speak of the higher transformation of *vision* into a *look* and then to a *point of view* that takes place the moment we rise from the rabbit to Man, with all his surrounding social factors. Till finally all this is synthesised into a world-outlook, a philosophy of life.

How the eyes are placed—in the given instance the eyes of thought. How those eyes see. Unusual eyes.

The eyes of Chaplin.

Eyes, able to see Dante's Inferno or Goya's Capriccio theme of 'Modern Times' in the forms of careless merriment?

With what eyes does Charlie Chaplin look on life?

'The Secret of his Eyes' is undoubtedly revealed in *Modern Times*. As long as he was concerned with the pleiad of the most beautiful of his comedies, of the clash of good and evil, of big and little, his eyes as if accidentally and simultaneously lighting on the poor and the rich—laughed and cried in unison with his theme. But they apparently went contrary to their own theme when in the most modern times of American depression the good and evil 'Uncles' turned out to be the real representatives of uncompromising social groups, at which the eyes of Chaplin first

10. *Modern Times*

blinked, then narrowed, but continued obstinately to look at modern times and phenomena in the old way. This led to a break in the style of things. In thematic treatment—to the monstrous and distorted.

In the inner aspect of Chaplin himself—to a complete revelation of the secret of his eyes.

In the following deliberation I do not at all wish to say that Chaplin is indifferent to what is happening around him or that Chaplin does not understand it (even maybe partly).

I am not interested in *what* he understands.

I am interested in how he perceives. How he looks and sees, when he is lost 'in inspiration'. When he comes across a series of images of phenomena, which he is laughing at, and when laughter at what he perceives is remoulded into the forms of comic situations and tricks: and with what eyes one must look at the world, in order to see it as Chaplin sees it.

A group of delightful Chinese children are laughing.
One shot. Another. Close up. Mid shot. Again close up.
What are they laughing at?
Apparently at a scene taking place in the depths of the room.
What is taking place there?
A man sinks back on a bed. He is apparently drunk.
And a tiny woman—a Chinese slaps him on the face furiously.
The children are overcome with uncontrollable laughter.
Although the man is their father. And the little China-woman their mother. And the big man is not drunk. And it is not for drunkenness the little wife is hitting him on the face.
The man is dead . . .
And she is slapping the deceased on the face precisely because he died and left to a hungry death, she and the two little children, who laugh so ringingly.

That, of course, is not from one of Chaplin's films. These are passing strokes from that wonderful novel of André Malraux *The Condition of Human Existence.*

In thinking of Chaplin, I always see him in the image of that merrily laughing little Chinese, seeing how comically the hand-slaps of the little woman make the head of the big man wobble from side to side. It is not important that the Chinese woman—is the mother. That the man—is the father. And it is not at all important that in general he is dead.

In that is the secret of Chaplin.

In that is the secret of his eyes.

In that is his inimitability.

In that is his greatness.

To see things most terrible, most pitiful, most tragic through the eyes of a laughing child.

To see the images of these things spontaneously and suddenly—outside their moral-ethical significance, outside valuation and outside judgment and condemnation—to see them as a child sees them through a burst of laughter.

In that Chaplin is outstanding, inimitable and unique.

The sudden immediacy of his look gives birth to a comic perception. This perception becomes transformed into a conception. Conceptions are of three kinds:

A phenomenon genuinely inoffensive. And Chaplin's perception clothes it with his inimitable Chaplinesque buffoonery.

A phenomenon personally dramatic.—And Chaplin's perception gives birth to the humorous melodrama of the finest images of his individual style—the fusion of laughter with tears.

The blind girl will call forth a smile when, without noticing it, she throws water over Charlie.

The girl with her sight restored might appear melodramatic when in touching him with her hand she does not fully realise that before her is the one who loves her and gave her back her sight. And then within that very incident the melodrama may be comically stood on its head—the blind girl repeats the episodes with the 'Bon-vivant', saved by Charlie from suicide: in which the 'Bon-vivant' only recognises his saviour and friend when he is 'blind'-drunk.

Finally, *socially-tragic phenomena*—no longer a childish amusement, not a problem for a mind, not a child's plaything—the comical—childish vision gives birth to a series of terrible shots in *Modern Times*.

The ability to *see as a child*—is inimitable, irrepeatable, inherent in Chaplin personally. Only Chaplin sees this way. What astounds is this very quality of Chaplin's sight to see piercingly and immutably through all the workings of professional cunning.

Always and in everything: From the trifle *A Night at the Show* to the tragedy of contemporary society in *Modern Times*.

To see the world thus and have the courage to show it thus on the screen is the attribute of Genius alone.

Incidentally, he doesn't even need courage.

For that is the way, and the only way, he sees.

We are grown-ups, and maybe have lost the ability to laugh at the comic without taking into consideration its tragic significance and content.

We are grown-ups, who have lost the time of 'lawless' childhood, when there were as yet no ethics, morals, higher critical values, etc., etc., etc.

Chaplin plays up to actuality itself.

It is the bloody idiocy of war in the film *Shoulder Arms*. The modern era of the most modern times in *Modern Times*. Chaplin's partner—is by no means the big, terrible, powerful and ruthless fat man, who, when not filming, runs a restaurant in Hollywood.

Chaplin's partner, throughout his repertoire—is another. Still bigger, still more terrible, powerful and ruthless. Chaplin and actuality itself, partners together, a pair in harness, play before us an endless string of circus acts. Actuality is like a serious 'white' clown.

He seems clever and logical. Observant and foresighted. But it is he finally who remains the fool and is laughed at. His simple, childlike partner Charlie comes out on top. Laughing carelessly, without being aware that his laughter kills his partner.

Chaplin works 'in a pair' with actuality. And that which a satirist is obliged to introduce into the given production by means of two shots, the comedian Chaplin does in one shot. He laughs spontaneously. Satiric indirectness is created by a 'mix' of the grimaces of Chaplin back on to the conditions which gave birth to them.

'You remember the scene in *The Kid* where I scatter food from a box to poor children as if they were chickens?'

This conversation takes place on board Chaplin's yacht. We have been his guest for three days on the waters near Catarina Island, surrounded

11. *City Lights*

by sea-lions, flying fish and undersea gardens, which we look at through the glass bottoms of special little boats.

'You see I did that because I despise them. I don't like children.'

The creator of *The Kid*, which five-sixths of the world cried over, because of the fate of an orphan child, does not like children. He is a 'Beast'!

But who *normally* does not like children?

Only—children themselves.

Six months later, on the day I was leaving Mexico, Chaplin showed me the rough cutting copy, as yet without sound, of *City Lights*.

I sit on Chaplin's own black oilcloth chair. Charlie himself is busy: At the piano, with his lips he fills in the missing sound editing of the picture. Charlie (in the film) saves the life of a drunken Bourgeois who tries to drown himself. The saved only recognises his saviour when he is drunk.

Funny?—tragic.

That is Saltykov-Schedrin.[1] That is Dostoyevsky.

The big one beats the little one. He is beaten up.

At first—man by man. Then more—man by society.

Once, long ago, there was a widely popular photograph either in the London *Sketch* or the *Graphic*.

'Stop for his Highness the Child!' was the title under it.

The photograph depicted an impetuous flood of street traffic, in Bond Street, Strand or Piccadilly Circus, suddenly freezing at the wave of a 'Bobby's' hand.

Across the street goes a child, and the flood of traffic humbly waits, until his Highness the Baby crosses from pavement to pavement.

'Stop for His Highness the Child!' one wants to shout to oneself, when attempting to approach Chaplin from a social-ethical and moral position in the widest and deepest sense of these words.

'Stop.'

Let's take His Highness as he is!

1946
(Translated by Herbert Marshall)

---

[1]Michael Saltykov, who wrote under the name of Schedrin, a writer of genius, and one of the world's greatest satirists.

Letter: *The Birth of a Nation*

D. W. GRIFFITH

My attention has been directed to Mr Peter Noble's attack against myself and certain of my films (*The Birth of a Nation*, etc.) in the Autumn, 1946, issue of *Sight and Sound*. This attack charges me with having projected in these films bias against, and hatred of, the Negro race.

I have also read an advance copy of a reply which Mr Seymour Stern, author of the Griffith Index and my biographer, has written to Mr Noble refuting his charges. Mr Stern informs me that this reply is scheduled for publication this Spring in *Sight and Sound*.

Mr Stern has, I believe, presented the facts adequately and effectively. I have nothing to add to them, but for myself, I will take this occasion of Lincoln's birthday to request that you permit me to say just this:

I am not now and never have been 'anti-Negro' or 'anti' any other race. My attitude towards the Negroes has always been one of affection and brotherly feeling. I was partly raised by a lovable old Negress down in old Kentucky and I have always gotten along extremely well with the Negro people.

In filming 'The Birth of a Nation', I gave to my best knowledge the proven facts, and presented the known truth, about the Reconstruction period in the American South. These facts are based on an overwhelming compilation of authentic evidence and testimony. My picturisation of history as it happens requires, therefore, no apology, no defence, no 'explanations'. I regret that Mr Noble, whose remarks do not appear to be based either on historic fact or personal experience, has made even this statement of the self-evident truth of my film necessary. [...]

Beverly Hills,
California.

Very truly yours,
DAVID WARK GRIFFITH

12 February 1947

Oscar Night in Hollywood

RAYMOND CHANDLER

Five or six years ago a distinguished writer-director (if I may be permitted the epithet in connection with a Hollywood personage) was co-author of a screen play nominated for an Academy Award. He was too nervous to attend the proceedings on the big night, so he was listening to a broadcast at home, pacing the floor tensely, chewing his fingers, taking long breaths, scowling and debating with himself in hoarse whispers whether to stick it out until the Oscars were announced, or turn the damned radio off and read about it in the papers the next morning. Getting a little tired of all this artistic temperament in the home, his wife suddenly came up with one of those awful remarks which achieve a wry immortality in Hollywood: 'For Pete's sake, don't take it so seriously, darling. After all, Luise Rainer won it twice.'

To those who did not see the famous telephone scene in *The Great Ziegfeld*, or any of the subsequent versions of it which Miss Rainer played in other pictures, with and without telephone, this remark will lack punch. To others it will serve as well as anything to express that cynical despair with which Hollywood people regard their own highest distinction. It isn't so much that the awards never go to the fine achievements as that those fine achievements are not rewarded as such. They are rewarded as fine achievements in box office hits. You can't be an All-American on a losing team. Technically, they are voted, but actually they are not decided by the use of whatever artistic and critical wisdom Hollywood may happen to possess. They are ballyhooed, pushed, yelled, screamed, and in every way propagandised into the consciousness of the voters so incessantly, in the weeks before the final balloting, that everything except the golden aura of the box office is forgotten.

The Motion Picture Academy, at considerable expense and with great efficiency, runs all the nominated pictures at its own theatre, showing each picture twice, once in the afternoon and once in the evening. A nominated picture is one in connection with which any kind of work is nominated for an award, not necessarily acting, directing, or writing; it may be a purely technical matter such as set-dressing or sound work. This running of pictures has the object of permitting voters to look at films which they may happen to have missed or to have partly forgotten. It is an attempt to make them realise that pictures released early in the year and since overlaid with several thicknesses of battered celluloid, are still in the running and that consideration of only those released a short time before the end of the year is not quite just.

The effort is largely a waste. The people with the votes don't go to these showings. They send their relatives, friends, or servants. They have had enough of looking at pictures, and the voices of destiny are by no means inaudible in the Hollywood air. They have a brassy tone, but they are more than distinct.

All this is good democracy of a sort. We elect Congressmen and Presidents in much the same way, so why not actors, cameramen, writers, and all the rest of the people who have to do with the making of pictures? If we permit noise, ballyhoo, and bad theatre to influence us in the selection of the people who are to run the country, why should we object to the same methods in the selection of meritorious achievement in the film business? If we can huckster a President into the White House, why cannot we huckster the agonised Miss Joan Crawford or the hard and beautiful Miss Olivia de Havilland into possession of one of those golden statuettes which express the motion picture industry's frantic desire to kiss itself on the back of the neck? The only answer I can think of is that the motion picture is an art. I say this with a very small voice. It is an inconsiderable statement and has a hard time not sounding a little ludicrous. Nevertheless, it is a fact, not in the least diminished by the further fact that its ethos is so far pretty low and that its techniques are dominated by some pretty awful people.

If you think most motion pictures are bad, which they are (including the foreign), find out from some initiate how they are made, and you will be astonished that any of them could be good. Making a fine motion picture is like painting 'The Laughing Cavalier' in Macy's basement, with a floorwalker to mix your colours for you. Of course, most motion pictures are bad. Why wouldn't they be? Apart from its own intrinsic handicaps of excessive cost, hypercritical bluenosed censorship, and the lack of any single-minded controlling force in the making, the motion picture is bad because 90 per cent is a little too virile and plain-spoken for the putty-minded clerics, the elderly ingenues of the women's clubs, and the tender guardians of that godawful mixture of boredom and bad manners known more eloquently as the Impressionable Age.

The point is not whether there are bad motion pictures or even whether the average motion picture is bad, but whether the motion picture is an artistic medium of sufficient dignity and accomplishment to be treated with respect by the people who control its destinies. Those who deride the motion picture usually are satisfied that they have thrown the book at it by declaring it to be a form of mass entertainment. As if that meant anything. Greek drama, which is still considered quite respectable by most intellectuals, was mass entertainment to the Athenian freeman. So, within its economic and topographical limits, was the Elizabethan drama. The great cathedrals of Europe, although not exactly built to while away an afternoon, certainly had an æsthetic and spiritual effect on the ordinary man. Today, if not always, the fugues and chorales of Bach, the symphonies of Mozart, Borodin, and Brahms, the violin concertos of Vivaldi, the piano sonatas of Scarlatti, and a great deal of what was once rather recondite music are mass entertainment by virtue of radio. Not all fools love it, but not all fools love anything more literate than a comic-strip. It might reasonably be said that all art at some time and in some manner becomes mass entertainment, and that if it does not it dies and is forgotten.

The motion picture admittedly is faced with too large a mass; it must please too many people and offend too few, the second of these restrictions being infinitely more damaging to it artistically than the first. The people who sneer at the motion picture as an art form are furthermore seldom willing to consider it at its best. They insist upon judging it by the picture they saw last week or yesterday; which is even more absurd (in view of the sheer quantity of production) than to judge literature by last week's ten best sellers, or the dramatic art by even the best of the current Broadway hits. In a novel you can still say what you like, and the stage is free almost to the point of obscenity, but the motion picture made in Hollywood, if it is to create art at all, must do so within such strangling limitations of subject and treatment that it is a blind wonder it ever achieves any distinction beyond the purely mechanical slickness of a glass and chromium bathroom. If it were merely a transplanted literary or dramatic art, it certainly would not. The hucksters and the bluenoses between them would see to that.

But the motion picture is *not* a transplanted literary or dramatic art, any more than it is a plastic art. It has elements of all these, but in its essential structure it is much closer to music, in the sense that its finest effects can be independent of precise meaning, that its transitions can be more eloquent than its high-lit scenes, and that its dissolves and camera movements, which cannot be censored, are often far more emotionally effective than its plots, which can. Not only is the motion picture an art, but it is the one entirely new art that has been evolved on this planet for hundreds of years. It is the only art at which we of this generation have any possible chance to greatly excel.

In painting, music, and architecture we are not even second-rate by comparison with the best work of the past. In sculpture we are just funny. In prose literature we not only lack style but we lack the educational and historical background to know what style is. Our fiction and drama are adept, empty, often intriguing, and so mechanical that in another fifty years at most they will be produced by machines with rows of push buttons. We have no popular poetry in the grand style, merely delicate or witty or bitter or obscure verses. Our novels are transient propaganda when they are what is called 'significant', and bedtime reading when they are not.

But in the motion picture we possess an art medium whose glories are not all behind us. It has already produced great work, and if, comparatively and proportionately, far too little of that great work has been achieved in Hollywood, I think that is all the more reason why in its annual tribal dance of the stars and the big-shot producers Hollywood should contrive a little quiet awareness of the fact. Of course it won't. I'm just daydreaming.

Show business has always been a little overnoisy, overdressed, overbrash. Actors are threatened people. Before films came along to make them rich they often had need of a desperate gaiety. Some of these qualities prolonged beyond a strict necessity have passed into the Hollywood mores and produced that very exhausting thing, the Hollywood manner, which is a chronic case of spurious excitement over absolutely nothing. Nevertheless, and for once in a lifetime, I have to admit that Academy Awards night is a good show and quite funny in spots, although I'll admire you if you can laugh at all of it.

If you can go past those awful idiot faces on the bleachers outside the theatre without a sense of the collapse of the human intelligence; if you can stand the hailstorm of flash bulbs popping at the poor patient actors who, like kings and queens, have never the right to look bored; if you can glance out over the gathered assemblage of what is supposed to be the elite of Hollywood and say to yourself without a sinking feeling, 'In these hands lie the destinies of the only original art the modern world has conceived'; if you can laugh, and you probably will, at the cast-off jokes from the comedians on the stage, stuff that wasn't good enough to use on their radio shows; if you can stand the fake sentimentality and the platitudes of the officials and the mincing elocution of the glamour queens (you ought to hear them with four martinis down the hatch); if you can do all these things with grace and pleasure, and not have a wild and forsaken horror at the thought that most of these people actually take this shoddy performance seriously; and if you can then go out into the night to see half the police force of Los Angeles gathered to protect the golden ones from the mob in the free seats but not from that awful moaning sound they give out, like destiny whistling through a hollow shell; if you can do all these things and still feel next morning that the picture business is worth the attention of one single intelligent, artistic mind, then in the picture business you certainly belong, because this sort of vulgarity is part of its inevitable price.

Glancing over the programme of the Awards before the show starts, one is apt to forget that this is really an actors', directors', and big-shot producers' rodeo. It is for the people who *make* pictures (they think), not just for the people who work on them. But these gaudy characters are a kindly bunch at heart: they know that a lot of small-fry characters in minor technical jobs, such as cameramen, musicians, cutters, writers, soundmen, and the inventors of new equipment, have to be given something to amuse them and make them feel mildly elated. So the performance was formerly divided into two parts, with an intermission. On the occasion I attended, however, one of the Masters of Ceremony (I forget which—there was a steady stream of them, like bus passengers) announced that there would be no intermission this year and that they would proceed immediately to the *important* part of the programme.

Let me repeat, the *important part of the programme.*

Perverse fellow that I am, I found myself intrigued by the unimportant part of the programme also. I found my sympathies engaged by the lesser ingredients of picture-making, some of which have been enumerated above. I was intrigued by the efficiently quick on-and-off that was given to these minnows of the picture business; by their nervous attempts via the microphone to give most of the credit for their work to some stuffed shirt in a corner office; by the fact that technical developments which may mean millions of dollars to the industry, and may on occasion influence the whole procedure of picture-making, are just not worth explaining to the audience at all; by the casual, cavalier treatment given to film-editing and to camera work, two of the essential arts of film-making, almost and sometimes quite equal to direction, and much more important than all but the very best acting; intrigued most of all, perhaps, by the formal tribute which is invariably made to the importance of the writer, without whom, my dear, dear friends, nothing could be done at all, but who is for all that merely the climax of the *unimportant* part of the programme.

I am also intrigued by the voting. It was formerly done by all the members of all the various guilds, including the extras and the bit players. Then it was realised that this gave too much voting power to rather unimportant groups, so the voting on various classes of awards was restricted to the guilds which were presumed to have some critical intelligence on the subject. Evidently this did not work either, and the next change was to have the nominating done by the specialist guilds, and the final voting only by the members of the Academy of Motion Picture Arts and Sciences.

It doesn't really seem to make much difference how the voting is done. The quality of the work is still only recognised in the context of success. A superb job in a flop picture would get you nothing, a routine job in a winner will be voted in. It is against this background of success-worship that the voting is done, with the incidental music supplied by a stream of advertising in the trade papers (which even intelligent people read in Hollywood) designed to put all other pictures than those advertised out of

12. *The Best Years of Our Lives*: Oscar-winner, 1946

your head at balloting time. The psychological effect is very great on minds conditioned to thinking of merit solely in terms of box office and ballyhoo. The members of the Academy live in this atmosphere, and they are enormously suggestible people, as are all workers in Hollywood. If they are contracted to studios, they are made to feel that it is a matter of group patriotism to vote for the products of their own lot. They are informally advised not to waste their votes, not to plump for something that can't win, especially something made on another lot.

I do not feel any profound conviction, for example, as to whether *The Best Years of Our Lives* was even the best Hollywood motion picture of 1946. It depends what you mean by best. It had a first-class director, some fine actors, and the most appealing sympathy gag in years. It probably had as much all-round distinction as Hollywood is presently capable of. That it had the kind of clean and simple art possessed by *Open City* or the stalwart and magnificent impact of *Henry V* only an idiot would claim. In a sense it did not have art at all. It had that kind of sentimentality which is almost but not quite humanity, and that kind of adeptness which is almost but not quite style. And it had them in large doses, which always helps.

The governing board of the Academy is at great pains to protect the honesty and secrecy of the voting. It is done by anonymous numbered ballots, and the ballots are sent, not to any agency of the motion picture industry, but to a well-known firm of public accountants. The results, in sealed envelopes, are borne by an emissary of the firm right on to the stage of the theatre where the Awards are to be made, and there for the first time, they are made known. Surely precaution could go no further. No one could possibly have known in advance any of these results, not even in Hollywood where every agent learns the closely guarded secrets of the studios with no apparent trouble. If there are secrets in Hollywood, which I sometimes doubt, this voting ought to be one of them.

As for a deeper kind of honesty, I think it is about time for the Academy of Motion Picture Arts and Sciences to use a little of it up by declaring in a forthright manner that foreign pictures are outside competition and will remain so until they face the same economic situation and the same strangling censorship that Hollywood faces. It is all very well to say how clever and artistic the French are, how true to life, what subtle actors they have, what an honest sense of the earth, what forthrightness in dealing with the bawdy side of life. The French can afford these things, we cannot. To the Italians they are permitted, to us they are denied. Even the English possess a freedom we lack. How much did *Brief Encounter* cost? It would have cost at least a million and a half in Hollywood; in order to get that money back, and the distribution costs on top of the negative costs, it would have had to contain innumerable crowd-pleasing ingredients, the very lack of which is what makes it a good picture.

Since the Academy is not an International tribunal of film art it should stop pretending to be one. If foreign pictures have no practical chance whatsoever of winning a major award they should not be nominated. At the very beginning of the performance in 1947 a special Oscar was awarded to Laurence Olivier for *Henry V*, although it was among those nominated as the best picture of the year. There could be no more obvious way of saying that it was not going to win. A couple of minor technical awards and a couple of minor writing awards were also given to foreign pictures, but nothing that ran into important coin, just side meat. Whether these awards were deserved is beside the point, which is that they were minor awards and were intended to be minor awards, and that there was no possibility whatsoever of any foreign-made picture winning a major award.

To outsiders it might appear that something devious went on here. To those who know Hollywood, all that went on was the secure knowledge and awareness that the Oscars exist for and by Hollywood, their standards and problems are the standards and problems of Hollywood, their purpose is to maintain the supremacy of Hollywood, and their phoniness is the phoniness of Hollywood. But the Academy cannot, without appearing ridiculous, maintain the pose of internationalism by tossing a few minor baubles to the foreigners while carefully keeping all the top drawer jewellery for itself. As a writer I resent that writing awards should be among the baubles, and as a member of the Motion Picture Academy I resent its trying to put itself in a position which its annual performance before the public shows it is quite unfit to occupy.

If the actors and actresses like the silly show, and I'm not sure at all the best of them do, they at least know how to look elegant in a strong light, and how to make with the wide-eyed and oh, so humble little speeches as if they believed them. If the big producers like it, and I'm quite sure they do because it contains the only ingredients they really understand— promotion values and the additional grosses that go with them—the producers at least know what they are fighting for. But if the quiet, earnest, and slightly cynical people who really make motion pictures like it, and I'm quite sure they don't, well, after all, it comes only once a year, and it's no worse than a lot of the sleazy vaudeville they have to push out of the way to get their work done.

Of course, that's not quite the point either. The head of a large studio once said privately that in his candid opinion the motion picture business was 25 per cent honest business and the other 75 per cent pure conniving. He didn't say anything about art, although he may have heard of it. But that *is* the real point, isn't it?—whether these annual Awards regardless of the grotesque ritual that accompanies them, really represent anything at all of artistic importance to the motion picture medium, anything clear and honest that remains after the lights are dimmed, the minks put away, and the aspirin is swallowed? I don't think they do. I think they are just theatre and not even good theatre. As for the personal prestige that goes with winning an Oscar, it may with luck last long enough for your agent to get your contract re-written and your price jacked up another notch. But over the years and in the hearts of men of good will? I hardly think so.

Once upon a time a once very successful Hollywood lady decided (or was forced) to sell her lovely furnishings at auction, together with her lovely home. On the day before she moved out she was showing a party of her friends through the house for a private view. One of them noticed that the lady was using her two golden Oscars as doorstops. It seemed they were just about the right weight, and she had sort of forgotten they were gold.

1950

Bicycle Thieves

RICHARD WINNINGTON

De Sica's *Bicycle Thieves*, like Rossellini's *Paisà* came to London with a fabulous reputation to live up to, and, in a way, to live down. To *Paisà*, a film made in a state of almost feverish immediacy, the two-year gap between continental and London showings was costly. The crudities inseparable from Rossellini's hotfoot production methods took on larger proportions, the film's courageous humanity had lost perhaps some of its heat in retrospect. In any case, the London critics found cause to lower the film's status. Public audiences had fewer quibbles.

The word 'great' was affixed to De Sica's film by Clair, Becker, Lean, Cavalcanti, Ustinov and numbers of travellers from Italy as long as a year ago, when a percipient British exhibitor could have bought it for a quarter of the price (£5,000) eventually paid. Confronted with a reputed masterpiece that turned out to be a masterpiece, the British Press came fairly clean. There were little murmured warnings about 'slightness', and a ludicrous belittlement from a prominent critic who smelled communism—the self-same critic, it will be remembered, who gave Vigo's *Zéro de Conduite* 'zero for achievement and one for trying'. But the reviews, guarded or otherwise, were sufficient to start *Bicycle Thieves* on what may well be the most successful record of any foreign film in British cinemas.

Bicycle Thieves is a wholly satisfying film in that De Sica has so simplified and mastered the mechanics of the job that nothing stands between you and his intention. It can be likened to a painting that is formed in an intensity of concentration, and is as good as finished before it reaches the canvas. In fact, *Bicycle Thieves*, as a film properly should, relates to plastic and in no sense to dramatic or literary art. De Sica displays this with the opening compilation of visuals, which at once places his family in an environment of slow, sapping industrial poverty, where the bicycle and the bed linen represent the last claims of domestic pride, and where the pawnshop and the tenement fortune-teller batten on misery. It is, needless to say, a Rome the visitor sees though seldom penetrates, but where, before the war, he might have admired the triumphs of Mussolini's industrial architecture.

At the same time and with the same economy, De Sica draws his family portrait group. An unemployed artisan with baffled dreams of security, a young wife with fading looks and breaking temper, a small boy full of premature knowledge who mingles criticism of his father with worship, and clownish innocence with precocious responsibility. De Sica may have been lucky with this amazing child (Enzo Staiola), with the father and with nearly all the rest of his unprofessional cast, but he spent a long time and used a rare instinct in finding them.

For all that, by some process of magnetism, De Sica has drawn from this boy an unparalleled child performance, it is the man who is his symbol of the human plight. He is the helpless individual, herded with, yet isolated from his fellows, who is caught in a situation. To De Sica and many Italians who have absorbed their Kafka and Sartre, this is the general theme of the century. It might be said to parallel the situation of Italy herself.

The story of that heartrending Sunday search after the stolen bicycle is

13. *Bicycle Thieves*

now too familiar to bear retelling. Its simplicity, far from being evidence of slightness, is the outcome of a discipline that has rigorously set itself against any facile effects of 'poetry', but has evolved a complex pattern of mood and incident. The ironies, humours, oddities and heartbreaks of this adventure in the modern jungle connect with the experience of any town-dweller who has been isolated at some time or times by misfortune, great or small, and finds his familiar world suddenly hostile and strange.

Bicycle Thieves is the true genre movie, and a superlative exercise in screen realism. Starting with his conception of the man and the boy, De Sica spent a year preparing the film. When it came to shooting, he found he had no need to refer to the script; the whole thing was clear in his mind. The fluid crowd scenes, so beautifully composed and natural, were obtained by roping off the streets with the help of the police, and enlisting the passers-by. The casual effects were all calculated.

De Sica's lifetime of experience in the theatre and cinema as a leading man and comedian (which led him to abjure the professional actor) may account for his power to compel those flawless performances from his amateurs. But it is a painter's instinct, probably inherited from his mother, which enriches his films with such comprehensive detail. His detached compassion, his sense of irony, his tolerant understanding, are the fruits of long study of his fellow men in difficult times. Anger does not show in his films, and anger is a concomitant of hope. Yet I do not find the conclusion of *Bicycle Thieves* wholly pessimistic. Comradeship did to some extent sustain this man and doubtless, one feels, will do so again.

With *Bicycle Thieves*, De Sica considers he has sufficiently exploited 'realism' for the moment. An artist who has found his true medium somewhat late in life, he possesses an unpredictable capacity for development. And in Cesare Zavattini he has found the scriptwriter who can play Prévert to his Carné. Their next film (the third of the trilogy which *Shoeshine* started), will essay a new form—'irrealism'. De Sica claims that in this film, *The Poor Disturb*, he will make 'the unreal seem real, the improbable seem probable, and the impossible seem possible' without the use of camera tricks. This could mean plain fantasy or, preferably, an experimental attempt to go beyond literal vision in the way Jean Vigo did. But the structure will be realistic, the actors non-professional, and their milieu the slums of Milan. De Sica believes in poor people.

1950

Sunset Boulevard

JAMES AGEE

Charles Brackett and Billy Wilder have a long and honourable record in bucking tradition, breaking rules, and taking risks, according to their lights, and limits. Nobody thought they could get away with *Double Indemnity*, but they did; nobody thought they could get away with *The Lost Weekend*, but they did; apparently nobody thought they could get away with *Sunset Boulevard*, but they did; and now, one gathers, the industry is proud of them. There are plenty of good reasons why *Sunset Boulevard* (a beautiful title) is, I think, their best movie yet. It is Hollywood craftsmanship at its smartest and at just about its best, and it is hard to find better craftsmanship than that, at this time, in any art or country.

It is also, in terms of movie tradition, a very courageous picture. A sexual affair between a rich woman of fifty and a kept man half her age is not exactly a usual version of boy meets girl; nor is it customary for the hero and his best friend's fiancée to fall in love and like it; nor, as a rule, is a movie hero so weak and so morally imperfect that he can less properly be called a 'Hero' than an authentic, unlucky and unadmirable human being. 'Unhappy endings' are not so rare, by now, but it is rare to find one as skilful, spectacular and appropriate as this one. Besides all that, *Sunset Boulevard* is much the most ambitious movie about Hollywood ever done, and is the best of several good ones into the bargain.

It is unlikely that any living men know Hollywood better than Brackett and Wilder; most of their portrait is brilliantly witty and evocative, and much of it is also very sharp. It seems to me, however, that this is essentially a picture-maker's picture. I very much enjoy and respect it, but it seems significant to me that among other interested amateurs there is a wide difference of reaction, ranging from moderate liking or disappointment all the way to boredom, intense dislike, or even contempt. Judging by that it is hard to imagine that it will do very well before the general audience, interesting and exciting as it is, unless through some miracle of ballyhoo. I suspect that its main weakness as popular art lies not so much in unconventionalities of story or character, as in its coldness. And if it falls short of greatness—and in my opinion it does—I suspect that coldness, again, is mainly responsible. However that may be, I am willing to bet that it will be looked at and respected long after most of the movies

14. *Sunset Boulevard* (Gloria Swanson)

too easily called great—not to mention the 'heartwarmers'—have been sat through and forgotten. However that may be, it is certainly something for anyone interested in movies to see here and now. It may not be all it might have been, but it is completely faithful to its own set, intelligent terms and, within those terms, all but perfect.

A moderately corrupt script-writer (William Holden), down on his luck and in flight from trouble, dodges his car into a chance driveway and into a world as strange and obsolete as that of ancient Peru: a home and grounds which are Hollywood of the mid-twenties in extremis, now in irremediable decay. The chatelaine is a great ex-star (Gloria Swanson). Half mad, suicidal, with the obsessed narcissistic arrogance of the once adored and long forgotten, for years she has been working on the awful script in which she plans her return to glory. Her only companion, her servant (Eric von Stroheim), was once a director as brilliant in his way as she, and was her first husband; he devotes his wrecked life to mending the leaks in her delusions. In part because of his need for a hideout, but fully as much because he is bewitched by curiosity, incredulity and a gradual crystallisation of awe and pity, the writer stays on in this hermetic world, as script-doctor, as half-imprisoned house-guest, ultimately as gigolo. He watches, while the woman is deluded into the belief that her return to the screen is only a matter of weeks; he watches while she uses every art and science available to Hollywood in her effort to turn fifty years into a camera-proof twenty-five; he watches while she sinks her talons and her desperate needs so deeply into him that escape, or the mere truth, without tragedy, becomes inconceivable. Meanwhile he carries on as best he may his effort to write a script of his own, with his best friend's girl (Nancy Olson); another love affair develops. The whole business culminates, inevitably, in a head-on collision between illusion and reality and between the old Hollywood and the new; and in staring madness, and violent death.

There is no use pretending to discuss all the virtues, or even all the limitations, of this picture: it is one of those rare movies which are so full of exactness, cleverness, mastery, pleasure, and arguable and unarguable choice and judgment, that they can be talked about, almost shot for shot and line for line for hours on end. The people of the present and their world are handled with a grimly controlled, mock-easy exactness which seems about as good as a certain kind of modified movie naturalism can get; this exactness is also imposed on the obsoletes and their world, but within that exactness they are treated always, with fine imaginativeness and eloquence, as heroic grotesques. Mr Holden and his girl and their friend (Jack Webb), not to mention Fred Clark acting a producer, are microscopically right in casting, direction and performance. Miss Swanson, required to play a hundred per cent grotesque, plays it not just to the hilt but right up to the armpit, by which I mean magnificently. Mr von Stroheim, with the one thoroughly sympathetic role, takes every advantage of that which is permissible to an artist's honour, and is probably the best single thing in the show. Miss Swanson's lonely New Year's Eve party, and the loud, happy little party to which Mr Holden escapes, are two of dozens of smashing proofs of mastery in conveying, and evoking, the living and the posthumous Hollywood.

Much of the detail is marvellously effective and clever; Miss Swanson watching her young face in an old movie and standing up into the murderous glare of the projector to cry: 'They don't make faces like that any more!' (they certainly don't and it is our loss); or the lighted swimming pool, so nicely calculated for the ultimate catastrophe. Sometimes the picture is a shade too clever for its own good: von Stroheim playing Bach on the organ, with gloves on, is wonderful in a way but possibly too weird, even for the context; and now and then a camera set-up or a bit of business or a line is so over-calculated, so obviously cherished, that it goes a little sour, much as the same thing can happen in prose which has gone rigid with overtraining. Yet one of the oddest and most calculated moments in the picture is also one of the best: the lingering, silent, terribly close close-up in which a soft, sleek clerk whispers to the slightly nauseated kept man: 'After all, if the lady is paying . . .' The intense physical and spiritual malaise of the young man's whole predicament is registered, through this brilliantly indirect shot, as it can never be, even in so bravely intransigent a movie, in a scene between him and Miss Swanson; and the clerk (and his casting) are as much to be thanked for that, as the man who conceived the shot.

Movies about Hollywood have always been better than novels about Hollywood (barring only Nathanael West's) because they are made by people who know the world and the medium they are talking about instead of by people who don't, and who have dropped in only to visit, hack or, in their opinion, slum. But almost inevitably, the view from inside is also limited. The manner of telling the story is apt to be gimmicky or too full of mere 'effectiveness' because that is apt to become a habit with nearly anyone who works in movies for long. Superficially, the self-examination and self-criticism are often a lot of fun and sometimes amount to more than that, but essentially they are apt to be easygoing or even complacent, because that seems nearly always to happen to those who work in movies long enough to know their business really well. (Literary standards, to be sure, are as seldom higher; but literary men who write about Hollywood seldom know—or care—how little they know, and perhaps accordingly, feel all the better qualified as annihilative critics.) It seems to me that the makers of *Sunset Boulevard* are at times too gimmicky, contriving, and 'effective'; on self criticism I am confused, as perhaps they are.

Largely through what is done with Miss Swanson, the silent era, and

15. *Sunset Boulevard* (William Holden, Gloria Swanson)

art, are granted a kind of barbarous grandeur and intensity, but the inference seems to be that they are also a good deal hammier than they actually were at their best. Further inference appears to be that the movies have come a long way since then. In many ways they have; in many other and important ways, this is open to argument and no such argument appears in this picture. On the other hand a great deal of truthfulness is achieved virtually without pointing or comment, by the people themselves. The lost people are given splendour, recklessness, an aura of awe; the contemporaries by comparison, are small, smart, safe-playing, incapable of any kind of grandeur, good or bad; and those who think they can improve or redeem the movies are largely just a bunch of what Producer Fred Clark aptly calls Message Kids, and compares with the New York critics. This is certainly a harsh picture of Hollywood; too harsh, considering some of the people who work there. By still quieter inference, of course, Hollywood is still essentially all right because it can produce such a picture as *Sunset Boulevard*; and with that, the considerable distance it goes, one is bound to agree.

Various observers have objected that the picture is 'lifeless'; that the characters are unsympathetic; that neither tragedy implicit in the story—that of the obsolete artist, or that of the obsolete woman—is sufficiently developed, or explored, or is even risen to. Some of this seems to me true, some I disagree with; most of it, I think, comes from a temperamental unwillingness to accept Messrs Brackett and Wilder as the kind of artists they happen to be. They are evidently much more concerned to make a character interesting, than sympathetic, and the interest itself is limited by the quality of their insight, which is intelligent and exceedingly clever, rather than profound. But the interest is real, and so far as I was concerned, sympathy developed accordingly; moreover, I am deeply grateful to artists who never try to cheat, coerce or seduce me into sympathy, and such artists are particularly rare in movies. On the charge of lifelessness I can only say that in my opinion there are two main kinds of life in art, not just one. The warmer, richer kind comes, invariably, from the kind of artist who works from far inside himself and his creatures. For the other kind, we can thank the good observer. Brackett and Wilder apparently have little if any gift for working from inside, but they are first-rate observers, and their films are full of that kind of life. It is true, I think, that they fail to make much of the powerful tragic possibilities which are inherent in their story; they don't even explore much of the deep anguish and pathos which are still more richly inherent, though they often reveal it, quickly and brilliantly. But this does not seem to me a shameful kind of failure, if indeed it is proper to call it a failure at all: they are simply not the men for such a job, nor was this the kind of job they were trying to do. But they are beautifully equipped to do the cold, exact, adroit, sardonic job they have done; and artists who, consciously or unconsciously, learn to be true to their limitations as well as to their gifts, deserve a kind of gratitude and respect they much too seldom get.

1950

Toby Jug and Bottle

KEN TYNAN

If you had been visiting Philadelphia in the winter of 1892, and had wanted to buy a newspaper, you would have stood a good chance of having mild hysterics, and a story to dine out on in after years. W. C. Fields, then a frowning urchin of thirteen, was spending a few halcyon months peddling papers; and his manner of vending contained already the germs of a technique which later made him one of the two or three funniest men in the world. While other lads piped about wars and football, Fields would pick on a five-line fill-in at the bottom of a page and, quite disenchantedly, hawk it at the top of his voice. 'Bronislaw Gimp acquires licence for two-year-old sheepdog!' he would bellow at passers-by, adding unnecessarily: 'Details on page 26!' And by the tone of his voice, his latest biographer[1] tells us, you would gather that Gimp was an arch criminal, for Fields trusted no one. A flabby scowl sat squarely on his face—the same scowl that we see in the curious portrait with which John Decker celebrated the comedian's sixtieth birthday: with a doily on his head and a silver salt-cellar balanced on top of that he sits, squinting dyspeptically at the camera, perfectly well aware of the profanity of the caption: 'Sixty Years a Queen'. Fields disliked and suspected most of his fellow-creatures to the end of his life: his face would work in convulsive tics as he spoke of them. For sixty-seven years he played duck's back to their water, until on Christmas Day, 1946, the 'fellow in the bright nightgown' (as he always referred to death) sneaked up on him and sapped him for good.

W. C. Fields, His Follies and Fortunes is certainly the best book we are likely to see about this droll and grandiose comic. Robert Lewis Taylor is a graduate of the New Yorker, and thus a master of the Harold Ross prose style—pungent and artless, innocently sly, superbly explicit: what one would call low-falutin'. Like all the New Yorker's best profiles, this picture of Fields is composed with a sort of childish unsentimentality, the candour of a liquorous quiz kid. Taylor, having inscribed Fields' name glowingly on the roll of fame, beats him over the head with it. Except that he sometimes calls a mistress a 'friend', he spares us little. We learn of

---

[1] W. C. Fields, His Follies and Fortunes, by Robert Lewis Taylor.

Fields' astonishing consumption of alcohol (two quarts of gin a day, apart from wines and whiskey); of his quite sincere cruelty (his favourite sequence was one in which he took his small niece to a fun fair and parked her 'for safety' in the shooting gallery); of his never wholly-cured habit of pilfering (on his first visit to England he strolled around stealing poultry hanging out in front of shops; it was his tribute to the salesmanship of the proprietors and, as he indignantly added: 'You don't think I'd have stolen chickens in the Balkans, do you?'); of his jovial callousness towards his friends, towards most women, and towards the clergy. One rainy night Fields, fairly far gone, was driving home waving a gin bottle in his free hand, and generously gave a lift to a hitch-hiker. The man was outraged when Fields offered him a drink and, explaining that he was a clergyman, went on to deliver a free sermon to the comedian—'I'll give you my number four,' he said, 'called "The Evils of Alcohol".' He was well into his stride when Fields nonchalantly pulled up alongside a hedge, kicked the man out, dropped a bottle of gin after him, and roared: 'That's my

16. 'And how is my little brood mare?': W. C. Fields, Mae West in *My Little Chickadee*

number three—"How to keep warm in a ditch"!' Equally savage was his exchange with a bartender in *My Little Chickadee*. 'You remember the time I knocked down Waterfront Nell?' he said. The barman, pretty angrily, replied: 'Why, you didn't knock her down, *I* did.' 'Well,' Fields went on, unperturbed; 'I started kicking her first.' He once genially condescended to teach an acquaintance of his, against whom he bore some slight grudge, a simple juggling trick requiring two paring knives. 'I hope he worked at it,' said Fields afterwards: 'because if he did, he was almost certain to cut himself very painfully.'

Some of the managements for whom he worked complained about such jests as these. Fields never lost his temper on such occasions. 'We must strive,' he would say thoughtfully, 'to instruct and uplift as well as entertain.' And eyeing them carefully, he would light a cigar.

About all this Mr Taylor is quaintly frank; and he is even better at describing (for nobody could ever explain) the mysterious caverns of private humour in which Fields delighted. There was the two-reeler entitled *The Fatal Glass of Beer* which he did for Mack Sennett: it opened with Fields sitting on a campstool in a far Northern shack, wearing a coonskin coat and crooning to himself. From time to time he would get up, open the door, and cry: "'Tain't a fit night out for man nor beast!', whereupon an extra would pelt him in the face with a handful of snow. There was hardly any other dialogue in the film.

Fields nearly always wrote his own stories (under pen-names such as Mahatma Kane Jeeves), and would drive studio chiefs to despair by his failure to understand that the fact that he appeared in every shot did not necessarily ensure continuity of plot-line. Still, he continued to scrawl plots on the backs of old laundry bills and get $25,000 a time for them.

Often he would wander through the streets wearing a false beard, his repulsive clip-in moustache and an opera cape, and amble into any party he saw in progress, introducing himself as 'Doctor Hugo Sternhammer, the Viennese anthropologist'. He first did this during the 1914–18 war. 'I remember telling one woman that the Kaiser was my third cousin,' he mused: 'she gave a little scream and ran like hell.' His treatment of women often bordered on the fantastic: finding strange, unaccountable depths of hilarity in the Chinese, he made one of his mistresses dress in satin slippers and a split black skirt, and always called her 'The Chinaman'. Many of his letters to his last mistress and devoted nurse, Carlotta Monti, start out 'Dear Chinese People', and are signed, even more bewilderingly: 'Continental Person', or 'Ampico J. Steinway'. He liked ordering Chinese meals in his films: in *International House* (for Paramount in 1932), he seated himself like a khan and blandly asked for : 'A couple of hundred-year-old eggs boiled in perfume'.

Fields enraged most people he worked with. Mae West still remembers how stunned she was when, in the middle of a take, he benignly adlibbed:

'And how is my little brood mare?' He worked first for Mack Sennett and later for Universal and MGM (most notoriously in *David Copperfield*, in which he was narrowly restrained from doing his entire juggling routine): but after he left Ziegfeld's 'Follies' in 1921, we are probably most indebted to Paramount, who suffered under him through twenty-one movies, including *Tilly and Gus, If I Had a Million, Six of a Kind, Mrs Wiggs of the Cabbage Patch, Mississippi* and *The Man on the Flying Trapeze*. Much of the time they had to fight to keep him from cursing during takes: in retaliation he devised two expressions, 'Godfrey Daniel!' and 'Mother of Pearl!', with which he baffled the Hays Office for more than a decade. They granted him a salary so spectacular that even Bing Crosby raised his eyebrows and, by their unearthly tolerance, they allowed him to turn out a series of films which must rank amongst the least money-making comedy classics in cinema history. At last he left them, his powers quite unimpaired, and went to Universal for his last four pictures, *You Can't Cheat an Honest Man, My Little Chickadee, The Bank Dick,* and the amazing *Never Give a Sucker an Even Break*—the last two of which probably represent the height of his achievement. They were made between 1938 and 1942, when Fields was moving reluctantly into his sixties. Someday they should be revived by the film societies, for in addition to being amongst the funniest films of a good period, they are splendid illustrations of the art of film-making without portfolio, or cinematic actor-management.

The function of a director in a Fields movie was clear right from the start. He either fought with or ignored them. He would reduce such men as Leo McCarey, Norman McLeod, George Marshall and even George Cukor to impotent hysterics of rage by his incorrigible adlibbing, his affectation of deafness whenever they suggested the slightest alteration in any of his lines or routines, and by his jubilant rudeness to anyone else who happened to be working in the neighbourhood. (Once, when it became known that Deanna Durbin was on a nearby lot and might be audible on clear days, Fields threatened 'to get a good bead from the upstairs balcony and shoot her'.) The only director to whose advice he ever paid attention was Gregory La Cava. 'Dago bastard!' he would growl as, fretfully, he listened to La Cava's analysis of his gifts: yet he admitted that the director was in the right when he implored Fields not to work too hard for his laughs. What La Cava said is worth quoting, for it is acute and provides some sort of key to Fields' later methods. 'You're not a natural comedian, Bill,' he said; 'You're a counter-puncher. You're the greatest straight man that ever lived. It's a mistake for you ever to do the leading. When you start to bawl out and ham around and trip over things, you're pushing. I hate to see it.' He said that in 1934.

La Cava was correct, as Fields' maturer films show. Fields quiescent and smouldering is funnier than Fields rampant and yelling. He played straight man to a malevolent universe which had singled him out for siege and destruction. He regarded the conspiracy of fate through a pair of frosty little blue eyes, an arm flung up to ward off an imminent blow, and his shoulders instinctively hunched in self-protection. It is hard to imagine him without the 'As I suspected' look with which he anticipates disaster. Always his face looked injured (as indeed it was: the nose was ruddy and misshapen not through drink, but from the beatings he received in his youth); he would talk like an old lag, watchfully, using his antic cigar almost as a cudgel. Puffy, gimlet-eyed, and magnificently alarmed, he would try to outwit the agents of calamity with sheer pomp, and invariably fail. Everything he says, even the most crushing insult, is uttered as if it were a closely guarded secret: he *admits* a line rather than speaks it. Only his alcoholic aplomb remains unpersecuted: that they cannot touch, these imps who plague him. Fields breakfasting with his screen family behaves with all the wariness of Micawber unexpectedly trapped in Fagin's thieves' kitchen. His face lights up only rarely, at the sight of something irresistibly and universally ludicrous, like a blind man. One remembers his efforts, in the general-store sequence of *It's a Gift*, to prevent a deaf and blind customer from knocking over things with his stick while Fields is attending to other clients. It was unforgettable, the mechanical enthusiasm of those brave, happy cries: 'Sit down, Mr Muckle, Mr Muckle, please sit down!' (a stack of electric light bulbs crashes to the floor). 'Mr Muckle, honey, *please sit down!*'

His nose, resembling a doughnut pickled in vinegar or an eroded squash ball, was unique; but so, too, was his voice. He both looked and sounded like a cement mixer. He would screw up his lips to one side and purse his eyes before committing himself to speech; and then he would roll vowels around his palate as if it were a sieve with which he was prospecting for nuggets. The noise that finally emerged was something quietly raucous, like the crowing of a very lazy cock. (If you substitute 'Naw' for 'No, Sir', and cast Fields as Johnson, most of Boswell becomes wildly amusing, as well as curiously characteristic.) Fields' voice, nasal, tinny, and massively bored, is that of a prisoner who has been uselessly affirming his innocence in the same court for centuries: when, in *It's a Gift*, he drives a carload of people straight into a large reproduction of the Venus de Milo, his response as he surveys the fragments is unhesitating. 'Ran right in front of the car,' he murmurs, a little wearily.

The recent revival at the Carlton of *It's a Gift* (Norman McLeod for Paramount, 1934) was received gratefully by students of Fields' middle period. He does little heavy wooing in it, and robs surprisingly few people, but most of his other traits are well represented. The cigar is there; so is the straw hat, which nervously deserts him at moments of crisis, and has to be retrieved and jammed back on to the large, round head which squats, Humpty-Dumpty-like, on the oddly boyish shoulders. There is

17. 'Sit down, Mr Muckle': *It's a Gift*

Fields' old rival, Baby LeRoy, to spill a barrel of molasses, described by the comedian in a famous line as 'spreadingest stuff I ever saw in m'life'. (To a friend who enquired the name of his new co-star, Fields replied: 'Fellow named LeRoy. Says he's a baby'. He once put half a pint of gin into the child's orange juice, inducing a total collapse which Fields greeted with shouts of: 'Walk him around! Send him home! The kid's no trouper!') There is Kathleen Howard, the Fieldsian equivalent to Margaret Dumont, sneering with her wonderful baritone clarity at his 'scheme to revive the celluloid collar'. And there is the long and savoury sequence in which Fields, driven by Miss Howard's nocturnal scolding to seek sleep on the verandah, is kept awake by such things as a coconut rolling down a fire-escape, a squeaking clothes-line, an insurance salesman (who asks 'Are you a Mr Karl LaFong, capital K small A small R small L capital L small A capital F small O small N small G?'), the whirr of bottles in a milk-crate, a 'vegetable gentleman' selling calabashes, and, of course, by Baby LeRoy, who drops grapes from above into the comedian's mouth. 'Shades of Bacchus!' mutters Fields, removing the eleventh.

In the same programme as *It's a Gift* was a revival of *Monkey Business*, which the Fields section of the audience took in glacial silence, because this is scriptbound comedy, the comedy of quotability. Groucho owes much to Perelman: Fields owes nothing to anyone, except dubiously

Harry Tate. Fields strolls out of the frame into the theatre, while the Brothers remain silhouettes. Fields' fantasy has its roots in the robust soil of drunken reverie: theirs are in the hothouse of nightmare. They will resort to razors and thumbscrews to get laughs which Fields would have got with a rolled-up newspaper. Their comic style is only comparable with his in that, as Mr Taylor notes, 'most people harbour a secret affection for anyone with a low opinion of humanity'. It is nowhere recorded what Fields thought of them, but it is possible to guess. Hearing them described: 'Possibly a squad of gipsies,' he would grunt, pronouncing the 'g' hard as in gruesome.

Fields is pre-eminently a man's comedian. Women never become addicts of his pictures, and it is no coincidence that his friends (John Barrymore, Ben Hecht, Gene Fowler, Dave Chasen, Grantland Rice) were all men. He belongs inseparably to the poolroom and the bar-room—

18. Fields and children: *Bank Dick*

though rarely to the smoking-room; and though he looked like a brimming Toby Jug, it was always clear that no mantelpiece would hold him. Few wives drag their husbands to see his films, which may partly explain their persistently low profits. Like Sid Field, he rejected pathos to the last, even when working with child stars: he refused to tap the feminine audience by the means which Chaplin used in *The Kid*. It is appalling, indeed, to reflect what Fields might have done to Jackie Coogan, a less resilient youth than LeRoy. Perhaps it is a final judgment on him that no self-respecting mother will ever allow her children to read Mr Taylor's brilliant book—a chronicle of meanness, fraud, arrogance and alcoholism.

We know, by the way, Fields' opinion of Chaplin. Late in life he was lured to a cinema where some of the little man's early two-reelers were being shown. The laughter inside was deafening, and halfway through Fields uneasily left. His companion found him outside in the car at the end of the show, and asked what he thought of Chaplin's work. 'The son of a bitch is a ballet dancer,' said Fields.

'He's pretty funny, don't you think?' his friend went on doggedly.

'He's the best ballet dancer that ever lived,' said Fields, 'and if I get a good chance I'll kill him with my bare hands.'

1951

Who Wants True?

> *Scenario Editor:* 'I was looking through another story
> you wrote. . . . I liked it. . . . It was true, and moving—'
>   *Embittered (and broke) scriptwriter:* 'Who wants true?
> Who wants moving?'
>
>   *Sunset Boulevard*

'Some opinions come from the heart, and if a man has no fixed opinion he
has no fixed sentiments,' a French moralist observed; fixed sentiments are
seldom forthcoming from critics today. Admittedly they are rather
unfashionable, perhaps because one has seen sentiment so frequently
abused or degraded, and admittedly few modern works of art are
'committed'—there is a convenience as well as a *chic* in concealed
allegiances. At least, though, most arts have a tradition of fixed
sentiments from which to deviate; disconsolate, one can go back—to
earlier periods, happier climates, larger feelings, for a yardstick of human
expression.

The difficulty is that the heart, as has so often been remarked, cannot be
mapped or charted. Indefinability exposes the expression of sentiment to
all kinds of falseness and evasion. One is on safer ground with analysis,
social or political commentary, any kind of polemic. The times have
produced an enormous number of aesthetic tracts, in which even praise
takes the form of logical dissection; the bareness lies not in the analysis,
but in its isolation, which seems to spring from the fear, or dislike, or
mistrust, of admitted passion. 'Think before you speak is criticism's
motto; speak before you think creation's.' Thus, E. M. Forster on the
raison d'être of criticism in the arts—and if any *raison d'être* is to be found,
the two methods must at least be reconciled on the common ground of the
work of art in question. Passion without analysis won't help, but nor will
analysis without passion, which is nothing if not 'committed'. If one
wants true and moving in the cinema, in a more than lip-service sense,
then commitments are vital.

Younger than the other arts, the cinema has suffered more than they on
account of the climate in which it operates. The subject of as many tracts
as the drama or the novel, it has known no other continuity of critical
approach. From the first, its voices were those of argumentation rather

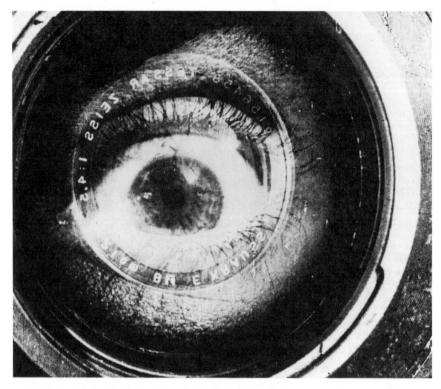

19. Point of view: the camera eye in *The Man with a Movie Camera*

than instinct. With a new medium, preoccupation with techniques, conditions and effects were valuable and inevitable, and if one surveys the bulk of film criticism, one is struck by the amount of excellent theorising on how films should be made—analysis of their stylistic properties, of the relations between artists and businessmen, the cinema's contribution to international understanding, its social effects, and so on. But if one looks further, for judgments on what has been or can be expressed in human terms by film makers, the prospect is disconcertingly bleak.

There have been only two widely formulated points of view in the cinema, and they were in many respects identical. The Soviet cinema, based on explicit social and political ideas, used the medium to convey these to its audience: Grierson's 'creative interpretation of actuality', again based on political and social convictions, less doctrinaire in themselves but equally exclusive, was developed to the same end. Both movements were concerned to discover some kind of aesthetic of propaganda, and in both the leading film makers were also the leading critics. As Eisenstein described the spirit of himself and his contemporaries—'our spirit urged us towards life—amidst the people, into the surging actuality of a regenerating country'—so Grierson was emboldened to compare the role of the cinema in public relations with that of the *Congrégation de Propaganda Fide*, and the patronage of talent by the Empire Marketing Board with that of Leonardo and Michelangelo by the Medici.

Public relations: the term is self-descriptive and self-limiting, like the phrase used by Grierson to clinch his comparison with Renaissance Italy, 'institutional advertising' being applied to the work of its painters and sculptors. One can't help feeling this to be more picturesque than apt, and to prove the limitations of a particular aesthetic. It is echoed in a different form today, however, by Richard Griffith, probably the most distinguished exponent of the school of social conscience. Stressing the necessity for the film maker to have the common touch, he writes: 'An artist may use what virtuoso methods he likes in his films so long as his subjects are emotionally important to the majority; if they are not, he cannot work at all.'

Eisenstein was aware of the antithesis between the Soviet cinema and that of other countries, just as Grierson opposed himself to current practices—the triviality in form and content of many studio-made films,

20. An aesthetic of propaganda: Eisenstein's *Strike*

which he (questionably) attributed to their form rather than their makers. The documentary thesis was also suspicious of 'aesthetic' views of cinema, and gained a notable convert, in fact, in Paul Rotha. In the preface to his revised version of *The Film Till Now*, Rotha emphasised that his original concern with films was primarily aesthetic; the book is an exploration of style and technique. The 1949 preface records the changeover. 'The screen's reflection of a people's character and ideals and traditions, its unlimited power to create goodwill and promote understanding, its unequalled importance as a medium for public communication are motives which have been largely overlooked in the scramble to monopolise this universal show business.' This is more flexible than 'institutional advertising', but still preoccupied with the relationship between a film and its audience, and not with what is surely the more vital relationship: a film and its maker.

One can extend this by saying that the emphasis is all general, all cerebration, and no particular, no passion. A major difference between the two movements was that Eisenstein and Pudovkin and their colleagues were concerned also with developing personal styles (often widely varying) for the expression of a collective ideal, while the tendency of propagandists elsewhere was to develop a collective style. Consequently, personal or human qualities were discussed, when at all, in general terms. An article by Rotha on 'The Development of Cinema' (in *For Filmgoers Only*) begins by dividing films into four categories: Story, Documentary, Cartoon and Absolute. (It seems a sign of the times that 'Absolute' should be defined as 'experimental abstract expression'.) The tendency to generalise about the personal continues today amongst critics interested more in the film-audience than the film-maker relationship, sometimes confusingly. In 'The Missing Element in the Cinema' (1948), Richard Winnington sums up the creative problem: 'The missing element is the artist himself, and we will find him not as a director or producer, but as a writer who inscribes on paper, with a completely visual power of writing, the thing that will be put down into celluloid by craftsmen.'

The preface to *The Film Till Now*, however, offers a different emphasis: 'Only the director can be the main creative mind that really gives life and breath and emotion and meaning to the writer's ideas.'

Who wants true? Who wants moving? A pendulum of reaction has swung from the extreme of form to the limit of content, and not yet paused with sureness between them. Thirty years ago the cinema's stylistic possibilities were new and exciting; the propagandists reacted against the limitations of over-concern with form, but the total result of their work, though strong in collective purpose, appears lacking in individuality. It is difficult not to feel sometimes that one is in a waiting-room while, across the corridor, the cinema is laid on an operating table, receiving transfusions of social conscience, injections of location work, and having various industrial tumours removed. One writes and talks too much about 'the cinema'. It is too abstract. Even as an abstraction, the cinema is too complex to contain all the generalisations it invites. In its most vital sense, besides, it is not 'the cinema', but a number of films made by individual artists of fixed sentiments. Since the fixed sentiments of the Soviet cinema and of Grierson's movement have, creatively, contracted, one's attention is focused even more sharply on the individual. This is a situation unlikely to change for, as Rotha acutely pointed out nearly twenty years ago: 'So many craftsmen have turned to the documentary propaganda cinema as offering a fuller scope for their ability. But again it is rare to find propaganda which is in accord with the mind of the director. It is no solution. It is a compromise.' The solution comes, for the film maker and the critic, when the sentiment is fixed in himself.

At the point where style becomes most closely merged with the artist's whole personality—and the most interesting, most rewarding styles are usually the least detachable—criticism becomes most difficult. One is reminded of Dr Johnson being asked to define poetry. 'Why, Sir, it is much easier to say what it is not. We all *know* what light is, but it is not easy to *tell* what it is.' And he never did. Tastes, preferences, pleasures, spring from the particular and can only be described with frequent reference to it. The advantage of theory is its explicitness; its disadvantage, the lack of intimacy and passion which is the substance of the finest imaginative work. In his films and his critical writing Eisenstein made plain what he intended. 'Mastering the elements of filmic diction, the technique of the frame and the theory of montage ... called upon to embody the philosophy and ideology of the victorious proletariat' is lucid if chilling. Grierson's well-known 'creative interpretation of actuality', by no means the aim or prerogative of documentary exclusively, is less revealing than his simpler statement: 'The ordinary affairs of people's lives are more dramatic and more vital than all the false excitements you can muster. That has seemed to me something worth spending one's life over.' If the false excitements of 'institutional advertising' had not intervened, ordinary people's lives might have been, in fact, more fully explored.

It is significant that the two great doctrinaire movements of the cinema encompassed, but could not contain, a poetic talent with sympathies and responses more personal than the doctrines. Dovzhenko seems to me the most completely gifted of the famous Soviet directors, and perhaps Humphrey Jennings was really the only example of 'the new kind of artist' called for by Grierson, though he may not have been what Grierson originally had in mind. The brilliance of Eisenstein, the application of Pudovkin, look respectively a little cold and a little stolid by the side of Dovzhenko's genius: *Arsenal*, with its rapt symbolism, *Earth*, with its transfixed lyrical slowness, its quiet revelation of character and living, would seem to personify the 'attack of individualism' against which Eisenstein was on his guard. Dovzhenko, indeed, writing in the 30s, revealed different methods and intentions. For him, 'through the smallest amount of material which is at hand, is expressed the greatest quality of ideas and social emotions'. In the same way, *A Diary for Timothy* is a personal film in a collective atmosphere, and with its sometimes capriciously private emphasis, its ground of association and intuition, not a public relations achievement at all. (The collective, again, made its inroads on Flaherty, whose *Industrial Britain*, *Man of Aran* and *Elephant Boy* remain his least distinguished work.)

Sacrifices to ideology or doctrine can be no less harmful than sacrifices to commerce, and the first issue must always be the motive of the artist in approaching his material. Enough good films exist unimpaired, or relatively unimpaired, to speak for their makers. At their most successful, the best film makers have created their own conditions and methods—of working inside or outside studios, for governments, film or oil companies, of accepting chores as the price of occasional freedom, of using professional or non-professional actors or both . . . No serious critic, naturally, is uninterested in these problems, and most will come to the same conclusions. Not so, though, on the greater problem, less discussed but more fiercely contested. The serious critic subscribes to an abstract idea of 'good' films, and of audiences more ready to accept them than many producers believe. Pressure to define 'good' films usually results in the compilation of competitive lists—probably the only possible way. If one has compiled such a list, it should always be in one's head; there is no other yardstick as certain.

When *City Lights* was revived eighteen months ago, Richard Winnington appended the following list to his column in the *News Chronicle*. 'My list of the world's greatest films, fought out with colleagues Gavin Lambert and Lindsay Anderson, amounts to nine (we cannot decide on the tenth). They are *Childhood of Maxim Gorki*, *The Grapes of Wrath*, *Earth*, *The Road to Life*, *Zéro de Conduite*, *Le Jour se Lève*, *Bicycle Thieves*, *Italian Straw Hat*, *City Lights*.' The list makes its preferences plain enough; it includes among the elect, Chaplin, Ford, Vigo, Dovzhenko, De Sica, Donskoi, Carné and Prévert, Clair, all of whom have, or had, the bond of human affections, who wanted true and who wanted moving. They shot in studios, on location, used all kinds of players, worked for different companies and organisations. (Two absentees with an equal right to inclusion, to whom the same applies, are Flaherty and Renoir.) They are all also artists of fixed sentiments—fixed roughly at the same point, though some, like Chaplin and Carné, have moved away from it. The list, in fact, points the existence of more than half a dozen first-rate directors in the first fifty years of cinema who have been humanists and

21. Humanist cinema: Carné's *Le Jour se Lève*

who, even when despondent—as in the case of *City Lights,* or *Le Jour se
Lève,* or *Bicycle Thieves*—managed, as Renoir writes in this issue, not to see
people like a tourist looking at crowds from a hotel balcony, but to portray
them with love.

How affections are nourished and expressed under present conditions
is something of a miracle. The motive force of Chaplin, De Sica, Carné,
seems to have been an emotional bond with the poor, the dispossessed,
the downtrodden; in different ways, the treasured experiences of
childhood and youth liberated the imagination of Vigo, Donskoi,
Dovzhenko; allegiance to traditional virtues, the search for simple
solidarities, inspired Ford; curiosity and delight travelled with Flaherty
and, in more sophisticated regions, with Renoir. As for the miracle itself,

the business of the critic is to record, not to explain, it: the films are their own explanation.

A simple, in itself unoriginal confession like Renoir's on the necessity of affection and goodwill, or De Sica's—'To see is very useful to an artist. Most men do not want to see, because often the pain of others troubles them. We, on the contrary, want to see. Our one aim is to see'—is something for which we may be peculiarly grateful. The worst danger of film criticism, or any kind of criticism, today is that of slipping over into relative values. One doesn't want or expect an exclusive diet of masterpieces, but one does need principles. Without them, all kinds of things get overpraised—at the moment, the meretricious American 'sociological' film. Without particular allegiances, not just to be brought out when compiling lists of Great Films, but as something permanent and sustaining, the adroit contractions and distortions of human experience typified in, say, *Ace in the Hole*, or *Pinky*, or *The Well*, may well be accepted with the dutiful reserved clichés of praise. Yet what is 'outspoken' in making a film about intense contemporary situations and resolving them in a claptrap of melodrama and sentimentality? Comparisons, on the whole, are a just and inevitable method of criticism; one exposes the essential puerility of Wilder's 'bitterness' most compactly by setting it against Buñuel's *Los Olvidados*.

Individual films and individual film makers are the critic's treasure-house, and the only true renovation of his spirit. 'Culture is on the horns of this dilemma; if profound and noble it must remain rare, if common it must become mean,' Santayana observed in a sentence which should make us all cautious, particularly before treating *Quo Vadis* or *The Greatest Show on Earth* too lightly. Thousands of people see thousands of films, and most people see bad films, because most films are bad. The critic and anyone who loves films has always to resist the invitations of mediocrity, which can be subtle and persuasive. Audiences will not suddenly change their tastes, nor film companies their standards. In the presence of so much anonymity, the need for personal response, personal contact, becomes all the greater. Directives for 'the cinema' are apt to exhaust themselves while certain film makers and certain films remain. Response, new and renewed, to these is the only thing which can save the convert and convert the unregenerate.

1952

Hedda Hopper: *From Under My Hat*

ARAMINTA TEAS

In our quiet metropolis the film gossip column is still a growing child—but already cutting its first strong, pointed teeth and flexing its terrible muscles.

In America, the child is already a giant. Its food is sex and salaries, major indiscretions and private rather than professional reputations. Facts, or near-facts about these topics, when related to stars and published before denials appear in other newspapers, are known as scoops. The two scoop-queens of Hollywood, as ruthless, feared and hung about with propitiatory gifts as any other tribal goddesses, are, of course, Mesdames Hopper and Parsons.

Miss Hopper has now dammed the torrent of her exuberant life within the restricting confines of a book, *From Under My Hat*, which tells of her rise from humble origins as Miss Elda Furry, of Hollidaysburg, Pennsylvania, to her present eminence as a national figure of broadcasting and the daily newspaper column 'Hedda Hopper's Hollywood'.

Miss Hopper is not just a strong personality; she is Attila, Genghis Khan and Little Nell all rolled into one. Under those staccato sentences, that frenetic whirl of events (the time-scheme is sometimes pretty hard to follow, and you have to watch Miss Hopper like a hawk or she's off on a chatty story before you know whether you're in the reign of Fairbanks or Tyrone Power)—under the furious ambition and the annihilating vitality, there beats a warm heart, bumping away like some dread dynamo. She doesn't much love Charlie Chaplin or Rex Harrison, and didn't care for the way Gene Tierney announced her pregnancy to Parsons at the same party as Hopper got to hear about it. But Dietrich is a great girl, and so is Norma Shearer and Joan Crawford, and William Randolph Hearst was a good pal too.

Miss Hopper's career took in agency work, a certain amount of hard labour for that other daughter of the American revolution, Elizabeth Arden, and of course the acting profession itself. Though her columnist's success is now at its height, the book seems to indicate that the world still owes the author something, and one hopes they will finish up all square.

There are frequent illustrations of Miss Hopper wearing different hats to visit Errol Flynn, Clark Gable, Merle Oberon, Deborah Kerr and Sabu, greeting our present Queen and Princess·Margaret at Ealing Studios in 1945, telephoning at her desk (without her hat), and acting in several films—specially appealing, a downcast pose in ropes of pearls and evening gown, under the frantic gaze of Edwin Arden in *Virtuous Wives*.

If you hope for scandalous revelations, Miss Hopper's book will disappoint. It is after all dedicated 'To my mother, who was an angel on earth,' and closes with the news that not only did Miss Hopper's mother, the courageous Mrs Furry, pray for her daughter every night, but that, since Mrs Furry's death, the well-known musical comedy star Trixie Friganza has taken over that laudable task and intercedes for Hedda devoutly and regularly. For those not content to browse through Norma, Doug, Coop and Ingrid, there are some nice bits about a sterling character called Dema Harshbarger, Hedda's agent, and a very disturbing story about J. M. Barrie calming Maude Adams' acute shyness by wrestling round the room with a huge dog.

'Miss Adams tossed her audience a timid smile, full of April light, and added, "If you sometime have a visitor who is shy, try putting him or her at ease by doing that."'

We'll think it over.

1953

Some Ideas on the Cinema[1]

CESARE ZAVATTINI

No doubt one's first and most superficial reaction to everyday reality is that it is tedious. Until we are able to overcome some moral and intellectual laziness, in fact, this reality will continue to appear uninteresting. One shouldn't be astonished that the cinema has always felt the natural, unavoidable necessity to insert a 'story' in the reality to make it exciting and 'spectacular'. All the same, it is clear that such a method evades a direct approach to everyday reality, and suggests that it cannot be portrayed without the intervention of fantasy or artifice.

The most important characteristic, and the most important innovation, of what is called neo-realism, it seems to me, is to have realised that the necessity of the 'story' was only an unconscious way of disguising a human defeat, and that the kind of imagination it involved was simply a technique of superimposing dead formulas over living social facts. Now it has been perceived that reality is hugely rich, that to be able to look directly at it is enough; and that the artist's task is not to make people moved or indignant at metaphorical situations, but to make them reflect (and, if you like, to be moved and indignant too) on what they and others are doing, on the real things, exactly as they are.

For me this has been a great victory. I would like to have achieved it many years earlier. But I made the discovery only at the end of the war. It was a moral discovery, an appeal to order. I saw at last what lay in front of me, and I understood that to have evaded reality had been to betray it.

Example: Before this, if one was thinking over the idea of a film on, say, a strike, one was immediately forced to invent a plot. And the strike itself became only the background to the film. Today, our attitude would be one of 'revelation': we would describe the strike itself, try to work out the largest possible number of human, moral, social, economic, poetic values from the bare documentary fact.

We have passed from an unconsciously rooted mistrust of reality, an illusory and equivocal evasion, to an unlimited trust in things, facts and people. Such a position requires us, in effect, to excavate reality, to give it a power, a communication, a series of reflexes, which until recently we

---

[1]This article is based on an interview with Zavattini which was originally published by the Italian journal *La Rivista del Cinema Italiano*.

had never thought it had. It requires, too, a true and real interest in what is happening, a search for the most deeply hidden human values; which is why we feel that the cinema must recruit not only intelligent people, but, above all, 'living' souls, the morally richest people.

The cinema's overwhelming desire to see, to analyse, its hunger for reality, is an act of concrete homage towards other people, towards what is happening and existing in the world. And, incidentally, it is what distinguishes 'neo-realism' from the American cinema.

In fact, the American position is the antithesis of our own; while we are interested in the reality around us and want to know it directly, reality in American films is unnaturally filtered, 'purified', and comes out at one or two removes. In America, lack of subjects for films causes a crisis, but with us such a crisis is impossible. One cannot be short of themes while there is still plenty of reality. Any hour of the day, any place, any person, is a subject for narrative if the narrator is capable of observing and illuminating all these collective elements by exploring their interior value.

So there is no question of a crisis of subjects, only of their interpretation. This substantial difference was nicely emphasised by a well-known American producer when he told me: 'This is how *we* would imagine a scene with an aeroplane. The plane passes by . . . a machine-gun fires . . . the plane crashes. . . . And this is how *you* would imagine it. The plane passes by. . . . The plane passes by again . . . the plane passes by once more . . .' He was right. But we have still not gone far enough. It is not enough to make the aeroplane pass by three times: we must make it pass by twenty times.

What effects on narrative, then, and on the portrayal of human character, has the neo-realist style produced?

To begin with, while the cinema used to make one situation produce another situation, and another, and another, again and again, and each scene was thought out and immediately related to the next (the natural result of a mistrust of reality), today, when we have thought out a scene, we feel the need to 'remain' in it, because the single scene itself can contain so many echoes and reverberations, can even contain all the situations we may need. Today, in fact, we can quietly say: give us whatever 'fact' you like, and we will disembowel it, make it something worth watching.

While the cinema used to portray life in its most visible and external moments—and a film was usually only a series of situations selected and linked together with varying success—today the neo-realist affirms that each one of these situations, rather than all the external moments, contains in itself enough material for a film.

Example: In most films, the adventures of two people looking for somewhere to live, for a house, would be shown externally in a few moments of action, but for us it could provide the scenario for a whole film, and we would explore all its echoes, all its implications.

Of course, we are still a long way from a true analysis of human situations, and one can speak of analysis only in comparison with the dull synthesis of most current production. We are, rather, still in an 'attitude' of analysis; but in this attitude there is a strong purpose, a desire for understanding, for belonging, for participating—for living together, in fact.

Substantially, then, the question today is, instead of turning imaginary situations into 'reality' and trying to make them look 'true', to make things as they are, almost by themselves, create their own special significance. Life is not what is invented in 'stories'; life is another matter. To understand it involves a minute, unrelenting, and patient search.

Here I must bring in another point of view. I believe that the world goes on getting worse because we are not truly aware of reality. The most authentic position anyone can take up today is to engage himself in tracing the roots of this problem. The keenest necessity of our time is 'social attention'.

Attention, though, to what is there, *directly*: not through an apologue, however well conceived. A starving man, a humiliated man, must be shown by name and surname; no fable for a starving man, because that is something else, less effective and less moral. The true function of the cinema is not to tell fables, and to a true function we must recall it.

Of course, reality can be analysed by ways of fiction. Fictions can be expressive and natural; but neo-realism, if it wants to be worthwhile, must sustain the moral impulse that characterised its beginnings, in an analytical documentary way. No other medium of expression has the cinema's original and innate capacity for showing things, that we believe worth showing, as they happen day by day—in what we might call their 'dailiness', their longest and truest duration. The cinema has everything in front of it, and no other medium has the same possibilities for getting it known quickly to the greatest number of people.

As the cinema's responsibility also comes from its enormous power, it should try to make every frame of film count, by which I mean that it should penetrate more and more into the manifestations and the essence of reality.

The cinema only affirms its moral responsibility when it approaches reality in this way.

The moral, like the artistic, problem lies in being able to observe reality, not to extract fictions from it.

Naturally, some film-makers, although they realise the problem, have still been compelled, for a variety of reasons (some valid, others not) to 'invent' stories in the traditional manner, and to incorporate in these stories some fragments of their real intuition. This, effectively, has served as neo-realism for some film-makers in Italy.

For this reason, the first endeavour was often to reduce the story to its most elementary, simple, and, I would rather say, banal form. It was the beginning of a speech that was later interrupted. *Bicycle Thieves* provides a typical example. The child follows his father along the street; at one moment, the child is nearly run over, but the father does not even notice. This episode was 'invented', but with the intention of communicating an everyday fact about these people's lives, a little fact—so little that the protagonists don't even care about it—but full of life.

In fact *Paisà*, *Open City*, *Sciuscià*, *Bicycle Thieves*, *La Terra Trema*, all contain elements of an absolute significance—they reflect the idea that everything can be recounted; but their sense remains metaphorical, because there is still an invented story, not the documentary spirit. In

22. Neo-realism: *Umberto D*

other films, such as *Umberto D.*, reality as an analysed fact is much more evident, but the presentation is still traditional.

We have not yet reached the centre of neo-realism. Neo-realism today is an army ready to start; and there are the soldiers—behind Rossellini, De Sica, Visconti. The soldiers have to go into the attack and win the battle.

We must recognise that all of us are still only starting, some farther on, others farther behind. But it is still something. The great danger today is to abandon that position, the moral position implicit in the work of many of us during and immediately after the war.

A woman is going to buy a pair of shoes. Upon this elementary situation it is possible to build a film. All we have to do is to discover and then show all the elements that go to create this adventure, in all their banal 'dailiness', and it will become worthy of attention, it will even become 'spectacular'. But it will become spectacular not through its exceptional, but through its *normal* qualities; it will astonish us by showing so many things that happen every day under our eyes, things we have never noticed before.

The result would not be easy to achieve. It would require an intensity of human vision both from the creator of the film and from the audience. The question is: how to give human life its historical importance at every minute.

In life, in reality today, there are no more empty spaces. Between things, facts, people, exists such an interdependence that a blow struck for the cinema in Rome could have repercussions all over the world. If this is true, it must be worthwhile to take any moment of a human life and show how 'striking' that moment is: to excavate and identify it, to send its echo vibrating into other parts of the world.

This is as valid for poverty as for peace. For peace, too, the human moment should not be a great one, but an ordinary daily happening. Peace is usually the sum of small happenings, all having the same moral implications at their roots.

It is not only a question, however, of creating a film that makes its audience understand a social or a collective situation. People understand themselves better than the social fabric; and to see themselves on the screen, performing their daily actions—remembering that to see oneself gives one the sense of being unlike oneself—like hearing one's own voice on the radio—can help them to fill up a void, a lack of knowledge of reality.

If this love for reality, for human nature directly observed, must still adapt itself to the necessities of the cinema as it is now organised, must yield, suffer and wait, it means that the cinema's capitalist structure still has a tremendous influence over its true function. One can see this in the growing opposition in many places to the fundamental motives of neo-realism, the main results of which are a return to so-called 'original'

23. 'Everyone must be his own actor': *La Terra Trema*

subjects, as in the past, and the consequent evasion of reality, and a number of bourgeois accusations against neo-realist principles.

The main accusation is: *neo-realism only describes poverty*. But neo-realism can and must face poverty. We have begun with poverty for the simple reason that it is one of the most vital realities of our time, and I challenge anyone to prove the contrary. To believe, or to pretend to believe, that by making half a dozen films on poverty we have finished with the problem, would be a great mistake. As well believe that, if you have to plough up a whole country, you can sit down after the first acre.

The theme of poverty, of rich and poor, is something one can dedicate one's whole life to. We have just begun. We must have the courage to explore all the details. If the rich turn up their noses especially at *Miracolo a Milano*, we can only ask them to be a little patient. *Miracolo a Milano* is only a fable. There is still much more to say. I put myself among the rich, not only because I have some money (which is only the most apparent and immediate aspect of wealth), but because I am also in a position to create oppression and injustice. That is the moral (or immoral) position of the so-called rich man.

When anyone (he could be the audience, the director, the critic, the

State, or the Church) says, 'Stop the poverty,' i.e. stop the films about poverty, he is committing a moral sin. He is refusing to understand, to learn. And when he refuses to learn, consciously or not, he is evading reality. The evasion springs from lack of courage, from fear. (One should make a film on this subject, showing at what point we begin to evade reality in the face of disquieting facts, at what point we begin to sweeten it.)

If I were not afraid of being thought irreverent, I should say that Christ, had He a camera in His hand, would not shoot fables, however wonderful, but would show us the good ones and the bad ones of this world—in actuality, giving us close-ups of those who make their neighbours' bread too bitter, and of their victims, if the censor allowed it.

To say that we have had 'enough' films about poverty suggests that one

24. Neo-realism: *Sciuscià*

can measure reality with a chronometer. In fact, it is not simply a question of choosing the theme of poverty, but of going on to explore and analyse the poverty. What one needs is more and more knowledge, precise and simple, of human needs and the motives governing them. Neo-realism should ignore the chronometer and go forward for as long as is necessary.

Neo-realism, it is also said, does not offer solutions. The end of a neo-realist film is particularly inconclusive. I cannot accept this at all. With regard to my own work, the characters and situations in films for which I have written the scenario, they remain unresolved from a practical point of view simply because 'this is reality'. But every moment of the film is, in itself, a continuous answer to some question. It is not the concern of an artist to propound solutions. It is enough, and quite a lot, I should say, to make an audience feel the need, the urgency, for them.

In any case, what films *do* offer solutions? 'Solutions' in this sense, if they are offered, are sentimental ones, resulting from the superficial way in which problems have been faced. At least, in my work I leave the solution to the audience.

The fundamental emotion of *Miracolo a Milano* is not one of escape (the flight at the end), but of indignation, a desire for solidarity with certain people, a refusal of it with others. The film's structure is intended to suggest that there is a great gathering of the humble ones against the others. But the humble ones have no tanks, or they would have been ready to defend their land and their huts.

The true neo-realistic cinema is, of course, less expensive than the cinema at present. Its subjects can be expressed cheaply, and it can dispense with capitalist resources on the present scale. The cinema has not yet found its morality, its necessity, its quality, precisely because it costs too much; being so conditional, it is much less an art than it could be.

The cinema should never turn back. It should accept, unconditionally, what is contemporary. *Today, today, today.*

It must tell reality as if it were a story; there must be no gap between life and what is on the screen. To give an example:

A woman goes to a shop to buy a pair of shoes. The shoes cost 7,000 lire. The woman tries to bargain. The scene lasts, perhaps, two minutes. I must make a 2-hour film. What do I do?

I analyse the fact in all its constituent elements, in its 'before', in its 'after', in its contemporaneity. The fact creates its own fiction, in its own particular sense.

The woman is buying the shoes. What is her son doing at the same moment? What are people doing in India that could have some relation to this fact of the shoes? The shoes cost 7,000 lire. How did the woman happen to have 7,000 lire? How hard did she work for them, what do they represent for her?

And the bargaining shopkeeper, who is he? What relationship has developed between these two human beings? What do they mean, what interests are they defending, as they bargain? The shopkeeper also has two sons, who eat and speak: do you want to know what they are saying? Here they are, in front of you ...

The question is, to be able to fathom the real correspondences between facts and their process of birth, to discover what lies beneath them.

Thus to analyse 'buying a pair of shoes' in such a way opens to us a vast and complex world, rich in importance and values, in its practical, social, economic, psychological motives. Banality disappears because each moment is really charged with responsibility. Every moment is infinitely rich. Banality never really existed.

Excavate, and every little fact is revealed as a mine. If the gold-diggers come at last to dig in the illimitable mine of reality, the cinema will become socially important.

This can also be done, evidently, with invented characters; but if I use living, real characters with which to sound reality, people in whose life I can directly participate, my emotion becomes more effective, morally stronger, more useful. Art must be expressed through a true name and surname, not a false one.

I am bored to death with heroes more or less imaginary. I want to meet the real protagonist of everyday life, I want to see how he is made, if he has a moustache or not, if he is tall or short, I want to see his eyes, and I want to speak to him.

We can look at him on the screen with the same anxiety, the same curiosity as when, in a square, seeing a crowd of people all hurrying up to the same place, we ask, What is happening? What is happening to a real person? Neo-realism has perceived that the most irreplaceable experience comes from things happening under our own eyes from natural necessity.

I am against 'exceptional' personages. The time has come to tell the audience that they are the true protagonists of life. The result will be a constant appeal to the responsibility and dignity of every human being. Otherwise the frequent habit of identifying oneself with fictional characters will become very dangerous. We must identify ourselves with what we are. The world is composed of millions of people thinking of myths.

The term neo-realism—in a very latin sense—implies, too, elimination of technical-professional apparatus, screen-writer included. Handbooks, formulas, grammars, have no more application. There will be no more technical terms. Everybody has his personal shooting-script. Neo-realism breaks all the rules, rejects all those canons which, in fact, only exist to codify limitations. Reality breaks all the rules, as can be discovered if you walk out with a camera to meet it.

The figure of a screen-writer today is, besides, very equivocal. He is usually considered part of the technical apparatus. I am a screen-writer trying to say certain things, and saying them in my own way. It is clear that certain moral and social ideas are the foundation of my expressive activities, and I can't be satisfied to offer a simple technical contribution. In films which do not touch me directly, also, when I am called in to do a certain amount of work on them, I try to insert as much as possible of my own world, of the moral emergencies within myself.

On the other hand, I don't think the screenplay in itself contains any particular problems; only when subject, screenplay and direction become three distinct phases, as they so often do today, which is abnormal. The screen-writer as such should disappear, and we should arrive at the sole author of a film.

Everything becomes flexible when only one person is making a film, everything continually possible, not only during the shooting, but during the editing, the laying of tracks, the post-synchronisation, to the particular moment when we say, 'Stop'. And it is only then that we put an end to the film.

Of course, it is possible to make films in collaboration, as happens with novels and plays, because there are always numerous bonds of identity between people (for example, millions of men go to war, and are killed, for the same reasons), but no work of art exists on which someone has not set the seal of his own interest, of his own poetic world. There is always somebody to make the decisive creative act, there is always one prevailing intelligence, there is always someone who, at a certain moment, 'chooses', and says, 'This, yes,' and 'This, no,' and then resolves it: reaction shot of the Mother crying Help!

Technique and capitalist method, however, have imposed collaboration on the cinema. It is one thing to adapt ourselves to the imposed exigencies of the cinema's present structure, another to imagine that they are indispensable and necessary. It is obvious that when films cost sixpence and everybody can have a camera, the cinema would become a creative medium as flexible and as free as any other.

It is evident that, with neo-realism, the actor—as a person fictitiously lending his own flesh to another—has no more right to exist than the 'story'. In neo-realism, as I intend it, everyone must be his own actor. To want one person to play another implies the calculated plot, the fable, and not 'things happening'. I attempted such a film with Caterina Rigoglioso; it was called 'the lightning film'. But unfortunately at the last moment everything broke down. Caterina did not seem to 'take' to the cinema. But wasn't she 'Caterina'?[1]

[1]Zavattini has now begun work on this film again, as one of the episodes in a new film journal called 'The Spectator'. Various Italian directors (among them Antonioni, Emmer and Lattuada) are contributing to the first number, *Amore in Città*, each sketch of which deals with an aspect of life in a great city. Zavattini's story of Caterina Rigoglioso tells of a few hours in the life of a woman before she decides to abandon her baby.

Of course, it will be necessary to choose themes excluding actors. I want, for example, to make a report on children in the world. If I am not allowed to make it, I will limit it to Europe, or to Italy alone. But I will make it. Here is an example of the film not needing actors. I hope the actors' union will not protest.

Neo-realism does not reject psychological exploration. Psychology is one of the many premises of reality. I face it as I face any other. If I want to write a scene of two men quarrelling, I will not do so at my desk. I must leave my den and find them. I take these men and make them talk in front of me for one hour or for twenty, depending on necessity. My creative method is first to call on them, then to listen to them, 'choosing' what they say. But I do all this not with the intention of creating heroes, because I think that a hero is not 'certain men' but 'every man'.

Wanting to give everyone a sense of equality is not levelling him down, but exalting his solidarity. Lack of solidarity is always born from presuming to be different, from a *But*: 'Paul is suffering, it's true, I am suffering, too, *but* my suffering has something that . . . my nature has something that . . .' and so on. The *But* must disappear, and we must be able to say: 'That man is bearing what I myself should bear in the same circumstances'.

Others have observed that the best dialogue in films is always in dialect. Dialect is nearer to reality. In our literary and spoken language, the synthetic constructions and the words themselves are always a little false. When writing a dialogue, I always think of it in dialect, in that of Rome or my own village. Using dialect, I feel it to be more essential, truer. Then I translate it into Italian, thus maintaining the dialect's syntax. I don't, therefore, write dialogue in dialect, but I am interested in what dialects have in common: immediacy, freshness, verisimilitude.

But I take most of all from nature. I go out into the street, catch words, sentences, discussions. My great aids are memory and the shorthand writer.

Afterwards, I do with the words what I do with the images. I choose, I cut the material I have gathered to give it the right rhythm, to capture the essence, the truth. However great a faith I might have in imagination, in solitude, I have a greater one in reality, in people. I am interested in the drama of things we happen to encounter, not those we plan.

In short, to exercise our own poetic talents on location, we must leave our rooms and go, in body and mind, out to meet other people, to see and understand them. This is a genuine moral necessity for me and, if I lose faith in it, so much the worse for me.

I am quite aware that it is possible to make wonderful films, like Charlie Chaplin's, and they are not neo-realistic. I am quite aware that there are Americans, Russians, Frenchmen and others who have made masterpieces that honour humanity, and, of course, they have not wasted film.

I wonder, too, how many more great works they will again give us, according to their particular genius, with actors and studios and novels. But Italian film-makers, I think, if they are to sustain and deepen their cause and their style, after having courageously half-opened their doors to reality, must (in the sense I have mentioned) open them wide.

1953

'The Lighter People'

DAVID ROBINSON

The future of comedy is, like claret, unpredictable. *Punch* is the popular example of how one generation's humour will sour on the next, and later, perhaps, return to taste and favour. The same is true of comedy on the screen. The Marx Brothers, Keaton, Langdon—even, to some extent, Chaplin—were forgotten in the 'forties, and have now returned to grace, while the oblivion of Semon and Griffith seems permanent. Among the larger talents, Laurel and Hardy still remain outside the pale of the intelligentsia's recognition.

They had their day of cultural respectability; and some have never deserted them. After *Laughing Gravy* (1931), *The Music Box* (1931) and *County Hospital* (1932), hats were respectfully raised. But Mickey Mouse and Silly Symphonies forced them into feature-length comedies, which at first their invention could not sustain. Many turned their backs then, too soon to notice the success of the best features—*Way Out West*, *Fra Diavolo*, *Swiss Miss*. We took their huge output (two hundred films in twenty years) for granted, and at last forgot them, so that their final unhappy attempts at film-making and their disappearance from the screen passed almost unnoticed.

This is ingratitude. Laurel and Hardy have made too many films. They have made bad films; and they admit it themselves. They are neither of them geniuses. But they are very, very good clowns. And they have made a real, and characteristically unassuming, contribution to screen comedy.

When the partnership was formed, in 1927, Laurel was already thirty-seven and Hardy thirty-five. Each had learnt his job through twenty years' solid experience of the theatre and cinema. Stan Laurel (born Stanley Jefferson, at Ulverston, Lancashire, in 1890) began his theatrical career as a child; after hard years in the British music-halls, he finally joined the Karno Sketch Company, with which he went to America. When the company disbanded there in 1913, Chaplin, another member, went to work for Sennett, while Laurel went back to touring in vaudeville. In 1917 he, too, entered films, with Broncho Billy (G. M. Anderson) at Universal. His success as Rhubarb Vaselino in *Mud and Sand*, combined with Broncho Billy's irregular payments, led to a contract with Hal Roach. With Roach, he took an increasing interest in the technique of film direction, finally giving up a successful career as a solo screen comic to devote himself entirely to direction.

'Babe' Hardy (born in Harlem, Georgia, 1892, Oliver Norvell Hardy) began his theatrical career as a singer, having been originally intended for the law. In 1913 he was engaged by the Lubin Company, and, after various engagements, found himself at Vitagraph, where he acted and directed with Larry Semon. After Semon's death, Hardy, too, joined Roach.

Laurel and Hardy had acted together for Broncho Billy; about 1917 Hardy played the heavy in a comedy with Stan Laurel (*A Lucky Dog*, directed by Jess Robins). Their teaming, however, was the result of an accident. Stan was directing one of Roach's All-Star Series pictures, in which Babe was playing comic lead. Shooting began on Monday, but on Friday Babe burnt his arm with boiling fat (the scars have survived with the partnership). Unwillingly, Stan, who had congratulated himself that his acting days were over, took his place. Babe returned before the picture was completed, and Roach decided that they should both stay in the film. Despite Stan's reluctance to resume an acting career, Roach persuaded them to make another film, this time as a team. 'And then,' they say, 'another . . . and another . . .'

Their earliest films were made towards the end of the silent period; yet even the first seem to belong to the age of talking pictures. Their technique outdates by years that of their comic contemporaries. Such a film as *Leave 'Em Laughing* (directed by Clyde Bruckman, who made *Feet First* and *Movie Crazy*) looks forward with such determination to the talking 'thirties that it is necessary to keep reminding oneself that the film is, in fact, silent. The innovation is in the relaxation of the pace. Laurel had constantly fought to slow down silent comedy; in his earliest films there is evident an attempt to break loose from the furious cross-cutting inherited from later Sennett days; already he is experimenting with easy, lingering shots, depending upon leisurely and graceful mime. Teamed with Hardy, he slowed down slapstick two-reelers still more. The peculiar style of their comedy demanded this relaxed pace; Hardy may, for example, require as much as sixty feet of film to register a change of expression, and any acceleration of the process would spoil the comedy.

A year after their partnership began, sound came, Jolson sang, and the rest talked twenty to the dozen. Laurel and Hardy rode the wave imperturbably. With characteristic good sense, they asked themselves just why they should talk any more than they had been used to, merely because they could now be overheard. Not that they failed to make use of the new medium. The shrieking and groaning jangles of the piano which they haul and drop down the interminable stairway in *The Music Box* is the last, the very last, word on the use of sound.

25. 'Stanley . . . stands by unharmed': *Way Out West*

These were their great days. But this was also the time of their first feature-length films (*Jail Birds, Pardon Us,* 1931), and the first suggestions that their comic invention could not support a full-length feature. The suggestions were to be disproved. *Way Out West* is not only one of their most perfect films, but ranks with the best screen comedy; and others run it close—*Our Relations, Fra Diavolo, Swiss Miss, Blockheads.*

After *Blockheads* (1938), Roach ceased to produce for MGM, for whom all their films had been made since 1929. Other producers had not the imagination to leave them to their own wayward, extravagant but productive methods of creation. Without Roach they became like nomads; moved to RKO to make *The Flying Deuces*; then two final films with Roach, *A Chump at Oxford* and *Saps at Sea*; for Fox they made *Great Guns* and *A-Haunting We Will Go*; and then returned to make one more film for MGM—*Air Raid Wardens*. They went back to Fox, but never fulfilled their contract. After five more films, none particularly successful (the best from this period of decline was *The Big Noise*, made in 1944 by Malcolm St Clair), they left the company. Their last film was made in France, with a French cast. Laurel and Hardy were horrified by the dilatory methods of production; Laurel was seriously ill during most of the time it was being made. It is not from modesty that he calls the film—*Atoll K* (*Robinson Crusoeland*)—'that catastrophe'.

The team is itself a joke, a cause of laughter. It is the old gag of Falstaff and his page—'the sow that hath overwhelm'd all her litter but one'—Belch and Aguecheek, the Walrus and the Carpenter, Herbert Campbell and Dan Leno. And besides the fun inherent in their teaming, there is a constant striving after the grotesque—in their costumes and funny wigs, the donkeys they ride in *Fra Diavolo*, the pony sled in *Way Out West* on which the mountainous Olly is drawn by Stan and a minute donkey.

The contrast between the characters could scarcely be greater. Oliver is fine, round and juicy; Stan little and dried up. Oliver is a grand, leisurely man with an elegant accent derived from the Southern States. Stanley is a fidgety, uncertain, timid little creature with an indefinable Lancashire-Cockney-Hollywood accent which only the English music-hall could father. 'The battle . . . of Dither versus Dignity' the contrast has been described; but the association is too complementary ever to be accurately described as a battle.

Oliver Hardy—his basic costume and make-up were based on a cartoon character, 'Helpful Henry'—always proposes and leads every enterprise. (It is interesting that the form of the majority of their films is the proposition of an enterprise; the progressive frustration of its execution; and its final catastrophic abortion, which leaves them where they were at the beginning, or even one unhappy step backwards.) Oliver gives the orders, explaining each step with a much-tried patience. He always knows best ('Well, I'm *bigger* than he is, so I think I *should* know best,' he explains). As the 'brains' of the partnership, he generally delegates the dirty jobs to Stan. Yet finally, sadly, inevitably, the misfortunes and ruin fall upon Oliver. Stanley—whose fault everything usually is—stands by unharmed, looking with helpless amazement upon the havoc he has innocently caused.

In contrast to Stanley's light-footed shamblings, Oliver is all elephantine elegance. His walk is assured, head in the air (with the consequences one might expect). His huge hands affect an elaborate grace; he has a way of ringing a doorbell which is like a courtly bow, and a courtly bow beyond comparison. He loads a cannon (*The Chimp*) with the same shop-madam delicacy as he brushes down the crumbling, moth-bald fur coat he wears in *Swiss Miss*. His conversation has the same elegance, and his small-talk is magnificent: 'A lot of weather we've been having lately . . .' A benign smile, and a pause. 'Only four months to Christmas!' Pause. '. . . Do you believe in Santa Claus?' (*Way Out West*).

Most of Oliver's misfortunes are due to his inability to bend to circumstances. Instead he faces them full square; and usually falls flat on his back as a result. He remains magnificently unaltered in all situations. Up to his neck in water (*Way Out West*), he folds his arms in a typical gesture of annoyance.

Stanley is a clown in a much more recognisable comic tradition. His descent can be traced back at least to Grimaldi, with his 'melancholy cast', grotesque costumes and greeting of 'How are you tomorrow?'—recognisably in Laurel's vein of simple humour. The likeness between Stan and Dan Leno is remarkable; and we have actually seen Stan—unconsciously—perform one of Leno's gags: where Leno climbed on to a stable roof, thereby to enter and poison a horse—explaining to his unimaginative sister, who tells him the door is open, that no real burglar ever goes through a door. More remarkable still is this dialogue, which Shakespeare (or for that matter one of their own scenarists) might well have written for Laurel and Hardy:

Sir Andrew: Sir Toby Belch,—How now, Sir Toby Belch?
Sir Toby: Sweet Sir Andrew!
Sir Andrew: Bless you, fair shrew.
Maria: And you too, sir.
Sir Toby (aside): Accost, Sir Andrew, accost.

26. Mutual destruction: *Big Business* (with James Finlayson)

Sir Andrew: What's that?
Sir Toby: My niece's chambermaid.
Sir Andrew: Good Mistress Accost, I desire better acquaintance.
Maria: My name is Mary, sir.
Sir Andrew: Good Mistress Mary Accost. . . .

(Alec Guinness's interpretation of the part of Sir Andrew emphasised this likeness.)

Yet Laurel's truth to the tradition is not conscious. Of Leno, he says: 'No, I never saw him; I've seen pictures, of course; he must have been a funny little guy. Yes, they tell me I look rather like him; but I never saw him.' The likeness is not complete. Stan would never address an audience so familiarly as Dan: 'Goodnight! Don't look so stupid! Don't!' For Stan is the extreme of clownish humility. He is the pure simpleton, to all appearances utterly vacuous. Well aware of his own limitations, he is content to teeter along behind his big companion and repeat and accept all his instructions. His witticisms and his moments of enlightenment are as accidental as his *sottises*—and surprise him quite as much. They surprise Oliver, too, who expects only nonsense from his partner, and so is never able to profit from his moments of light.

Unfortunately, as happens in real life, it is upon the more slender shoulders that responsibility is thrust. That is why it is always Stan who has left the key at home; Stan who is always accused: 'That's another fine mess you've gotten me into.' And it is he who, with a look of the utmost self-satisfaction, will demonstrate his knowledge by telling the thieves where his money is hidden; who tumbles over the furniture and turns on the radio when they are themselves robbing a house at dead of night.

Stan is not, perhaps, so much a fool as a child. (In *Be Big* his preparations for a day in Atlantic City consist in packing his toy yacht.) This child's innocence is a quality which Hardy shares with him, and which is, perhaps, the leading distinction of their comedy work. They are the most innocent of all the clowns; more innocent than Buster Keaton's single-minded hero, than Raymond Griffith, Lloyd or Leno; certainly more innocent than Langdon, in his slightly improper moments of first experiment. The motives which impel them have a childish logic; their jealousies and meannesses (they have been known to deceive each other) are mere babyishness. When Stan drinks (it is always Stan who drinks) it is about as vicious as a cigarette in the bathroom. In their films they are often given wives; but to them a wife is no more nor less than a kind of starchy, unyielding, unsympathetic governess, to be deceived (in simple things), outwitted and escaped for the afternoon. Stan and Olly are, of course, always recaptured. Extra-marital interests are on the erotic level of taking an apple for the lady teacher.

Their world is not intended for innocents, however. 'In this case the meek are not blessed. They do not inherit the earth. They inherit chaos. Chaos most active and violent and diabolical takes advantage of their inhibitions.'[1] Tacks exist to be trodden on; banana skins to be slipped on; roofs to be fallen off; trousers to tear; beds to collapse; pianos to fall downstairs; windows and doors to be trapped in. But this is none of their seeking. They deplore it. 'They are perhaps the Civil Servants of comedy. Nothing on earth would please them more than a quiet permanence in all things.'[2] Admittedly, they are loved for their technique of mutual destruction: 'for instance, as when they smash up Finlayson's house while Finlayson destroys their car. This technique is very elaborate, for each side waits patiently for the other to complete each item, thus ensuring a perfectly equal balance of destroyed property.'[3] But this is not of their choice. *That* is Finlayson's fault; it is merely that they have not the finesse to escape such a situation. The destruction may be inevitable, even dutiful, but never orgiastic.

The things that happen in their world are above all things funny in themselves. James Agee has described the famous situation in *Swiss Miss*: 'simple and real . . . as a nightmare. Laurel and Hardy are trying to move a piano across a narrow suspension bridge. The bridge is strung over a sickening chasm, between a couple of Alps. Midway they meet a gorilla.' The same piano had earlier run amok through an hotel, careering of its own accord (perhaps Hardy had pushed it) across the top floor, down the stairs, through the lounge and entrance hall, out of the front door, down the steps and along the road, with Oliver roaring and Stanley whimpering after it.

The success of all this comedy and nonsense is due, finally, to conscientiousness as much as talent. They propound a few basic comic principles, which they mean and which they stick to: 'Keep a semblance of belief, however broad. Let your gags belong to the story; you must have a reason to motivate everything,' says Laurel. Some years ago was published a brief dialogue, in which they put forward their theories of the basis of comedy:

> O.H.: The fun is in the story situations which make an audience sorry for the comedian. A funny man has to make himself inferior . . .
> S.L.: Let a fellow try to outsmart his audience and he misses. It's human nature to laugh at a bird who gets a bucket of paint smeared on his face—even though it makes him miserable.

---

[1] John Grierson in *Grierson on Documentary*.
[2] *ibid*.
[3] Basil Wright: 'Blest Pair of Sirens' (*World Film News*, June, 1937). James Finlayson (?1887–1953) appeared in many of their films: 'snouty James Finlayson, gleefully foreclosing a mortgage, with his look of eternally tasting a spoiled pickle' (James Agee).

27. *Hog Wild*

O.H.: A comedian has to knock dignity off the pedestal. He has to look
small—even I do—by a mental comparison. Lean or fat, short or tall,
he has to be pitied to be laughed at.

S.L.: Sometimes we even feel sorry for each other. That always gets a
laugh out of me. When I can feel sorry for 'Babe'.

O.H.: Me, too, when I can feel sorry for Stan.

A joke of Laurel and Hardy's is no transient thing. It is sniffed and
savoured before use, then used, squeezed dry and squeezed again;
smoothed out, folded up with care and put away ready for the next time.
The same jokes recur again and again. *Be Big* was expanded into
Fraternally Yours; the joke about shooting one's own foot sticking up at the
end of the bed, under the impression that it is a foreign hand, turns up
two or three times, and so on.

There are two reasons why Laurel and Hardy succeed in avoiding monotony, while employing such a limited range of material. Firstly, they appeal particularly and consciously to the pleasures of *recognition* which have always been especially exploited in the music hall—in the use of catchphrases, of dialogue which becomes comic through its very familiarity. Laurel and Hardy's famous lines 'Hard-boiled eggs and nuts', 'Another fine mess'; Stan's cry, or the frequent sight of Oliver, prostrated and turning up his face in speechless appeal, may seem unfunny at first acquaintance, but gradually grow upon one until they are hilarious, irresistible, looked for and cherished.

Secondly, there is their seemingly infinite capacity for variation on a simple theme. Basil Wright described one example: 'In *Aerial Antics* the attempt to fix a wireless aerial on the roof of Laurel's house precipitated Hardy off the roof into a goldfish pond at least five times. Each time a different gag-variation appeared, until the comedy passed into the realms of cutting, and the final fall was but a flight of birds and the sound of an almighty splash. Eisenstein would have been proud to do it.'

The Music Box is better known. Throughout two reels they struggle to get a piano up a tremendous flight of steps. At last they reach the top, where a postman tells them it would have been easier for them to bring it up the back way. Gratefully they thank him, and toil back down the stairs to bring the piano up the easy way.

For all this, and though they themselves never altered, the quality of their pictures did decline. Their technique of film-making demanded conditions of the greatest independence. It is now known—as was long suspected—that the principal creative force behind the films was Stan Laurel. The ideas invariably betray the common influence. He always took a forceful hand in the direction, and it appears that the so-called director, particularly in the early days, was principally required to stand behind the camera while Stan himself was on the set. Finally, he closely supervised the editing.

Laurel considers that it is not possible to make a slapstick comedy by the usual method of discontinuous shooting. Therefore their films for Roach were generally shot in continuity—which must have been an expensive method. They went on the set with a basic idea and an outline of the 'business' they were to introduce; but the main work of creation was done on the set. The actual 'business' and its timing were worked out in accordance with the reactions of the informal audience of technicians and the like who were on the set.

Laurel's editing technique was unusual, and made possible only by his method of continuous shooting. The film was fairly finely cut as it was shot; so that at every stage Laurel and Hardy could see an approximation to the final version, up to the point they had reached in shooting. The timing and editing of the final version were reached, however, only after the reactions of preview audiences had been carefully studied.

The aim of Laurel's film technique appears therefore to have been to approximate the conditions of creation to those of the live theatre. Roach alone seems to have recognised the eventual economy of giving them the degree of freedom demanded by such methods; and in the big studios they were frustrated. With writers and directors haphazardly delegated to their films, regardless of their suitability or sympathy, the decline was inevitable.

Laurel and Hardy make no films today, though they would almost certainly be prepared to start again, given the chance to make them in their own way. They are both sexagenarians, men of great charm and courtesy, both seeming much younger than their real age in their gaiety and continued interest in their work. Each retains, after nearly thirty years, a boundless admiration for the comicality of the other. In refutation of Basil Wright's surmise that their film-making 'must be a solemn, serious and probably bad-tempered process', they describe the shooting of *Leave 'Em Laughing*. 'We had a scene where we're together on a bed. We went on the lot the first day, got up on the bed and started laughing. We laughed so much we couldn't stop. So we weren't able to shoot anything that day. Next day we went back, got up on the bed, and the same thing happened again. So we weren't able to shoot anything that day either.'

At the moment they are in the course of a prolonged music hall tour of this country—their third since the war. And it is amazing to see how little, if at all, they are forgotten by their public, after their long absence from the screen. In the Palaces and Empires their first appearance—wandering in and out of two doors, always just missing each other, Olly waving his bulbous umbrella in greeting to the audience, Stan smiling coyly—is invariably greeted with yells of joyful and loving recognition. And Laurel and Hardy seem to regard that as gratitude enough.

1954

The Seven Samurai

TONY RICHARDSON

Akira Kurosawa's brilliant new film is a long episodic reconstruction of an incident in 16th century Japan. A peasant village is harried by brigands; in despair the villagers decide to hire professional soldiers to defend them; after recruiting difficulties, seven are collected; they organise the village's defence and succeed in wiping out the bandits completely. This basically simple plot Kurosawa elaborates in two ways. He introduces a profusion of incidents and subplots—the youngest samurai falling in love with a village girl disguised by her mistrustful father as a boy, the attempts of a wandering, humorous braggart to be accepted by the others as a samurai; and he gives to each of the many characters an intensely differentiated individual personality—the mature, kindly, selfless leader, the unassuming but obsessive professional swordsman, the traditional braggadoccio.

In *The Seven Samurai*, and in the light it throws back on *Rashomon*, Kurosawa's method and personality emerge clearly. He is, above everything else, an exact psychological observer, a keen analyst of behaviour—in a fundamentally detached way. His handling of the young lovers is typical of this. He notes and traces with precision and truth their first, half-terrified awareness of each other sexually, the growth of mutual attraction, the boy's *gauche* admiration, the girl's aching and almost frantic abandonment; what he fails to do is to convey any feeling for, or identification with, the individuals themselves. He strives for this, he uses other images to heighten their scenes—the flower-covered hillside, the sun filtering through the tops of trees (an echo of its more successful use as an orgasm metaphor in *Rashomon*), the dappled light swarming like insects over them as they lie together in a bamboo hut—but somehow these remain perfunctory, a little cold, lacking in real poetry.

In this it is not unrewarding to compare Kurosawa with Ford—by whom, report has it, he claims to have been influenced. There are many superficial resemblances—the reliance on traditional values, the use of folk ceremonies and rituals, the comic horseplay—to Ford in particular and to the Western in general. The fast, vivid handling of the action sequences, the staccato cutting, the variety of angles, the shooting up through horses rearing in the mud, are all reminiscent of recent films in this genre. But the difference is more revealing. The funeral of the first samurai, killed in a preliminary skirmish, is exactly the sort of scene to which Ford responds, with all his reverence and honour for times past and the community of beliefs and feelings which they embodied. Kurosawa uses the scene in two ways, first as a further observation of the character of the 'crazy samurai'—who, in a defiant attempt to satisfy his own feelings of frustration and impotence, raises the flag the dead man had sewn—and secondly, as an effective incident for heightening the narrative tension: the bandits launch their first onslaught during the funeral. One of the love scenes is used in a similar way, and in both cases one feels an ultimate shying-away from any direct, committed emotion—except anger.

Of course, to say Kurosawa is not Ford is critically meaningless; the comparison has value only in so far as it is a way of gauging the film's intentions, and its realisation of them. What made *Rashomon* so unique and impressive was that everything, the subject, the formal structure, the playing, even perhaps the period, allowed for this exterior approach to behaviour. In *The Seven Samurai* Kurosawa is striving for something different, a re-creation, a bringing to life of the past and the people whose story he is telling. Here, for all the surface conviction of period, the perceptive observation, the raging vitality and the magnificent visual style, the film doesn't quite succeed. All the elements are there except the depth and the generosity of life. One feels that each incident is too carefully worked into the texture as a whole. The Donskoi of the *Gorki* trilogy is a much simpler and, in many ways, more ordinary personality; but he achieved, almost without realising it, what Kurosawa labours for. Life itself seems to have taken over from Donskoi, carrying him along on its great stream, but Kurosawa has engineered a stunning aqueduct along which it must flow. Only in his handling of the 'crazy samurai' does it occasionally overflow. Toshiro Mifune, gibing at the samurai, waving, in mocking triumph, a fish caught in a stream, and—another Falstaff—bullying his hopeless recruits, brings to his portrayal a reckless and at moments out-of-hand gusto. It is a splendid performance, losing no opportunity, and it only fails to integrate a gratuitously introduced class motivation—he is really a peasant wanting to be a samurai. (The fault here lies with the script rather than the performer.) This is perhaps a momentary and rather glib contemporary analogy out of keeping with the rest.

These ultimate reservations should not, however, prevent us from recognising the film's astonishing qualities. Incident after incident is created with biting precision for the whole 2½ hour length (the exported version, incidentally, is an hour shorter than the original)—the villagers shunning the samurai on their arrival only to tumble towards them in panic as the alarm is sounded, the capture of a thief and, brilliantly suspended in slow motion, his death, a brief and wonderful sketch of a

28. *The Seven Samurai*: the villagers' revenge

farmer's wife abducted by the brigands stirring, guilty but sated, in her
sleep. On a different level, Kurosawa is a virtuoso exponent of every
technique of suspense, surprise, excitement, and in this he gives nothing
to his Western masters. Only in his handling of the series of battles is
there a hint of monotony. He knows exactly when to hold a silence; how
to punch home an extraordinary fact with maximum effect; and his use of
the camera is devastating—dazzling close-ups as the village deputation,
overawed and desperate in their quest for samurai, scan the crowded
street, or wild tracking shots as the drunken Mifune stumbles after his
assailant. Visually the film makes a tremendous impression. Kurosawa
can combine formal grace with dramatic accuracy, and many scenes
create a startling pictorial impact. The raid on the bandits' hideout, when
their slaughtered bodies are hurled, naked and haphazard, into the
muddied pools outside their burning hut, is not unworthy of the Goya of
Los Desastres. The final effect, indeed, of *The Seven Samurai*, is not unlike
that of 'Salammbo', a triumph of rage and artifice; and one's final
acknowledgment is not of the intrinsic fascination of the material but the
wrested skill of the artificer.

1955

Letter: Critical Attitudes

JOHN RUSSELL TAYLOR

Sir,—The contributors to *Sight and Sound*, like those to most responsible film periodicals these days, adopt a highly critical, even despairing, attitude to the current product in films. And, no doubt, rightly so, but whether for altogether valid reasons is quite a different question. It is instructive to compare the articles in the Summer number by Lindsay Anderson and Walter Lassally; there seems to be behind both their criticisms an implicit standard of judgment which is accepted as self-evidently 'true', though in fact highly arguable.

The demand behind both articles seems to be for the simple, the warm and human, varied occasionally by hard-hitting but unsensational social criticism. This is of course quite acceptable as a personal taste—perhaps even a personal prejudice—on the part of the critics concerned; but surely to erect it into an apparently abstract standard of judgment and judge all films accordingly is to carry things too far. It lays, the less committed critic might think, far too much stress on the subject-matter of the film, and far too little on the treatment. To say that, say, *Not as a Stranger* or *The Man with the Golden Arm* are bad because they 'contain this fundamentally unhealthy element, which seems to derive from a conviction that today's audiences simply will not take a straightforward, honest drama dealing with the lives of reasonably average men and women', is no doubt part of the story, but only a part. To me they seem bad simply because they are boring—over-long and over-leisurely in treatment for their subjects, variably acted and, most important, directed heavily, without imagination or individuality. The most sensational, blatantly one-sided view of things can be acceptable if handled with conviction and imagination—if it seems a true reflection of a point of view, however far that point of view may be from one's own. In this way, if we are fair, we must admit that an honest glorification of the good sides of war can be just as valid as a statement of complete disgust with the whole thing ... In the same way *Potemkin*, *The Triumph of the Will* and *Mr Smith Goes to Washington* all have a right to exist and a right to non-partisan, aesthetic judgment as works of cinema.

The trouble with a demand for 'commitment' in subject-matter is that it demands also the rejection of much that to the 'irresponsible' aesthete makes the cinema most worthwhile. In practice, to judge by the reviews that appear in your columns, it seems to involve a distrust of the film that demands a sophisticated, civilised response (*Member of the Wedding, Les Enfants Terribles, To Catch a Thief, Muerte de un Ciclista*, to cite a variety of cases), and a weakness for the unpolished and just-competent in direction. Ultimately it seems to approach the newsreel outlook; that is to say, that if in a newsreel one sees victims of famine one is moved, but one is moved simply by their plight, not by the artistic representation of famine. Many of your critics seem to regard this as the height of cinema art—the camera simply records, and nothing stands between the audience and the events portrayed. To me this seems a betrayal of film art—it is rather as if one were to say that efficient journalism is the height of literary achievement.

Take, for example, de Sica's much praised *Umberto D.*: some scenes in it, such as that of the maid's first chores around the kitchen, are exquisitely handled—camera-movement and lighting are at one with the subject and fuse together into an expressive whole. Other scenes, however, such as that in which Umberto D. tries to beg, rely on making something touching happen in front of the camera and then recording it. And we *are* moved, but surely, by the situation itself, not by its realisation in filmic terms.

Also the demand for commitment involves a number of snobberies. Critics forget that it is just as easy, and probably easier, to make a bad film ordinary shape, black and white, on a small budget and without stars as it is to make one in the full glory of CinemaScope and stereophonic sound, with five stars—and for that matter professional film-makers are usually professionals because they know more about it than amateurs. By all means let us praise enterprise and good intentions, but if necessary we should be ready to allow a film 'nought for achievement, one for trying'—as I felt, dare I admit it, to be the case with *Together*. Another favourite snobbery is the rejection of the period, costume film—on the principle, presumably, that something vital about human beings can only be said about people in modern dress, as if people are social counters and their reactions are entirely dependent on their immediate social milieu . . . And of course there is the fashionable despair over the pure entertainment film. But why bother to despair over science fiction, or *Hilda Crane*, or *The Rains of Ranchipur* or *Serenade*? They will mostly be forgotten in a few months, like the majority of films at any period, and the few survivors will be resurrected to critical praise in some five or ten years time . . .

By all means let critics prefer committed, humanist films on contemporary subjects, but such moral judgments should be presented as what they are—personal, subjective tastes, not the be-all and end-all of criticism. To present such moral judgments (which could often be reached just as well through reading a plot summary of the film without seeing it) does not absolve critics from the necessity of reaching some aesthetic judgment for the benefit of people who just happen to love the film for its own sake, and would rather, in the words of the late Richard Winnington, 'join the queue for a Mark Ostrer film or an American musical (much rather!) than see no films at all'.

Yours faithfully,
J. R. Taylor

1956

A Long Time on the Little Road

SATYAJIT RAY

I remember the first day's shooting of *Pather Panchali* [*The Little Road*] very well. It was in the festive season, in October, and the last of the big *pujas* was taking place that day. Our location was 75 miles away from Calcutta. As our taxi sped along the Grand Trunk Road we passed through several suburban towns and villages and heard the drums and even had fleeting glimpses of some images. Someone said it would bring us luck. I had my doubts, but I wished to believe it. All who set about making films need luck as much as they need the other things: talent, money, perseverance and so on. We needed a little more of it than most.

I knew this first day was really a sort of rehearsal for us, to break us in, as it were. For most of us it was a start from scratch. There were eight on our unit of whom only one—Bansi, the art director—had previous professional experience. We had a new cameraman, Subrata, and an old, much-used Wall camera which happened to be the only one available for hire on that particular day. Its one discernible advantage seemed to be a device to ensure smoothness of panning. We had no sound equipment, as the scene was to be a silent one.

It was an episode in the screen-play where the two children of the story, brother and sister, stray from their village and chance upon a field of *kaash* flowers. The two have had a quarrel, and here in this enchanted setting they are reconciled and their long journey is rewarded by their first sight of a railway train. I chose to begin with this scene because on paper it seemed both effective and simple. I considered this important, because the whole idea behind launching the production with only 8,000 rupees in the bank was to produce quickly and cheaply a reasonable length of rough cut which we hoped would establish our bonafides, the lack of which had so far stood in the way of our getting a financier.

At the end of the first day's shooting we had eight shots. The children behaved naturally, which was a bit of luck because I hadn't tested them. As for myself, I remember feeling a bit strung up in the beginning; but as work progressed my nerves relaxed and in the end I even felt a kind of elation. However, the scene was only half finished, and on the following Sunday we were back on the same location. But was it the same location? It was hard to believe it. What was on the previous occasion a sea of fluffy

whiteness was now a mere expanse of uninspiring brownish grass. W
knew *kaash* was a seasonal flower, but surely they were not tha
shortlived? A local peasant provided the explanation. The flowers, h
said, were food to the cattle. The cows and buffaloes had come to graz
the day before and had literally chewed up the scenery.

This was a big set-back. We knew of no other *kaash* field that woul
provide the long shots that I needed. This meant staging the action in
different setting, and the very thought was heartbreaking. Who woul
have known then that we would be back on the identical location exactl
two years later and indulge in the luxury of reshooting the entire scen
with the same cast and the same unit but with money provided by th
Government of West Bengal?

When I look back on the making of *Pather Panchali*, I cannot be su
whether it has meant more pain to me than pleasure. It is difficult t
describe the peculiar torments of a production held up for lack of fund
The long periods of enforced idleness (there were two gaps totalling
year and a half) produce nothing but the deepest gloom. The very sight
the scenario is sickening, let alone thoughts of embellishing it with detai
or brushing up the dialogue.

But work—even a day's work—has rewards, not the least of which
the gradual comprehension of the complex and fascinating nature c
film-making itself. The edicts of the theorists, learnt assiduously over th
years, doubtless perform some useful function at the back of your min
But grappling with the medium in a practical way for the first time, yo
realise (a) that you know rather less about it than you thought you did; (
that the theorists don't provide all the answers, and (c) that your approac
should derive not from Dovzhenko's *Earth*, however much you may lov
that dance in the moonlight, but from the earth, the soil, of your ow
country—assuming, of course, that your story has its roots in it.

Bibhutibhusan Bannerji's *Pather Panchali* was serialised in a popula
Bengali magazine in the early 1930s. The author had been brought up in
village and the book contained much that was autobiographical. Th
manuscript had been turned down by the publishers on the grounds tha
it lacked a story. The magazine, too, was initially reluctant to accept it, bu
later did so on condition that it would be discontinued if the readers of th
magazine so wished. But the story of Apu and Durga was a hit from th
first instalment. The book, published a year or so later, was a
outstanding critical and popular success and has remained on th
best-seller list ever since.

I chose *Pather Panchali* for the qualities that made it a great book: it
humanism, its lyricism, and its ring of truth. I knew I would have to do
lot of pruning and reshaping—I certainly could not go beyond the firs
half, which ended with the family's departure for Benares—but at th
same time I felt that to cast the thing into a mould of cut and drie

29. Satyajit Ray directing *Pather Panchali*

narrative would be wrong. The script had to retain some of the rambling quality of the novel because that in itself contained a clue to the feel of authenticity; life in a poor Bengali village does ramble.

Considerations of form, rhythm or movement didn't worry me much at this stage. I had my nucleus: the family, consisting of husband and wife, the two children, and the old aunt. The characters had been so conceived by the author that there was a constant and subtle interplay between them. I had my time span of one year. I had my contrasts—pictorial as well as emotional: the rich and the poor, the laughter and the tears, the beauty of the countryside and the grimness of poverty existing in it. Finally, I had the two natural halves of the story culminating in two poignant deaths. What more could a scenarist want?

What I lacked was first-hand acquaintance with the *milieu* of the story. I could, of course, draw upon the book itself, which was a kind of encyclopædia of Bengali rural life, but I knew that this was not enough. In

any case, one had only to drive six miles out of the city to get to the heart
the authentic village.

While far from being an adventure in the physical sense, the
explorations into the village nevertheless opened up a new a
fascinating world. To one born and bred in the city, it had a new flavour
new texture; and its values were different. It made you want to obser
and probe, to catch the revealing details, the telling gestures, tl
particular turns of speech. You wanted to fathom the mysteries
'atmosphere'. Does it consist in the sight, or in the sounds? How to cat
the subtle difference between dawn and dusk, or convey the grey hum
stillness that precedes the first monsoon shower? Is sunlight in Spring tl
same as sunlight in Autumn? . . .

The more you probed the more was revealed, and familiarity bred n
contempt but love, understanding, tolerance. Problems of film-makix
began to recede into the background and you found yourself belittling tl
importance of the camera. After all, you said, it is only a recordix
instrument. The important thing is Truth. Get at it and you've got yo
great humanist masterpiece.

But how wrong you were! The moment you are on the set tl
three-legged instrument takes charge. Problems come thick and fa
Where to place the camera? High or low? Near or far? On the dolly or t
the ground? Is the thirty-five OK or would you rather move back and u
the fifty? Get too close to the action and the emotion of the scene spi
over; get too far back and the thing becomes cold and remote. To ea
problem that arises you must find a quick answer. If you delay the si
shifts and makes nonsense of your light continuity.

Sound is a problem, too. Dialogue has been reduced to a minimum, b
you want to cut down further. Are these three words really necessary,
can you find a telling gesture to take their place? The critics may well ta
of a laudable attempt at a rediscovery of the fundamentals of sile
cinema, but you know within your heart that while there may be sor
truth in that, equally true was your anxiety to avoid the uninspirix
business of dubbing and save on the cost of sound film.

Cost, indeed, was a dominant determining factor at all time
influencing the very style of the film. Another important factor—anc
wouldn't want to generalise on this—was the human one. In handling n
actors I found it impossible to get to that stage of impersonal detachme
where I could equate them with so much raw material to be moulded ar
remoulded at will. How can you make a woman of eighty stand in the h
midday sun and go through the same speech and the same actions ov
and over again while you stand by and watch with half closed eyes ar
wait for that precise gesture and tone of voice that will mean perfection f
you? This meant, inevitably, fewer rehearsals and fewer takes.

Sometimes you are lucky and everything goes right in the first tak

Sometimes it does not and you feel you will never get what you are aiming at. The number of takes increases, the cost goes up, the qualms of conscience become stronger than the urge for perfection and you give up, hoping that the critics will forgive and the audience will overlook. You even wonder whether perhaps you were not being too finicky and the thing was not as bad or as wrong as you thought it was.

And so on and on it goes, this preposterous balancing act, and you keep hoping that out of all this will somehow emerge Art. At times when the strain is too much you want to give up. You feel it is going to kill you, or at least kill the artist in you. But you carry on, mainly because so much and so many are involved, and the day comes when the last shot is in the can and you are surprised to find yourself feeling not happy and relieved, but sad. And you are not alone in this. Everybody, from 'Auntie' for whom it has been an exciting if strenuous comeback after thirty years of oblivion, down to the little urchin who brought the live spiders and the dead toad, shares this feeling.

To me it is the inexorable rhythm of its creative process that makes film-making so exciting in spite of the hardships and the frustrations.

30. *Pather Panchali*

Consider this process: you have conceived a scene, any scene. Take the one where a young girl, frail of body but full of some elemental zest, gives herself up to the first monsoon shower. She dances in joy while the big drops pelt her and drench her. The scene excites you not only for its visual possibilities but for its deeper implications as well: that rain will be the cause of her death.

You break down the scene into shots, make notes and sketches. Then the time comes to bring the scene to life. You go out into the open, scan the vista, choose your setting. The rain clouds approach. You set up your camera, have a last quick rehearsal. Then the 'take'. But one is not enough. This is a key scene. You must have another while the shower lasts. The camera turns, and presently your scene is on celluloid.

Off to the lab. You wait, sweating—this is September—while the ghostly negative takes its own time to emerge. There is no hurrying the process. Then the print, the 'rushes'. This looks good, you say to yourself. But wait. This is only the content, in bits and pieces, and not the form. How is it going to join up? You grab your editor and rush off to the cutting room. There is a gruelling couple of hours, filled with aching suspense, while the patient process of cutting and joining goes on. At the end you watch the thing on the moviola. Even the rickety old machine cannot conceal the effectiveness of the scene. Does this need music, or is the incidental sound enough? But that is another stage in the creative process and must wait until all the shots have been joined up into scenes and the scenes into sequences and the film can be comprehended in its totality. Then, and only then, can you tell—if you can bring to bear on that detachment and objectivity—if your dance in the rain has really come off.

But is this detachment, this objectivity, possible? You know you worked honestly and hard, and so did everybody else. But you also know that you had to make changes, compromises—not without the best reasons—on the set and in the cutting room. Is it better for them or worse? Is your own satisfaction the final test or must you bow to the verdict of the majority? You cannot be sure. But you can be sure of one thing: you are a better man for having made it.

Paths of Glory

GAVIN LAMBERT

France, 1916, a few miles behind the front: upstairs, in the chateau commandeered by the French army as military headquarters, the orchestra plays a waltz for an officers' ball; and in the grandiose panelled library General Broulard has deserted his guests to sip brandy and talk with young Colonel Dax. 'Troops are like children. They need discipline . . .' The General believes in setting examples. Dax asks what kind of example and the old man gives an elegant, furtive shrug. 'Shooting a man,' he explains, 'now and then.'

In fact, three French soldiers are due to be shot as 'examples' in a few hours' time. On the previous day the Division Commander, General Mireau (at Broulard's hint that promotion will attend a success) ordered Dax to lead an attack on an obviously impregnable German position. When it failed the enraged Mireau first ordered the artillery commander to fire on his own men, which the commander refused to do, then after the battle insisted that three men should be chosen by lot from the division and be court-martialled for cowardice. Broulard, also feeling the honour of GHQ at stake, agreed. The trial took place and in spite of Dax's plea (in civilian life he was a criminal lawyer) the men were sentenced to death. As a last resort, Dax now brings to Broulard his knowledge that Mireau wanted to fire on his own men, but the old General still doesn't feel that this alters the case. He doesn't share Mireau's angry thirst for revenge, but he believes in discipline. Examples must be set.

The execution proceeds. Afterwards, at breakfast in the chateau, Broulard calmly turns on Mireau and tells him he will have to face an inquiry. Then he offers Mireau's position to Dax, explaining with a smile of complicity that he realises this is what Dax has been after all the time. When Dax explodes with rage and says all he has been after is human decency, the terrible old man is genuinely incapable of understanding him.

Paths of Glory, directed by Stanley Kubrick, has no lack, as you can see, of brutal ironies. It is based, incidentally, on a novel by Humphrey Cobb in turn drawn from an actual incident that occurred in the French army during World War One. Its epigraph might be von Clausewitz's remark: war is merely an extension of the policies of peace. There is much in the film that powerfully illustrates the physical horrors of war, but even more impressive and frightening is the study of its social structure. The world seems cruelly divided into the leaders and the led. The officers conduct their foxy intrigues in the elegant rooms of a great chateau, and the setting somehow emphasises their indifference to human life. The men go to the trenches and into battle as in peace-time they went to offices or factories. The sequence of the attack itself, done mainly in a series of vivid, inexorable, lateral tracking shots, is a fearful reminder that war, simply, kills a lot of people; and the film finds an eloquent visual contrast between the grim carnage of the battlefield and the spacious luxury of headquarters.

We are in fact a long way from the emotional pacifism of *All Quiet on the Western Front*, which was made twelve years after World War One. *Paths of Glory*, made twelve years after World War Two, never openly attacks war as an abstraction, neither does it examine causes. I suspect it will be the more lasting film, certainly it is difficult to imagine a film about war that could have a more stunning impact today. Seeing *All Quiet* again recently, I was as impressed as ever by the tragic realism of its battle sequences and the boldness of its protest, but occasionally appalled by the inadequacy of its arguments. (At one point two privates suggest that everything could be solved if the two opposing generals rolled up their sleeves and fought it out alone on the battlefield.) *Paths of Glory*, by showing the gulf between leaders and led fatally widened by the fact of war, shows war itself as an extended struggle for power, internal and external. It is the practical as opposed to the sentimental argument, and seems easily the more persuasive today, when one can't avoid feeling that if another war breaks out it will be for reasons completely remote from the lives of most people: another extension of the policies of peace, in fact, which when we read about them in the newspapers seem remote enough already. The visual contrast of, say, a 'Summit' conference and a hydrogen bomb exploding on a city, is only taking *Paths of Glory*'s contrast of the chateau and the trenches a stage further.

This is not only a film of unusual substance but a powerfully realised and gripping work of art. In *The Killing* Stanley Kubrick's talent was operating within the limits of familiar melodrama; *Paths of Glory* is meaningful as well as brilliant. The material is very well organised—the first fifteen minutes are a *tour de force* of complex exposition made clear and dramatic by resourceful handling—and the characterisations bitingly sharp. The two most memorable portraits are of the Generals Broulard and Mireau. Adolphe Menjou as the first, cynical, sly and incalculably corrupt, George Macready as the cold, vengeful, ambitious militarist, are beyond praise. Richard Anderson is also excellent as Mireau's lackey, Major Saint-Auban. Evil in fact, turns out not for the first time to be more dramatic than good. Kirk Douglas is sober and honest in the part of Dax,

31. *Paths of Glory*

but we know less about him than the others, and he remains more a spokesman for the audience's feelings than a fully explored character. At the end he is left on the brink of disgust for the human race—not only officers but men, who seem to forget their comrades' death all too quickly. A final incident convinces him that men are more than pigs, and when news comes that his division will be moved into action again next day, he is able to face it with equilibrium. This scene is effective in itself but loses some force because we see it through the eyes of a character never brought very close.

There is much violence and unsparing physical detail in the film, yet the final effect is somehow austere, because the horror has a moral force. For the dialogue sequences Kubrick uses a fluid probing technique recalling Max Ophuls (whom he especially admires) with more close-ups. At times he dispenses with the conventional syntax of fade or dissolve, which has the general effect of stretching the narrative line very tight and can also make a particular dramatic comment—a briefly held shot of the corpses of the three executed men, slumped against the wooden posts to which they have been tied, is followed by a cut to the two generals at breakfast in the dining-room, the table glittering with fine silver. The execution sequence itself—the soldiers drawn up in the chateau's formal garden, the priest embarrassedly countering the hysteria of one of the men with correct religious phrases, the three upright wooden posts, the coffins waiting in an open cart, the two generals erect and bemedalled nearby as if dressed up for a review, and a sudden twittering of birds as rifles are raised—is masterly.

It may be that some of the film's more relentless moments were a little too much for the censor; the version of *Paths of Glory* which has just opened in London is very slightly shorter than the American original.

1958

The Critical Question

PENELOPE HOUSTON

> The English critic, always protesting that the drama
> should not be didactic, and yet always complaining if
> the dramatist does not find sermons in stones and
> good in everything . . .
>
> BERNARD SHAW

Was Shaw right, and has the English critic a constant, if concealed, longing for the right-minded work, the play or film or novel with its moral lessons as firmly and unambiguously stitched in as those of a nineteenth-century sampler? Sometimes it seems so, when the nanny instinct that lurks somewhere in most critical consciences rises to the surface and the reader is warned off the cruel or the depressing in entertainment as though being counselled against taking sweets from strange men. (Only nanny, who has never had much of a sense of humour, could so signally have failed to see the joke of *Psycho*.) On the whole, though, nanny knows her place. The governing characteristic of English critical writing, rather, seems to be its empiricism, its innate distrust of theory and reluctance to draw demarcation lines. The aspiring critic naïve enough to ask advice is likely to be given it succinctly. His job: to make up his mind about what the artist was trying to do; then to consider how well he has done it. The third question is the dangerous one: was it really worth doing in the first place? To ask it implies that the critic is judging the work not 'on its own merits' (that favourite, elusive English phrase) but according to some system of values; that, in fact, he has a theory.

Exactly four years ago, Lindsay Anderson's article 'Stand up! Stand up!' was published in this magazine. In some quarters it was greeted as a significant statement of principle, its insistence that the dangerous third question could not be evaded being accepted as a statement of something self-evidently true although too often neglected. In other areas, Mr Anderson was welcomed rather like a bowler caught throwing in a test match. The method might take a wicket or two, but wasn't he trying to impose his own reading of the rules of the game? In any case, the argument about commitment was on; and it has been with us ever since. The commitment question still remains central to any discussion of a critical theory. But there has been so much misunderstanding and confusion about just what the expression ought to mean, more particularly about how Lindsay Anderson interpreted it and where people thought this interpretation was leading, that a certain restatement is still necessary.

'Stand up! Stand up!' called into question the not uncommon idea that a critic should somehow be able to separate the analytical, appreciative, professional side of his personality from the rest of his attitudes to life. In itself, of course, the idea is an illusion: there is no such thing as entirely objective, unbiased criticism; there is only critical writing (and not a great deal of it at that) which aspires to this condition. But the critic who will gaily admit his personal quirks of taste just because these help to build up his image, his personality as it addresses itself to the reader, will keep tactfully quiet about where he stands on the larger issues. He will make moral judgments (on films like *Peeping Tom*) more easily than social ones (on films like *The Angry Silence*). He will attack what he feels to be dangerously vicious while tolerantly letting pass what he knows to be as insidiously damaging in its encouragement of snap reactions and slipshod thinking.

Lindsay Anderson is not an Englishman, and he has none of the English respect for words like 'fair' and 'balanced' and 'impartial'. With all a Scot's distrust of compromise, he took the critical writing of four years ago to task for its undefined liberalism and asked it to declare its principles: he wanted values to be openly admitted. Some of the misunderstanding began here. How, he was asked, could he properly review a film such as the Nazi *Triumph of the Will* or the Catholic *Journal d'un Curé de Campagne*? These films' quality was in their 'use of the medium'; and wasn't a critic's expressed dislike of the ideologies they reflected going to cloud his perception? This sort of question in itself shows a striking lack of appreciation of how the disciplines of criticism operate. The critic does not have to agree with a case to know whether it is being well or badly stated; he does not have to find the Bernanos-Bresson ethos, with its masochistic self-questioning, a sympathetic one (he may even find it repellent) to appreciate that *Journal d'un Curé* is a masterpiece of resolute conviction. He can admire without agreeing and agree without admiring. And although this ought to be self-evident, apparently it has not been.

The belief—more often it looks like a pretence—that one can somehow write a sounder review of a film by keeping to style and method, by not bothering to work out what its motive force may be, is surprisingly influential. *Triumph of the Will* is the kind of film brought up as an example; and if ever an example boomeranged against those who introduce it, then this is the one. No critic can overlook the film's brilliance, its electric authority. Anyone who feels that it should be reviewed *primarily* in terms of technique rather than for its unique value as a document of Nazism triumphant has somehow failed to establish contact with the century in which he is living. Maybe there are those who prefer it that way.

There is no point in discussing here the arguments for committed criticism. They ought to be familiar enough by now. And Lindsay Anderson's article, in any case, was not only—was not perhaps even primarily—an attempt to elucidate a theory. It was also a call to arms, an appeal to the critics to stand up and be counted. Mr Anderson made no secret of his own commitments, which are Left Wing, though in the humane rather than the actively political sense; and, by implication, he has since made it apparent that he is not greatly concerned with other people's commitments unless they coincide more or less with his own.

Although the critical profession traditionally occupies a position somewhat left of centre, the critics as a whole did not relish being told that they ought to be radicals. In all the arts, in the eyes of its upholders and in those of its opponents, committed criticism effectively means Left Wing criticism. If you say that you are committed, you are also saying (or are thought to be saying) that you are a socialist; and this makes it impossible to consider the critical problem without relating it to some of the wider issues of life in this country.

'Stand up! Stand up!' was not simply an isolated article: it was part of an atmosphere which may be evoked through the names of half a dozen groups and organisations: the Royal Court Theatre, Joan Littlewood's Theatre Workshop, Free Cinema, *Universities and Left Review* (now the *New Left Review*), *Encore, Tribune*, the Aldermaston marches. During the last half of the Fifties, most of the creative and energetic thinking directed to that point where politics and culture meet has been orientated towards the Left. There has been nothing that could precisely be defined as a movement, but there has been constant interaction. Meanwhile, socialism in the country at large has steadily been losing ground. The 1959 election was a turning point; and the *New Statesman*'s election-eve comment that, whatever the result, the campaign would prove to have been a triumph for Labour, only underlined the distance between illusion and reality. Since the election, all the divisions within the Labour Party have been paraded before the electorate; a split of which rather less has been made is that between the young, radical, socially critical faction (who have their allies also on the Right) and the politicians of the Left. The gap between political practice and quasi-political thinking can seldom have been wider: the Young Left, which has found its Osbornes and Weskers, its Bergers and Tynans, has yet to find its politicians.

This is hardly the climate of optimism, which means that a brave, essentially hopeful gesture such as Arnold Wesker's attempt to interest the unions in the arts seems all the more encouraging. What Wesker is

attempting may not work, and he knows it, but the effort itself
magnificently positive. But Wesker gives the impression of having son
of the confidence that moves mountains; and there is not a great deal '
that around. Rather, there is an air of disillusionment, a soure
disapproving frustration, which is the mood least helpful not only '
creative endeavour but to good writing of any kind. The critic wr
appears a congenital nagger and disapprover, who tries to bully ar
hector art into following the path he would like it to take, is more of
liability than a help to his cause.

The worst enemy, it sometimes seems, of commitment in criticism
the writing of some of those who carry its banner. There is, for instanc
the lunatic theory, occasionally paraded, that art *only* becom
meaningful if it has something directly to say to the ordinary man. Mar
writers, in this magazine and elsewhere, have appealed for a cinema ar
theatre more closely related to life as we are currently experiencing it, *a*
appreciation of the ordinary as subject matter. But the idea that art cann
also afford to be difficult, esoteric, private, would take us into the sphe
of the cultural *gauleiters*. Then there is the theatre critic who will lambast
depressingly bad drawing-room comedy one week, because this
decadent bourgeois entertainment, and will find virtue next week in a r
less pitiful farce because this, at least, has the 'honest vulgarity' that tl
man in the street ,enjoys. This is the special pleading of criticism, tl
setting up of a double standard.

In the cinema, opponents of the committed approach claim that tl
double standard again operates. Technique, they say, is dangerous
devalued: a badly made film is forgiven its faults if its approach is four
sympathetic. This is difficult territory and one can only make a person
comment. Should the critic write a selling notice of a work which I
believes deserves encouragement, or should he be stringent in pointir
out its weaknesses? My own belief: enthusiasm is essential to the criti
and where he feels it he must communicate it. Incompetence deserves r
quarter, but when the promise is unmistakable, and the effort to grapp
with a subject not merely in terms of technique but of trying '
understand the truth about it, then the time to start making a major issu
of what went wrong is with the artist's second or third film.

Changes in critical attitudes are not merely inevitable but absolute
necessary, since art keeps alive through a constant process '
re-evaluation and reassessment. It is through this process that criticis
ought to stimulate creation; and it is through it that the 'masterpieces' th
take a clique or a critical group or a whole generation by storm a
revalued for the future. There should be no final judgments in criticisn

If a new generation is emerging in film criticism in this country, some
its first stirrings may be visible in an undergraduate magazine, *Oxfo.*

Opinion (it is now twelve years since *Sequence* came out of Oxford), in the letters that reach *Sight and Sound* from young writers or would-be writers, in more or less vague hints and indications. As might be expected, by the natural process of reaction, the new mood is directly opposed to the one that preceded it. Its allegiance is solely to the cinema; its heroes are directors also greatly admired by the younger generation of French critics (Nicholas Ray, Samuel Fuller, Douglas Sirk, Frank Tashlin); its concern is essentially with the cinema as a director's medium. The general attitudes are extremely close to those of the French critics, which are discussed in detail elsewhere in this issue; but some brief statement of them is necessary here.

Insisting that criticism as generally practised pays over-much attention to script, story, acting performances, subject generally, they have themselves swung to the opposite extreme. All this is irrelevant, something cinema shares with the other arts: what must be isolated is the special, elusive quality that is the cinema's own, and that can be found in the way a sequence is lit, the way space is manipulated, the way a mood can be transmitted through the choice of camera angles and the pacing of a scene.

So far, so good. Here is *Oxford Opinion* on Samuel Fuller, director of the current cult 'masterpiece' *The Crimson Kimono*: 'Fuller is at his best, i.e. most beautiful, when his ideas are at their least inspired—in *Steel Helmet*, the most exciting images came when he was producing total nonsense.' On *Comanche Station*, a B-Western very favourably reviewed: '*Comanche Station* does not use its structure as a framework for ideas. In fact it has almost nothing to say . . .' On Nicholas Ray's sense of composition: 'In *Party Girl* there is a shot of a girl lying with her hands dangling in a bath full of water which is red from the blood of her slashed wrists. Even by Ray standards it is outstandingly beautiful.' On Anthony Mann: 'He seems to me to be far worthier of a cult than John Ford; at least Mann never made a *dull* movie.' And, not unexpectedly, on *Sight and Sound*: 'It is only a pretty typical product of an approach to films that is fundamentally perverted . . .'

Perverted, perhaps, but not blind to what the new critical school—if that is not too pompous a phrase for it—are after. There are no good or bad subjects; affirmation is a word for boy scouts; social significance is a bore; don't expect a film to present you with sympathetic characters; don't even, if one takes it far enough, look for character; don't have any truck with anything that smacks of literature. Cinema, by this definition, means first and foremost the visual image; and the critic's response is to the excitement it can communicate.

A lot of this comes from *Cahiers du Cinéma*, along with the list of admired directors. And it is this list itself, as much as the way in which the films are discussed—don't look to these reviews for analysis, but rather for a series

32. Cult cinema? John Ford's *Wagonmaster*

of slightly breathless statements—that underlines fundamental diverg-
ences of viewpoint. A letter from Ian Jarvie, one of the more articulate of
the younger writers although not attached to the Oxford group, gave us a
hint two years ago: 'The young take odd, isolated, almost idiosyncratic
lines like: preferring later Hitchcock to the pre-war vintage, enjoying the
fast, tough (perhaps sadistic?) gangster film, rhapsodising over Nazi
films, being bored with neo-realism and Free Cinema . . .' Nicholas Ray or
Satyajit Ray? Samuel Fuller or John Ford?

Here, we are reaching the main area of disagreement. Methods of
criticism are not the most significant point, since no one, however
resolutely disinterested in subject matter, can avoid coming to grips
sooner or later with the question of what a film is about. The limitation of
the aesthetic approach, finally, is that it simply won't work: reviewing a
film in terms of half a dozen striking shots, and of what their emotional
impact and technical brilliance meant to you, is like walking in a fog
without a torch. The mist of images swirls around, landmarks are
obscured, without realising it one progresses in a series of circles. Cinema
is about the human situation, not about 'spatial relationships'.

What the young critics mainly admire, however, are films whose relation to the business of living is in itself somewhat precarious. You cannot write, for instance, about a film like *Pather Panchali* (or *Les Quatre Cents Coups*, or *The Tokyo Story*) without concerning yourself with the way in which certain truths about the relationships between people, and the place of these people in their society, are defined on the screen. The film is not enclosed within its circumference; it is not retreating behind any protective hedge of 'art'. *The Crimson Kimono*, however, which is pulp literature with (oddly enough) some stabs at a social conscience, is a film which can only be admired in terms of its immediate impact. We would be a prim and dismal lot if we denied admiration to this kind of cinema, though I would not myself choose *Crimson Kimono* as an example. But we all have a way of constructing general theories on the basis of particular admirations; and a theory of criticism constructed around an appreciation

33. Cult cinema? Nicholas Ray's *Party Girl*

of *Crimson Kimono,* or *Party Girl,* or *Written on the Wind,* seems to me distinctly barren one.

Extreme skill, working on subject matter of whatever banality, ca produce an intoxicating excitement of its own; and because the condition of film-making are such that almost no creative worker in the cinema ca be a full-time artist, we are all used to finding some of our excitement i part-time art—in seeing, that is, what the first-rate talent can do with th third-rate subject, even in watching how he can work against the subjec to communicate something of his own. In the American cinema especially, the big subject often intimidates; it is the casual glances a reality which are more telling. To pass from this, however, to a belief tha the subject itself is always irrelevant is to make a preposterous leap. Anc in this context, one suspects that the subjects are not as irrelevant as a that. 'Run out and get yourself a positive affirmation and cinematicall you're made,' says one of *Oxford Opinion*'s contributors about *The Grapes* Wrath. 'Fine; but don't ask me to sit through it.' Well, of course, on wouldn't. But one might ask whether it is the accretion of critical opinio that has built up around *Grapes of Wrath* or the film itself that is bein denigrated; whether the mistrust is of committed criticism or committe cinema.

Attitudes of this kind are, one suspects, fairly widespread. And the are understandable enough. To the generation which has grown u during the last few years, art is seen as something for kicks: films whic stab at the nerves and the emotions; jazz, and the excitemen surrounding it; Method acting, with its carefully sustained illusion c spontaneity. Violence on the screen is accepted as a stimulant an anything which can be labelled as slow or sentimental is suspec Conversely, though, there does not seem to be much appreciation for th consciously cynical and sophisticated. The attitude is far from being on of disillusionment or defeat: it is more simply a disinterest in art whic does not work on one's own terms, and an inevitable belief that thos terms are the only valid ones.

The gap between my own Oxford generation, the initiators of *Sequenc* and the present group of Oxford critics is only twelve years or so. Bu those of us who grew up during the war, when violence was perhaps to close to be also a handy stimulant, and whose attitudes to the cinem were being formulated at the time of the neo-realist experiment, of th general outburst of wartime and postwar realism, are not easily incline to divorce art and morality or art and society in our minds. At the sam time, this is the generation that made the critical discovery of Nichola Ray, helping to get his first film, *They Live By Night,* its London screening and that admired the 'black' Hollywood cinema of the post-war years. W liked (and still like) *The Big Sleep* and *Sunset Boulevard* and *Mildred Pierc* and not for their qualities of affirmation.

These, in any case, are the skirmishing rounds of criticism; the real battlefield is elsewhere. Criticism ought to be a perpetual questioning of values, a subjection of opinions and standards to pressure. And the weakness of the *Cahiers du Cinéma* school, both in its own country and among its exponents here, seems to be that it barely admits of experience which does not take place in the cinema. Its criticism too easily becomes shop talk for the initiated; its enthusiasms are self-limiting; it turns inward upon itself, so that a film's validity is assessed not in relation to the society from which it draws its material but in relation to other cinematic experiences. It is all a bit hermetic, as though its practitioners had chosen to live in the dark, emerging to blink, mole-like, at the cruel light, to sniff the chilly air, before ducking back into the darkness of another cinema.

The so-called commitment argument, by forcing the antagonists to take up extreme and impossible positions, has confused the real issues. These are not whether the social or moral standpoint of the artist or aesthetic values are more important, but whether the cinema can find its own mode of expressing essential truth.

Film Journal, Melbourne

What we mean by 'standards' is surely nothing that can be tabulated, but rather a general approach, a willingness to assess in detail the social and moral content of a film by analysing the impact it makes upon us. And such analysis presupposes a clear conception of the way the film medium works—i.e., an aesthetic.

Definition, London

The impasse in film-making and in film criticism is essentially the same as the impasse in radical thought. In both, old traditions have run their course . . . In both, vague and unsystematic new stirrings have begun.

Film Quarterly, San Francisco

These three quotations, taken from recent issues of film journals published in three continents, all reflect the same dissatisfaction. Film criticism is in search of an aesthetic, which will not be found in the narrower issues of committed versus anti-committed attitudes; and, as *Film Journal* says, this debate ceases to be illuminating when both sides are forced into taking up extremist positions. The unattractive truth, of course, is that there is plenty of reviewing and not nearly enough criticism (and a magazine such as this one must accept its share of the guilt); that the film, because it cannot be taken home and studied like a novel or a play, invites reactions and impressions rather than sustained analysis; that there has never really been an aesthetic of the sound cinema, and that most of the standard text books are useful only for those who still believe that cinema history virtually stops with *Blackmail* and *The Blue Angel*.

The contemporary cinema is moving, and moving fairly rapidly, in half a dozen directions at once: a state of affairs which increases the bewilderment of the critic who would like to hang on to an aesthetic like a life-belt in a stormy sea. An aesthetic that can encompass Resnais' constantly moving camera and Ozu's stationary one; the anti-dramatic cinema of Zavattini and the anti-dramatic cinema of Bresson; the intellectual refinements of a film by Antonioni and the sensuous impact of one by Renoir; the stripped down cinema of Buñuel and the dressed up cinema of Bergman . . . this is a tall order. I do not believe, in any case, that the elusive, will o' the wisp 'aesthetic of cinema' is suddenly going to emerge; and I can't believe that it greatly matters.

In the long run, the critic is still on his own, confronted with the work of art. His tools: his sensibility, his knowledge, his judgment, and his apparatus of values. There are fifty different ways of being a good critic, and again I do not believe it really matters—as the editors of *Definition* apparently do—that two critics 'who might be expected to share certain basic values' can arrive at judgments almost diametrically opposed. 'What are the differences in attitude, in presuppositions, in general view of life which can elicit conflicting responses to a single film?' enquires *Definition*. One might almost as profitably ask why two witnesses disagree about what really happened in a traffic accident.

Any theory one can formulate is of general value only in so far as it illuminates the general problem. And the main duty of criticism at present, as I see it, has little to do with the argument about form versus content, aesthetic values versus values of subject. If the film makes an impact, it does so through its style, using style here to mean the full force of the artist's personality as revealed in his work: there can be no argument here. Primarily, though, I would suggest that the critical duty is to examine the cinema in terms of its ideas, to submit these to the test of comment and discussion. That the cinema is an art is no longer in question; that battle is over and won. But if it is an art on the same plane as literature and the theatre, then it is the use of its special techniques for the expression of ideas that must make it so.

One is not asking here for an intellectual cinema, though some corrective to the present mistrust of intellect and over-emphasis on emotional content might not be a bad thing. And the content of a film in terms of ideas, naturally, is as much a matter of its attitude as its subject, since if there is no attitude there can be no idea worth speaking of. Beyond this, and beyond art, assumptions and ideas about the entertainment film are constantly changing; and the critic has here a responsibility to keep the entertainment cinema clearly in focus, to put assumptions to the challenge of analysis.

If these are the critic's jobs, what of his principles? Commitment, clearly, is inescapable, but commitment precisely to what? I find much contemporary 'committed' writing needlessly didactic, too readily

34. A questioning cinema: Alain Resnais' *Hiroshima mon amour*

prepared to lay down the law and to accept, unconsidered, such Brechtian dicta as the one that the only questions which can usefully be asked are those which can be answered.

Art has an inescapable relationship to politics, but the committed critic, in practice, tries too often to narrow it down: art must be related to *his* politics, and the relationship must be recognisable. There is a suspicion of the complexities of the artistic process and a preference for the subject which lays its cards on the table. Lionel Trilling, in his book *The Liberal Imagination*, writes of 'the dark and bloody crossroads where literature and politics meet. One does not go there gladly,' he adds, 'but nowadays it is not exactly a matter of free choice whether one does or does not go.' And he proceeds to an analysis of American critical attitudes to Henry James and Theodore Dreiser, of the 'fear of the intellect' which inhibited American critical responses to the complexities of James and the indulgence extended to Dreiser because 'his books have the awkwardness, the chaos, the heaviness which we associate with "reality"'. Over-simplification of the kind Trilling attacks is the ambush awaiting the critic who does not question his own commitments as severely as he does those of other people.

If cinema is the art we think it is, then it is entitled to the kind of critical analysis that has traditionally been devoted to the theatre and the novel: and the principles which seem most likely to be constructively useful remain the liberal ones. The socialist may argue that liberalism is not so much a commitment as a refuge from commitment; which is to say that the liberal label has been the excuse for any amount of escape from thought. On the level at which ideas are formulated, however, both about society and about art, I believe there is at present rather more conflict and disagreement about means than about ends; and liberalism, which ought to mean allegiance to principles but a certain flexibility of mind about assumptions, a readiness to subject them to the pressure of thought, is more valuable here than the rigidity of mind which believes that once the end is agreed on the means must be pre-determined. Again, one might profitably turn to Trilling: 'The job of criticism would seem to be to recall liberalism to its first essential awareness of variousness and possibility, which implies the awareness of complexity and difficulty.' The awareness of complexity; or the readiness, perhaps, to investigate the questions an artist chooses to ask rather than to expect him to answer those we would put to him.

In terms of our own medium: *Hiroshima mon Amour, L'Avventura, Nazarin* are concerned with questions; *Les Quatre Cents Coups*, or *The World of Apu*, have more to do with the answers. The recurring question: the difficulty of loving and the problem of communication. It would be entirely profitless to discuss which of these films is the 'best'; and hardly more useful to discuss whose approach is the most valid. But a tradition of criticism—and I believe it would necessarily be a liberal one—which looked to the cinema to extend our range of ideas rather than to confirm pre-conceived assumptions, could find some of its material here. We might not be able to pull down a film aesthetic out of the clouds, but we should be able to get closer to defining the cinema's place in the world we live in. And, while we are about it, we might try to rescue the word 'liberal' from its present implications of indecision and inertia.

1960

Saturday Night and Sunday Morning

PETER JOHN DYER

Generally speaking, there are two ways in which the British film-maker can treat life in Britain today. He can scratch its surface, or he can turn his back on it. Though directors like Val Guest and Joseph Losey are sometimes congratulated on doing the first, they are to all intents and purposes doing the second: even allowing for its quota quickie plot, there is something naggingly unreal about *The Criminal*, something evasive and self-indulgent, too, in Losey's gravitation to a prison milieu. As for the few films which have made the first grade (*Room at the Top*, *The Angry Silence*, *Look Back in Anger*, *The Entertainer*), there was still something contrived and journalistic about the first two; a hint of the histrionic about the Osborne adaptations.

Altogether more modest and straightforward, Karel Reisz, that least 'documentary' of Free Cinema directors, now introduces a third method. And if *Saturday Night and Sunday Morning* proves to be a film of more lasting impression than its predecessors, then the reason will undoubtedly lie in Reisz's attempt to interpret the spirit behind a large part of British life today, as well as to reproduce its surface. Hence the distaste, not to say alarm, openly admitted by several older generation reviewers. For its script, adapted by Alan Sillitoe from his own novel, is inconclusive. Not only that, but it has an unrepentant hero who measures success in terms of wife-poaching, drink and dukey suits, who regards his parents level-headedly as 'dead from the neck up', who actually dares to revel in life and the mischief he makes with dead rats and airgun pellets, and who ends up, not at the sinful Top (that at least would have been bearable) but throwing a stone at the housing estate where he plans to settle down at last and raise kids.

Reisz's main achievement, shared by his writer and his leading actor, Albert Finney, is the creation of a contemporary backyard-and-factory conscience. With more insight and instinct and spontaneity than Osborne and Tony Richardson, this trio has created a face, a voice, a habit of mind, true in every detail of a lifelong combatant against authority. With his jutting fighter's chin, drinker's jowl and watchful, moody eye, Finney exactly fulfils the part as written; with the tension and over-exuberance of inexperience, he somehow magnifies it into a figure brimming over with

35. *Saturday Night and Sunday Morning* (Albert Finney)

vitality, one who earns more and womanises more than his mates, who prides himself on having everyone 'summed up' and who frequently lies the same way he gambles, to put snap judgments to the test. The way he talks about everything, and about himself, and even to himself, is exactly right too; it is a portrait not without charm. So that the other characters, even when played by actors less obviously endemic to the Midlands than Finney, seem to respond with a similarly scrupulous honesty of being. Hylda Baker's shrewd aunt, Norman Rossington's cousin, above all Shirley Anne Field's quietly appealing, no-nonsense girl friend, have the same cardinal virtue of truth. If Rachel Roberts' married woman who must give up her lover and have his baby appears almost too poignant a cut-out against the strenuously unheroic tone of the rest, that is indirectly due to the heightening effect of compressing two of the novel's characters into one; the part is in fact beautifully played. Less satisfactory, though, is the handling of the potentially interesting figure of the passive husband, a dull stick here taken by the actor at Sillitoe's word; and the decline of Ma Bull, the street gossip, into an exploding balloon.

Saturday Night and Sunday Morning holds one principally as the portrait of a dimly dawning conscience, a boy-into-man metamorphosis too consistently honest to permit false ironies or heroics. But it has other distinctions. As a piece of story-telling, for instance, it holds from the start, having gathered together all that is of value in Sillitoe's novel and discarded the excesses—the negro soldier, the half-wit girl from the stocking factory, that unconvincing abortion. The film's opening sequence, introducing lover, husband, wife and family, is brilliantly cut and dried in a matter of minutes, and from then on Reisz never loses his judgment of pace, whether accelerating with Finney's anger or defiance or come-uppance, in street, pub and whirling round Goose Fair; or decelerating in the love scenes and along the river bank. If at times the punch seems too mechanical (a slammed-down dustbin lid comes over as the least effective of several forceful linking devices), certain camera set-ups a shade obvious, this is a negligible price to pay for the good taste of the whole. (There are, in any case, plenty of felicities to highlight the overall impression of self-effacing decency: witness the pleasant shock of surprise at the end, when the camera pans left to reveal that the lovers' voices on the sound-track come not from that receding couple in long-shot, but from a second couple, our couple, seated in the foreground. And, for that matter, has any British director ever handled a fight, or a bedroom scene, with quite as much tact and yet candour?)

Of course, it can be argued that this is not a film 'on a world level'. Certainly it lacks the sublimity and universality of *Pather Panchali* and *Tokyo Story*; even Tony Richardson's films were less insistent than *Saturday Night* on absolute authenticity of surface detail, being after something altogether more profound and fundamental. I'm not sure, though, that it's an argument that gets you very far. There has always been something notoriously inbred and exclusive about the British which tugs against the broader, deeper expressions of feeling—against, if you like, universality. And for all the originality achieved by *Look Back* and *The Entertainer*, they didn't—marred as they were by subjective falsity—carry that supremely genuine quality which stamps *Saturday Night* as a first-rate work of art. Why, in any case, should not the Nottingham wilderness of trade-marked houses and digital smokestacks be as likely a setting for important truths as Tokyo or Taormina? It would be a great pity if our sensibilities, our standards of what is major and minor art, should continue to be directed, despite the example of *Saturday Night and Sunday Morning*, by sophisticates and romantics, sceptics and theorists, of every shade and hue. Reisz's great virtue lies in his obvious disinclination to put a quart into a pint pot; his promise in the way in which he has brought to a provincial British film qualities of natural charm: a charm, furthermore, which remains valid under the keenest scrutiny. Grant us more such 'minor' films and directors. Then, and—in the context of contemporary British cinema—only then, can we start asking for something 'major'.

1961

Cinema of Appearance

GABRIEL PEARSON and ERIC RHODE

Without doubt, the best films of the New Wave have been associated with a radical change in film-making. Though their innovations are often startling, we should not be blinded by this from seeing them as part of a more general revolution in which our idea of art, or consciousness itself, may have been subtly transformed.

The Humanist's Approach

As humanists, our first reaction to the most extreme examples of this revolution—Godard's *Breathless* and Truffaut's *Shoot the Pianist*—is as much one of bewilderment as of pleasure; for these films, according to our theories, shouldn't work. They break most of the rules of construction; sequences are barely connected; moods veer violently and without explanation. Like a cat teasing a ball of wool, the thread of a tale may be arbitrarily picked up, played with, and just as suddenly dropped. As for morality (if there is a morality), we are given few indications of how we should understand its alien logic: characters apparently behave without motive, their feelings remain unpredictable. Moreover, we feel that this is a contingent art, created on every level by improvisation—a procedure which affronts our belief in the artefact as a contrived and calculated work. It is as though, having landed on the moon, we were confronted by a lunar art.

For our intensity of response confirms these films as works of art. And here we notice the first of two contradictions. Although apparently outraging every principle of organisation, they are not chaotic. On the contrary, they cohere beautifully. And second, though their very being is improvised, they move with a deftness and aplomb that is almost scornful.

The aim of this investigation is to explore these contradictions and try to resolve them, if only partially. This undertaking would be pedantic if it were restricted to *Breathless* and *Shoot the Pianist*, both of them relatively slight films. What interests us is that these two contradictions, expressed here in their most extreme form, are found to varying degrees in the most recent films of Antonioni, Resnais, Bresson and Wajda; in such plays as *The Connection* and *Waiting for Godot*; and, moving out into another field, in certain types of non-figurative painting. To investigate the New Wave, therefore, may throw back an unusual light on what at first seem a number of widely disparate works of art.

The critic must have some basis of understanding with a film before he can analyse it. Otherwise his comments, however intelligent, will be continually off the mark. As in politics, there must be a common language before negotiations can take place.

Jacques Siclier's article on New Wave and French cinema in the Summer number of *Sight and Sound* is a case in point. We have here an intelligent humanist who is unable to come to terms with the new movement. Lacking the vocabulary by which he can both define his response to these films and at the same time make evaluations from a humanist standpoint, his argument, though for the most part logical, remains at one remove from the subject. We see this most obviously in his conclusion: 'Progressively this young cinema is losing itself behind a curtain of smoke and dreams; and this cinema, which has been described as representative of its time, is in reality as remote from the actual as anything one can imagine.'

In using such phrases as 'losing itself behind a curtain of smoke and dreams' and 'remote from the actual', Siclier is taking certain assumptions for granted. But this makes his position extremely vulnerable, since it is on just these points that apologists for the New Wave would challenge him. Their argument would be that the humanist approach, though admirably decent, provides us with an unsatisfactory approach to criticism since it presupposes a stable reality (implied in such terms as 'actual') which we can no longer believe in. For many reasons, they would continue, reality has become as arbitrary as smoke and dreams. There is no curtain, and there is no 'actual' as Siclier would have it.

Faced by this challenge, the humanist critic may at first feel—as perhaps Siclier doesn't—that his position is so inadequate that he must abandon it. If he is more tenacious, however, he may hope to discover a vocabulary to resolve the deadlock between himself and the New Wave without a forced surrender of his position. Before he can achieve this, and in order to discover such a basis of understanding, he would first have to analyse his own assumptions. For the sake of clarity, we are summarising these in note form.

ASSUMPTIONS OF THE HUMANIST CRITIC

1. Great art is created out of certain conditions, and these conditions are limited. They are:

(*a*) That in this art both the inner world of the individual and the outer world in all its totality are stable and continuous; that their relationship is dynamic; and that man is equipped, by his reason and imagination, to understand both this world and himself.

(*b*) That this inner and outer world remain, despite disruptions, in harmony with each other.

(*c*) That, most important of all, the greatness of this art depends on the extent to which it illuminates the central human predicaments. This concept of centrality is a difficult one to define; for centrality in art, the critic usually points to such literary models as *The Odyssey* or *Anna Karenina*, or to such films as *The Childhood of Maxim Gorki* and *The World of Apu*.

(*d*) Finally, that this art matches up, however inadequately, to our sense of continuity in the real world. It achieves this by aspiring towards both maximum inclusiveness and maximum coherence. This is brought about by making connections. (See E. M. Forster's 'Only connect'.)

2. The stable yet dynamic relationship between inner and outer world can best be conceived of in dramatic terms (i.e., dialectically). Because of this a certain type of plot is most useful, a type of plot which develops from:

(*a*) *Antagonisms*: the most valuable of these play the stable world against some disruptive force—i.e. order against chaos, moderation against excess.

> Ulysses':
>> '*Untune that string,*
>> *And, hark, what discord follows!*'

describes the most serious development of that conflict.

Fortunately, such discord is usually followed by:

(*b*) A *dénouement* and *resolution*, in which the world returns to its natural harmony.

3. Having consented to this model of reality, we are then forced to accept further steps in the argument.

(*a*) The artist holds this balance between inner and outer world at his peril, for if he cannot sustain it in his work his vision of reality is impelled to become *either* a riotous, all-embracing fantasy in which his mind is the controlling authority *or* a 'scientific' construction of mechanistic laws in which men are seen as no more than biological automata. (cf. Naturalism.)

(*b*) Though these two deviations move in opposing directions, they do, when taken to an extreme, merge into each other and unify; for any aspect of reality becomes indistinguishably grotesque and arbitrary when taken out of total context.[1]

---

[1] The reason for this is complicated. If we sever the connection between an object and its

The misunderstanding between humanist critic and New Wave apologist begins to make itself clear. It arises, as misunderstandings often do, over a confusion of categories. The deadlock in fact is less over an aesthetic than over the theory of reality on which it depends.

In realising this, the humanist critic finds himself in an impossible position. If he is honest he will accept his opponent's point: that at our present state of knowledge we can no longer believe in a stable reality, since such a belief supposes a hierarchy of values based on a public morality—and none such now holds. This concession breaks the back of his argument. Without a centrality there can be no arbitrary and grotesque. Therefore the humanist has no reason to describe the New Wave films as failures: he must indeed accept them on their own terms.

This is the situation—stated too drastically, perhaps. Most humanist critics would probably go as far as admitting that they desired, rather than believed in, a stable reality, and that they willingly suspended disbelief as they went about their work. Unfortunately this scepticism does not extend to their critical language. If it did, we would be spared such presumptuous judgments as the *Sight and Sound* reviewer's faulting of *Pickpocket* because it didn't make 'the necessary connections', or the BBC critic's rejection of *Breathless* ('The best one can say of it is that it stinks') because its plot lacked conflict. Such comments reveal a failure to recognise how far these films have broken from their humanist prototypes in the nineteenth-century novel and play.

It is over this 'how far' that confusion has arisen. If the break had been complete from the start, the inadequacy of the humanist's vocabulary would have been obvious. The shift to a completely new kind of film has however been a gradual one; and the directors themselves seem to have been barely conscious of it. It is only now, with our complacency disturbed by the New Wave, that we can look back and see the process by which the meaning of such concepts as plot and action has been developed. One can usefully trace such a development from *Bicycle Thieves*, through *L'Avventura* to *Breathless*.

---

environment, we disrupt the harmony by which parts express wholes. A foot, severed for demonstration, remains significant within a physiological context. But lacking both this context and the body it expresses, the severed foot becomes thoroughly enigmatic and even sinister, as in W. F. Harvey's horror story in which a severed hand scuttles after its victims like a spider and strangles them. Perhaps such inexpressive objects become sinister because they provide a handy focus for phobias. By contrast, in *The Brothers Karamazov*, Grushenka's foot is for Dimitri almost over-expressive of her sensuality, becoming in fact a fetish.

The Mona Lisa was, for the nineteenth century, the supreme enigma. This was due less to the ambiguity of her famous smile than to her isolation from any usual context, amongst the rocks. Consequently, rather like the severed foot—though reinforced by mysterious feelings about the eternal feminine—she acted as focus for all and every feeling. Pater remarks that 'Lady Lisa might stand as . . . the symbol of the modern idea.' And indeed it looks as though this still holds. Could not the last shot of Jean Seberg's face in *Breathless* be its contemporary equivalent?

36. *L'Avventura* (Monica Vitti, Gabriele Ferzetti)

Bicycle Thieves is apparently conceived in terms of the nineteenth-century theatre. The plot exposes a typical conflict: a lone man pitted against the injustices of society. As in a Feydeau farce, De Sica uses objects to further the intrigue—the stolen bicycle is no more than an honourable equivalent of the stolen letter or double bed. Yet by the standards of the well-made play this plot is weak; for the intrigue is undermined by a current of aimless and seemingly irrelevant lyricism. The social conflict in fact is not the plot: it is no more than a theme. The true plot, miming the wayward drift of father and son lost in a labyrinth of streets and piazzas, is the futile search for the elusive thief. This search poses strange, unanswered questions. 'What do we mean by a thief, and how can we apply moral categories when we know the situation which makes him as he is?' There is an equally strange transference of guilt, by which the father-as-detective becomes the father-as-criminal. Such preoccupations, though never acknowledged fully, disrupt the plot's manifest action.

Yet it is still rewarding to approach *Bicycle Thieves* in terms of the humanist's idea of plot. This is not so with *L'Avventura*, in which such a plot is both a lure and an irrelevance. Critics have understandably been disturbed by the unexplained disappearance of Anna. As a device this can be justified: it enacts Antonioni's sense of the arbitrariness of experience—the unpredictable workings of memory and feeling. Yet in the last resort the device leaves us uneasy, since the conventions of the film do not prepare us for it. Although Antonioni has moved a long way from De Sica in his discovery of new techniques, he has not come to terms with their similar problem. His plot, too, does not conduct the film's true meaning.

Claudia, the critical and moral intelligence of the film, involves herself with a corrupt society and helps to define it, in much the same way that James's bright young things from America define the corruption of Europe. Yet Claudia, for many reasons, lacks their moral stability; hence the idea of corruption, as exemplified by Sandro and his circle, needs drastic qualification. The conflict is so blurred that moral judgment at first sight becomes impossible. To make sense of *L'Avventura*, in fact, one must initially discard this concept of corruption, with all its satisfying imprecision, in favour of the more neutral concept of failure. For it is surely part of Antonioni's intention, by doing as much justice as he can to the complexities of human relationships, to neutralise such self-approving moral categories.

But first, if only as a form of puzzle about technique, *L'Avventura* helps us to start asking the right questions. What are we to make of Antonioni's camerawork? Those beautiful dolly and tracking shots cannot be understood in terms of the narrative devices of the nineteenth-century novel, upon which so much previous camerawork has implicitly relied. Antonioni's tracking shots do not fulfil any obvious narrative requirement. Yet our aesthetic sense warns us that this ballet of movement is as much part of the film's meaning as the device of Anna's enigmatic disappearance. The difficulty here lies in relating our sense of the 'rightness' of these techniques to our general moral sense of what the film is about.

In *Breathless* this difficulty is at its most extreme, and for this very reason it should begin to point the way to a solution. Here there is no gradual shift of conventions to help us to readjust. We are launched immediately into anarchy. We have no apparent choice between blind acceptance and blind rejection. We cannot, as we could with *L'Avventura* and *Bicycle Thieves*, simply go on trying to read the film in our own terms. Here connections are difficult, almost impossible to discover: the camerawork, the editing and the behaviour of the characters appear alike random and unmotivated.

Yet the tensions between apparent plot and what actually happens on the screen are not so different from those of its two predecessors. The plot could best be described like this: Patricia is a Jamesian Daisy Miller involved with what one might quaintly call a corrupt young European, Michel. Here, however, the notion of corruption is not even questioned: it is rendered absurd and irrelevant. Michel's banditry and search for a mysterious colleague who owes him money by no means defines what Michel is. On the contrary, the whole notion of corruption is burlesqued, until it ceases to be in any way what the film is about. Hence the apparent plot, of which we could give a clear account in the conventional terms of the hounded thief, is utterly extraneous to the film's action. It becomes indeed what Godard would call *un gag*.

With so little connection between action and plot, all other connections begin to fail us. The usual let-out is symbolism; but here there is nothing like such a meaning. Indeed, as soon as we seize on some aspect of the film as containing symbolic significance, we are immediately contradicted by the action. To be symbolically satisfying, Antonio (the man with the money for whom Michel is searching) ought never to turn up. Yet, apeing the conventions of the B-thriller, up he duly pops with the money in the last reel, although he is too late. This too late evokes no irony, however. That sort of moral is not the subject of the film.

And so our confusion increases. Significance is like a chair continually being pulled from under us. We fall with an absurd bump, victims of *le gag*. The more we probe these films, the more enigmatic they appear. The more we try to penetrate their depths, the more we find ourselves involved in a series of shifting, ambiguous surfaces. We are like Alice, trying to walk away from the Wonderland cottage.

The Artist's Approach

The principal reason why the humanist critic has failed to realise the inadequacy of his vocabulary is that the artist himself has been barely conscious of a change in outlook. While ostensibly holding on to the humanist's belief in a stable reality, he has in fact been groping towards an expression which requires a quite different metaphysic.

Pirandello's plays give us a lead. We have here a writer whose artistic insights are ahead of a metaphysic to clarify them. Hence our impression of hesitancy in a playwright who employs many of the modern devices of improvisation. He is hesitant because, despite the utmost scepticism about the notion of centrality, he remains a humanist. Centrality, however illusory, exists for him, though he doubts our ability to recognise it. In his *Henry IV* he is still asking whether the madman is sane or the sane man mad, whether the twelfth century is eternally present or irredeemably past. The most challenging question for a humanist—as to whether a central reality exists or not, or whether there is only illusion and therefore an art which can only be illusion imitating illusion—remains unasked.

Six Characters in Search of an Author takes us a stage further. One notices here the title's pun: 'author' is both desired author in the ordinary sense and *auctoritas*—a coherent metaphysic which can establish hierarchies among the characters' modes of being and so evaluate and dignify their actions. Their terrible predicament, their anguished states of mind, are both heightened and nullified by the ironic framework within which Pirandello sets them. They are no longer figures of tragedy but specimens with tragic potentialities. In as much as the theatre has been turned into a laboratory, so they too have been turned into automata, puppets struggling desperately to be human. They protest—too much perhaps. But in this clinic of humanity their anguished clichés are seen to lack meaningful content; only in their enigmatic but terrible cry, in their very desire to become human, do they transcend this sorry state.

All we are left with is a cry, and the debris of a play. Pirandello's achievement is strangely moving; yet we may well ask why such a paraphernalia of construction yielded results so meagre and limited. The humanist critic, we remember, fails to account for the new aesthetic because he is blinkered by a theory of reality which cannot make sense of it. In Pirandello's case, the failure works in reverse.

The humanist assumes that (to use Sartre's image) experience is an onion from which one peels off layers and layers of illusion to expose a small white nub of reality at the centre. But if we shift to an existentialist view, we conceive of experience as an unending series of appearances, each of which is equally 'real'. Pirandello fails, then, because his idealist humanism, from which he ultimately derives his sense of form, cannot contain his existentialist insights.[1] We are left in the end with an impression not of controlled irony, but of bewilderment and contradiction.

The best films of the New Wave leave no such impression. Their existentialism may be partial and muddled but it does support their aesthetic. And since it is this philosophy that their language of smoke and dreams enacts, we need to know its main assumptions. Again, we are summarising these in note form.

ASSUMPTIONS OF THE NEW WAVE

1. A world in which all appearances are equally valid is a world of discontinuity. The self is a series of events without apparent connection: its past and future are a series of actions, but its present is a void waiting to be defined by action. The self therefore is no longer seen as stable. It is without an inner core—without essence.

---

[1] This failure to embody insights is to be found in a number of directors. In *Rocco*, Visconti fails to find a suitable form for those unmotivated bursts of violence which characterise his anarchistic vision of experience. Since he tries to develop these within the outworn formal husks of 19th-century literature, the result is not tragedy but grand opera. Ingmar Bergman too cannot find a form for his existentialist insights; and so resigns himself to describing rather than enacting them. His films contain much sophisticated by-play around a philosophy of appearance. They even produce symbols like the clock without hands. Yet the vision remains intellectualised, and the films fail to make their potentially powerful impact.

2. Other people are likewise without essence: since they too are a
infinite series of appearances, they remain unpredictable. Onl
objects—i.e. 'things' with an essence—can be understood. People remai
mysteries.

3. Since there is no longer a stable reality, traditional moralities prov
untrustworthy. They seek to essentialise appearances, order them so tha
they can be predicted, and so conceal from men their true condition in
discontinuous world—utter isolation. Each is responsible for improvisin
his moral imperatives; to accept any one role (i.e. to fix one's identity a
'bandit', 'pianist' or 'intellectual') is an evasion of responsibility an
becomes 'bad faith'. Such 'bad faith' dehumanises and turns man into a
object. Existentially, he dies.

4. Conversely, to avoid bad faith morality must be an endless, anguishe
process of improvisation. One no longer acts to fulfil ideals like goodnes
and decency, but to initiate one's own self-discovery, the only mor
'goal' left. Hence action is necessarily opportunistic.

5. In consequence, each act is unique and without social precedence, an
so to others will appear motiveless since there is no stable self on which t
pin a motive. From this arises the seemingly absurd notion of a motiveles
act (*l'acte gratuit*).

6. Our continuous re-creation in every act is the condition of ou
freedom. But such a continuous freedom demands total responsibility fo
all that we are, have been, and are to be. It is only theoretically possible t
live up to such a rigorous ideal, so that we seek to flee from it into th
passivity of being an object. To the man-as-object the world ceases to b
an infinite series of appearances and becomes an infinite series c
accidents.

The self is a void. Its past and future are a series of events waiting to b
filled in. To take on an identity is an act of bad faith: we become objects t
be used by others, we die existentially. The hero of *Shoot the Pianist* move
uneasily between such self-destructive roles. He can become Charlie, th
timid lover; Edouard Saroyan, the concert pianist; or a wild beast like hi
brothers. Though he knows that each of these choices is false, he is unab
to discover the authentic. In *Breathless* Michel has similarly disastrou
alternatives: finding himself cast as bandit, callow lover, or son of a
eminent clarinettist, he immediately tries to break out into freedor
Identity is a trap; and since sex is identity, he and Patricia try to sav
themselves by remaining androgynous. In the void of the self, thes
identities are deceptions; and they can teach us nothing. They ar
appearances, as 'real' only as the actor's role. To ask if Michel's father wa
indeed a great clarinettist is as naive and irrelevant as to ask the actor if h
was 'really' King Lear.

To believe we can learn from the past is also bad faith. Memories are a

37. 'Her face is still an enigma': *Breathless* (Jean Seberg)

ambiguous and deceptive as identity. So Sandro cannot learn from his previous *avventura*, nor can Charlie make sense of the murder in the snow. Was it a nightmare or did it take place? Such questions are meaningless. If, for the benefit of the doubt, he were to mourn the girl's death—and who knows if she, like Sandro's Anna, ever existed?—he would again be deceiving himself; for to become a mourner is again to take on an identity.

A world of appearances confronts us not with expressive faces and meaningful objects, but with enigmas and indecipherable images.[1] In

[1]The process by which morality breaks down into images can be traced most interestingly through the films of Andrzej Wajda. In direct relation to the director's increasing scepticism about their ideology, the plots disintegrate; to be replaced by an unaccounted for lyricism. In *Kanal* plot controls every element of structure, but by *Ashes and Diamonds* it barely contains

Breathless, Patricia seems to conceal her feelings behind her dark glasses, but when she removes them her face is still an enigma. And it is still the same enigmatic face she turns to us at the end of the film—the face of a beautiful sphinx. To all our questions she returns the same answer: her own cool features into which we can read all meaning or no meaning. The face of Charlie at the end of *Shoot the Pianist* is her male equivalent.

Of all enigmas the most inscrutable is suicide. Because of this inscrutability, and because it is the one act we have no adequate response to, suicide has haunted writers like Fitzgerald and Pavese, film directors like Antonioni and Truffaut. If we mourn a suicide we take on a role, so deceiving ourselves. All we can do is either hastily forget, or answer it with our own enigma. As the hero of *Il Grido* hurls himself down from the tower of a sugar refinery, his wife screams. As with Pirandello's characters, this cry is a last chance to assert her humanity against an inscrutable mystery. She tries to call his bluff by matching enigma against enigma.

In a world of appearances, responsibility lies in discovering one's own morality. Our intention is opportunistic. Since other people are unpredictable, our only chance of survival is to trap them into taking roles. Naturally they will behave in the same way to us. In such a game we can only hope to win by improvising the rules. Our principal trick will be *le gag*, the unpredictable quip or act which turns the tables. So Michel robs people, plays jokes on them, and knocks them down. In each case the result is the same: he turns them into objects. 'Have you anything against youth?' says a girl and flourishes a copy of *Cahiers*. 'Yes,' he counters, 'I like the old . . .' Distinctions between generations, class, or creed must be minimised: they are traps to be evaded by improvisation.

With Patricia this shadow-boxing takes on a disinterested intensity. 'A girl's a coward who doesn't light her cigarette the first time,' he improvises, and waits for her next move. She bluffs him magnificently by *un acte gratuit*; that is, by an act which is an enigma to him, but which is in terms of her own morality quite understandable. 'I stayed with you to see if I were in love. Now I know I am not, and I am no longer interested in you.' For the sake of her own freedom he must no longer exist; and it is therefore logical that she should betray him to the police and so indirectly bring about his death. As she says, 'Elephants vanish when they are unhappy.' Too bad that he should hold the last trump in the pack—death, and an inscrutable remark, *'Tu es dégueulasse.'*

A morality which requires us to be continually free and responsible at the same time is impossible; so we retreat into a passivity one of whose

---

certain lyrical sequences like the polonaise at dawn. In *Lotna*, his most recent film to be shown here, plot has collapsed completely into a twitter of trivial ironies. The only positive elements left are images—of a white horse, of a flaming emblem—which have no significant connection with the action.

forms is stoicism. The world in this position becomes a series of accidents, and we can do nothing about controlling it. Charlie is resigned to bearing his brothers' guilt; because of their crimes he too has become a criminal. Though this transference of guilt is mysterious, he makes no attempt to understand it. He is as stoical about it as he is about the inconsequentiality of life. Somehow for him action and intention never connect. In trying to be kind to the café *patron*, he murders him; respecting women, he kills the two he loves the most. In both this film and in *Breathless* there are long sequences shot from within a car. A jumble of lights and scenery whirls past. The characters look out, but they are cut off from this world, this senseless inanimate place. What can they do about it? Nothing. They shrug their shoulders and drive on.

This morality of course applies to more than the story on the screen. It conditions, too, the director's own relationship to his material. He no longer uses the film as a means of unveiling the reality behind illusion. Such penetration is out of place in a world of appearances, in which the cinematic shadows are as 'real' as the world outside. If there is no 'reality' art cannot be an illusion. Further, the director rejects the rules of film-making as bad faith. Both morality and aesthetic must be discovered through improvisation and our interest will lie in this process of discovery. Each director must create his own language of appearances, although his language is not one of shadows and dreams as Siclier would claim: shadows imply a reflecting object, dreams a waking reality; and these are assumptions rejected by the existentialist. The humanist critic should not be surprised if this improvisation fails to create a plot, for the plot is not now found within the film but in the director's relationship to his material. This is where the conflict and drama lie.

Such an aesthetic is neither new, nor developed to its full extent in the films of Truffaut and Godard. Harold Rosenberg in the *London Magazine* (July 1961) has described how such a theory finds its most extreme form in action painting. The action painter, he writes, does not work from a predetermined idea, but approaches his canvas as he would a person. He sets up a dialogue with his medium, and through improvisation tries to make discoveries about his own mind. 'To work from sketches arouses the suspicion that the artist still regards the canvas as a place where the mind records its contents—rather, it is itself the "mind" through which the painter thinks by changing the surface through paint.'

This is not to be seen as a form of self-expression: 'which assumes the acceptance of the ego as it is. It has to do with self-creation, self-definition, or self-transcendence.' This art is not 'personal', though its subject matter is the artist's individual possibilities. Painting here significantly approaches pantomime and dance.[1]

---

[1] The comparison here with the symbolist aesthetic is irresistible. It is only odd that painting

In the light of this we must be cautious of the way in which we consider the 'content' of *Breathless* and *Shoot the Pianist*. We cannot censure them for the banality of their material or the self-regarding nature of their humour. Gags, snippets from the B-feature thriller, Cocteauesque surrealism, and so on, are used not for their intrinsic merit but as a kind of vocabulary. It is only if they fail to find a diction or a style that one can fault their use. We can talk here of burlesque and quotation but not of parody, for parody implies a 'real thing' on which to depend.

Since we are not interested in content but in the mind handling it, the disruptions and disconnections of narrative no longer disturb us; for these features do not signal a failure on the director's part but, on the contrary, a success. Failure would lie in his forgetting this self-exploration and becoming involved in the bad faith of telling a tale. He achieves his success by freeing himself from this temptation, imposing his own mental gestures on us. This can best be contrived through camerawork and cutting. In *Shoot the Pianist*, for instance, there is a sequence of a girl walking up and down a corridor which is not edited for the sake of narrative economy, but for that of the maximum visual brilliance. Not enough that this scene, by the canons of traditional film-making, should be excessively obtrusive; but Truffaut must underline his pyrotechnics by developing them against a background of virtuoso violin playing. Cutting, too, is used to set up enigmas of troubling beauty. There is one device in particular which is favoured by these directors. In *L'Avventura* we see it in embryonic form. It begins in the island hut with a close-up of Claudia's face which fades into a shot of the turbulent sea. Before we can shriek pathetic fallacy, however, the camera pans and we see Claudia in long shot looking down at the waves. Since Antonioni makes no clear point with this device, it remains a trick. Godard, however, uses it continually and to a purpose. Michel raises his revolver to the sun. We cut to a shot of the sun, synchronised (apparently) with the sound of a pistol shot. Then Michel's voice is overlaid: 'Women,' he says, 'never drive carefully.' The gun shot has become the crash of car bumpers. At another moment Michel, looking ashamed, is seen in the back of a car. Just when we become certain that he has been arrested, he steps out of the car and pays the driver; and we have to reinterpret his expression. In a world of appearances, Godard seems to be saying, we must always be on our guard; for not only are our assumptions a form of bad faith—they also deceive us.

The director is no longer an interpreter: he is indeed a director, a

---

and the cinema should have taken so long to develop similarly. The paradox about this art is that the more successful it is, the more it will appear autonomous. Films like *Breathless* are similar to a symbolist poem in that they try to become an image from which one cannot generalise; and which sets up hazards to our doing so by reminding us that we are controlled by the artist's mind.

dictator. Though we may be privileged to enter his mind, we must pay a price in obeying its seemingly arbitrary movements. It is as if we too were inside the fast moving car; for we too have to accept the phantasmagoria outside as the total world. We are all—characters, audience and film—at the director's mercy. His disturbing treatment of his characters is typical. When Michel turns to us and we see how his dark glasses are without one lens, we laugh uneasily. We are laughing not only at his expense but at the expense of our previous assumptions.

We are not involved in the story, then, but with the director. Each time we try to identify ourselves with the narrative he will deliberately attempt to alienate us. Naturalistic effects therefore must be limited: the love scene is disinfected of possible associations, blood is conspicuously absent from Michel's death. The messiness of the world, all its pathetic and irrelevant demands on our attention, have to be tidied away. If they weren't, our attention might all too easily deviate from the play of the controlling mind.

Our two contradictions are now resolved. Since films like *Breathless* and *Shoot the Pianist* enact a philosophy of discontinuity, they can be disconnected on almost every level and yet cohere beautifully. Further, their improvisations do not appear hesitant, since the director, in making his self-discoveries, uses them purposively. If it is bad faith to believe that reality is predictable, improvisation will be the best way to show us how it is in fact a series of appearances in the process of Becoming. At the same time, improvisation rather dishonestly satisfies our naturalistic habits ('It's so like life!') and so dupes us. Too dazzled to notice the aggressive originality of these films, we watch them without our usual defensiveness towards experiment.

The Humanist Position Reconsidered

Despite its many insights, the Cinema of Appearance is inadequate, for reality is much richer than it makes out. To define its limitations we need a humanism reinterpreted by psycho-analysis; in the light of which the existentialist outlook is shown as psychotic and centrality, or the total rich vision, becomes closely linked with an idea of the 'integrated self'.

We have attempted so far to describe the new cinema without discussing its own standards of evaluation. How in fact would one of its defenders judge the worth of its films, know whether a film was good or bad? Their criteria are threefold: firstly, they would be concerned with the quality of the director's imagination; secondly, with his ability to avoid the bad faith of previous conventions, like narrative or plot; and thirdly, with his talent in creating a coherent style.

By these criteria, *Breathless* emerges as a better film than *Shoot the Pianist*, for Godard avoids bad faith and creates a self-contained style whilst Truffaut creates a poignant, uncertain style and hints at a lost centrality. By evoking an atmosphere similar to the *apache* world of *Casque d'Or*, Truffaut makes plain his nostalgia for the lost luminous place where all men are brothers, where love is given and received with unselfconscious gratitude. In his film the most haunting image is of people putting arms around each other, helping each other to bear a mutual pain. Behind these images lies a theme of man's desire for centrality, a theme which is established from the first moments of the film as Chico, the amiable gangster, listens to a stranger talking about marriage, and developed through Charlie, his brother, into a formidable criticism of the Cinema of Appearance.

As a great pianist, Charlie is unhappy not because his role is a form of bad faith, but because he knows it hinders him from being a complete man, from giving himself to others both through his talents and, especially, through his love for them. This failure is disastrous. His wife commits suicide when he is unable to give her the help she needs. As an act of reparation he retreats to a café, apparent centre of brotherhood, where his failure to be a total person leads to the murder of the *patron* and the death of a second girl he would like to love. Since he cannot be himself, he remains an enigma to others: people therefore try to create roles for him. The girl sees him as a means of escape from the sordid city; the *patron* as a catalyst for lustful fantasies in which all women become prostitutes. Charlie's self-mistrust becomes a denial of responsibility, so that instead of actions he breeds accidents. It is not without significance that he accidentally kills the *patron* at the moment when he embraces him; for to claim brotherhood without responsibility can only lead to death.

In taking refuge from himself in timidity, Charlie condemns himself to failure. Why then has he been forced into such an unhappy position? The two kidnappers supply an answer. 'Always prepare for the murderer at your door,' they say, 'and if it turns out to be only a burglar, you're lucky.' In making such a remark, these two clowns cease to be an arbitrary gag and—unlike the shadowy detectives of *Breathless* with whom Michel and Godard merely play—take on a sharp symbolic force. They begin to stand for all that is sordid, stupid and malignant in society, all that drives Charlie into flight from society and himself. If we accept this motivation, we see that Truffaut's film no longer embodies a philosophy of discontinuity, but has become a film about a man who suffers discontinuity and loss.

By existentialist canons, then, and unlike *Breathless*, this film breaks all the rules and fails. At the same time it approaches more closely than

38. 'A philosophy of discontinuity': *Shoot the Pianist* (Charles Aznavour, Marie Dubois)

Breathless to our own sense of reality's richness. Since in the last resort we must base our judgments on this response, we are forced to question the all-embracing claims of this New Cinema.

The Cinema of Appearance, we see, is a retreat from a total vision of reality. Though this retreat is honest (it takes courage to realise how lonely man is in a disconnected world where traditional consolations are useless), it is unable to articulate our sense of life's richness. Yet to argue failure in such terms is to leave oneself vulnerable to the charge of whimsical subjectivism. We need a public criterion. One of these is indicated by psycho-analysis, though this does not exclude others.

The terms we would use are those of Melanie Klein. According to her, the individual under stress moves either towards integration or disintegration—and this of course conditions his perception of the world. To achieve integration, he must work through the depressive (or mourning) phase in which he acknowledges, however unknowingly, the fact that he has destroyed his inner world by envy. By confronting this desolation, he begins to re-create the value and coherence of his inner world, and this in turn begins to give meaning to the outer world. If this desolation is too hard to bear, however, he will defend himself by 'splitting' himself, and thus cutting off the consciousness of depression. If he does this frequently he gradually becomes schizophrenic. The inner and outer world cease to relate and each in turn splits more and more.

By this view, *Breathless* exhibits all the symptoms of such a manic defence. It is no more than a splintered fragment of a splintered reality. Its hard, glossy clarity can be seen as an attempt to foil the onrush of reality with all its messy completeness. It constructs a relationship whose sole justification is to deny love, with its mutual knowledge and commitment, and substitutes instead a form of manic defence—narcissism—so that Michel and Patricia see each other as mirrors and not as people. It works towards no release, because it creates no solid, intractable stuff through which to work. The disturbing tensions between youth and age, class and creed, are deliberately excluded. Bodies never sweat. Objects hit, neither crunch nor thump. Hence death is denied its sole human significance— loss. For as there is nothing to lose, there is nothing to gain; as there is nothing to destroy, there is nothing to create. This is the anti-art of an anti-world; and all we are left to marvel at is the pyrotechnic flight of intellect through void.

Or so the director would have us believe. Yet even the most extreme manic defence is not impregnable. In *Shoot the Pianist* there is, obviously, a fumbling attempt to re-create a world where love and the desolation of reality are not feared. In *Breathless* the break in the defence is not so immediately apparent. It only begins to reveal itself when we look closely at its morality, which is a form of stoicism.[1]

Since traditional moralities have lost their sanctions, our only alternatives are either collapse or a manifestation of dignity simply at the process of being. This stoicism finds for itself a weird code of honour which runs counter to the improvised rules of the game. Michel, having murdered, must court death and endure without comment the neon headlines announcing his coming capture. Patricia, having betrayed, must go on betraying. As Michel says, 'Murderers murder, informers inform, and lovers love.' Michel imitates the tough man ethos—his idol is Humphrey Bogart—and mimes his set of aggressive gestures: which is ridiculous since a shadow world presents no objects. There is no point in being tough if there is nothing to be tough about. If this stoicism is inconsistent with the theory of the world as appearance, why then does Michel subscribe to it?

---

[1] Without a public morality our feelings lack sanction, and we become hesitant about their importance. Consequently we play them down: we develop a morality which is 'cool'. Our repressed energy, in compensation, finds release in violence, in living for 'kicks'.

In Kleinian terms one would say it was a defence against the tragic sense of life; of the fulness which love and gratitude can bring, and with it—since we cannot have one without the other—the desolation of death and destruction. One can only partially realise this knowledge, for a complete realisation would require more than human courage. To some degree we all have our defences; and all our defences in the light of this reality are absurd.

Michel's stoicism, however, is a defence not only against this awareness of tragedy but against the terrifying demands made by an existentialist morality; for this philosophy of appearance is in itself deeply psychotic. Instead of mourning it offers anguish, instead of the integrated self it offers flight from identity, and instead of reality it offers us a reality like a shattered mirror.

Yet Michel and Patricia cannot gag the tragic sense. It is there in the pregnancy they try to ignore, and it is there in Michel's desire to go to Rome, that old centre where all roads used to lead. It is even there in his jealousy, which contradicts his 'cool' creed of stoic indifference. A sense of loss does issue from this film as a note of wistfulness—the wilfulness of world-baffled children. And once we have caught this note, we begin to make sense of the film in humanist terms. However tentatively, the film begins to transform itself and take on the shape of drama. It begins to manifest plot. Up to now we have accepted Patricia's betrayal of Michel on its own terms as an *acte gratuit*. It now exposes itself to a different reading.

Throughout the film Patricia is bombarded with a series of misleading, gnomic and contradictory statements about the meaning of life. There is a spate of these at her airport interview with a celebrity. Finally she manages to get in her own question, which is both urgent and, in the context, rather stupid. 'What is your greatest ambition?' she asks. Though his reply—'to become immortal, and then to die'—might pass as an artist's insolent flourish, it cannot help her; and help is what she needs. Patricia is forced into fabricating naive formulae so that she can cope with life. In order to be independent of men, she claims, she has to earn a living. Yet she is waiting for some lead which she cannot discover. Her American friend baffles her with remarks she cannot understand about books she only boasts of having read. She would like to love Michel; but he makes her play his game which drains words of their meaning. Perhaps her hand really shook with emotion when she could not light her cigarette for the first time, but the rules force her to 'gag' back at the accusation. Michel might be sincere about his Rome invitation, but how is she to judge when he won't allow her to know him? He denies her the full choice of commitment and rejection and uses her simply to explore the spectrum of his own attitudes.

All she can do is retaliate. Her betrayal is a desperate attempt to force him to commit himself either one way or another. But he denies her even this gratification by the enigma of his death. She is left, at last, still unenlightened, still not knowing whether she is a sex machine waiting to be worked, or a woman waiting to be loved. Not knowing who she is, she cannot tell us; and so, in the final shot, she looks out at us enigmatically. Yet in psycho-analytic terms the enigma does betray a meaning. For is this not the face of the seventeen-year-old schizophrenic described by R. D. Laing in *The Divided Self*, in whom, beneath the vacancy and terrible placidity of the catatonic trance, there still lurked the desolation of irreparable loss, and of whom, though she was a hopeless case, the author could still conclude: 'There was a belief (however psychotic a belief it was, it was still a form of faith in something of great value in herself) that there was something of great worth deeply lost or buried inside her, as yet undiscovered by herself or by anyone. If one could go deep into the depth of the dark sea one would discover the bright gold, or if one could get fathoms down one would discover the pearl at the bottom of the sea.'?

1961

La Notte

GEOFFREY NOWELL-SMITH

Neo-realism at its purest, in De Sica, Visconti or De Santis, set out not only to describe life but to interpret history. But history refused to be rewritten, the revolution did not materialise, and neo-realism petered out. Antonioni is the inheritor of this failure. The elegant formal patterns of his films are not arbitrary, but the expression of the revolt of creative intelligence against reality—the reality of a historical situation which it needs more than a simple faith in God, Marx or Freud to interpret and criticise.

In *Rocco* Visconti brought his characters out of the world of conventional neo-realism into a new situation. Abject poverty gives way to comparative affluence, but whereas poverty creates its own conditions—attitudes to problems of religion, marriage, sex, crime, social status being crystallised in a way of life determined by economic necessity—affluence breaks up the pattern; and the traditional moral standards of Visconti's peasant family come into inevitable conflict with their new way of life, with tragic consequences. The rich of Antonioni's films, filling in time 'between the last coffee and the first apéritif' (Pavese), are in an aggravated version of the same predicament. A life which presents, instead of a fixed system of moral values, an unending series of apparently equally frivolous choices, is theirs by acquisition. But the solutions they have inherited from earlier generations are not adequate to their new condition. The world of their private thoughts and feelings is out of step with the world of material and scientific progress, and their attitudes to questions of personal relationships, sex and the condition of women, beneath a superficial modernity and much talk of the 'Scandinavian solution', are geared to another, older way of life.

Other artists, including Pavese, have used the same background for a similar investigation of more general problems, and like Antonioni treated of suicide as a possible answer to the frustrations of existence. In Antonioni's films, for suicides and survivors alike, the ultimate problem is the same, the inevitability of solitude. Against a background of alien townscapes and a hostile nature— a parallel rejection of progressive and romantic dreams—his characters stumble uncomprehending from crisis to crisis. In an alienated world communication becomes impossible; and love, the only antidote to solitude, is a momentary passion, without communication, bringing transitory happiness. Only the lingering sense of a hope that is occasionally and briefly fulfilled relieves the blackness of this pessimistic vision.

For us, however, spectators and not participants in this impossible existence, it is Antonioni's artistic sense and his profound feeling for physical beauty that provide the relief. We see the ideas incarnated in the form of a certain style, and respond to a development of the ideas across the development of the style right down to the last details of cinematic technique. In *La Notte* the technique increases in scope to carry a weight of generalisation new in Antonioni. His earlier films had a linear flow which was due largely to the fluidity of his camera movement, and his absolute rejection of cross-cutting and cut-away shots. The positive advantages of this style, which was carried over, with modifications, into *L'Avventura*, are retained in *La Notte*, but the montage has become crisper and cross-cutting is admirably (and unconventionally) used to break the flow and give a sense of abstract duration or sometimes a sculptural finality to the images. Many of the shots however still bear the traditional Antonioni trademark—dialogues with characters looking out of frame, abstract compositions of glass and concrete with a minuscule human being lurking in the background, reflections in water or in glass, wide pans which lose people and pick them up again. All these are parts of Antonioni's cinematic vocabulary and serve a clear expressive function. At their worst they are merely neutral features of language: at their best, as in the first shots of Monica Vitti and an unexpected track *back* from the face of Bernhard Wicki at a moment of crisis, they display an unpredictable genius equal to that of Welles.

The credit-titles come up against the background of an aerial shot of Milan taken from inside the lift of the Pirelli skyscraper. The camera tracks down, accompanied by a series of harsh, unrelated electronic sounds, and the city seems to rise up from the ground and engulf the camera. From this moment on the city, with all that it throws up by way of human and material flotsam, allows the characters no respite. More than a background, or (as in Bresson) a subjective emanation of the characters' spiritual condition, the landscape becomes a protagonist in the action and a co-actor in the human tragedy. Traffic piles up in the streets in a chaotic symphony of claxons: in a slum quarter a child cries and won't be comforted. Out in the *periferia*, on a wasteland, two men fight each other for no given reason: rockets are let off in a cornfield and sizzle up into a featureless sky. In an almost empty night-club a coloured woman does a striptease that is mechanical to the point of obscenity. All these are accidents of the city, but they act upon the characters, or are simply observed by them, and acquire in the process an explicit role in the development of the story.

The story is told allusively at first, with frequent background interpolations. It is only later, after a great many external impressions have been sifted and assimilated and the characters have defined themselves in their situation, that the film acquires its full concentration and intensity. Giovanni Pontano (Marcello Mastroianni), a successful young novelist, and his wife Lidia (Jeanne Moreau) pay a visit to their friend Tommaso dying in a modern hospital in the skyscraper quarter of Milan. To Giovanni Tommaso is just a colleague: to Lidia, it transpires later, he was a great deal more—a man who, some years back, had loved her, unlike Giovanni, without egotism, and whose love for that reason she was unable to return. For the moment the style is impressionistic, holding the characters at a certain distance, and we catch more than anything else the tense, uneasy atmosphere of the visit, and a feeling of frigid luxury about the décor. The impression is significant. In the same hospital, in a room which is a replica of the one in which Tommaso is dying, a girl—a nymphomaniac—is being slowly and methodically reduced from animality to nothingness. When Giovanni leaves alone, after Lidia, he is waylaid by the girl, and in a hallucinatory and horrific scene, which gives full expression to Antonioni's contempt for the complacent weakness of the Italian male and to his protest against the denaturing of human feeling, yields feebly but involuntarily to her violent assault.

Giovanni finds Lidia waiting for him, dwarfed against the great concrete wall of the hospital, and in a brief dialogue in the car, during a traffic jam, confesses to this first infidelity. Her reply is calm, lucid and ambiguous. 'It doesn't change anything.' But of course it does change something. However much—or however little—she may feel she loves her husband at that moment, she is going to be affected, and will eventually be forced into a complete revaluation of her life with Giovanni. She escapes from a smart cocktail party given to celebrate the publication of Giovanni's new novel, and begins a long, distracted wandering about the streets alone. Does she just want to be by herself for a bit? Or is she half hoping, at least subconsciously, for a sexual encounter that will in some way reassure her of her quality as a woman? Camera movement gives way to montage at this point, an evaluative montage of great precision and beauty. The images themselves are neutral, objective and flat—like the mysterious images of a dream translated into the cold formulae of a civil service report. She sees, successively, a child, men fighting, the rockets, images which on their own would be meaningless and incidental. It is the montage which gives them meaning and duration. As they succeed each other they evoke in her all her unsatisfied desires of maternity, sex, independence. Her estrangement from Giovanni becomes patent, and in the abstraction imposed by the montage and the indetermined locations, seems both inevitable and absolute.

Her wanderings take her outside the city, to Sesto, and here the memory, barely mentioned, of the days when she and her husband used to live there together, afflicts her with a nostalgic sense of her present solitude. She sends for him, but recrossing with her the once sympathetic landscape arouses no response in him. They return to Milan. The deadened intimacy of a bath scene, without the slightest quickening of sensuality (though she continues throughout this episode to try to reassert the attraction she once had for him), gives way to the mechanical frigidity of the night-club, before they set out together to an all-night party given by an industrialist, a rich, pretentious pseudo-Olivetti with a taste for tame intellectuals.

The succeeding sequences in or around the house of the industrialist, even out of context, are a prodigy of pure *mise en scène* comparable to the best moments of *Le Amiche* (but infinitely more sustained) and to the search on the island in *L'Avventura*. The rhythm accelerates as the film takes up the weight of significance acquired in the earlier part. The slow discovery of the differences, now explicit, that separate the couple has created an emotional tension which is maintained and intensified by the *mise en scène* as they play out, separately, the penultimate acts of their common drama. The appearance of the enigmatic Valentina, daughter of the industrialist (Monica Vitti), the news of Tommaso's death and Lidia's active reaction, then the confrontation of the two women: all this is plotted into a complicated texture of cross-cutting, camera movement and movement within the frame. Attitudes are reversed. Lidia despairingly incites Giovanni to flirt with Valentina, to force a clean break, and leaves the party in a sports car with a young man called Roberto. As Giovanni pursues his cat-and-mouse flirtation with Valentina, the car with Lidia and Roberto in it crawls slowly through the streets, stops by a hotel, then moves on. The dialogue is unheard; the faces, isolated from the world by torrential rain beating on the windscreen, almost invisible, but we feel the significance and finality of her decision. A night of love is no solution to the problem. Life has gone on before and will go on after. Lidia will return to Giovanni.

But the film is not over yet: the series of agonising *prises de conscience* receives a last twist which seems to draw out the agony interminably. Out on a golf course, just within earshot of the cool jazz being blown across from the party, Lidia reads Giovanni a letter he once wrote to her and which he has now forgotten. The slow rhythm of the cutting freezes the couple against a grey dawn, as they resuscitate the truth about the past. Giovanni pushes Lidia down on to the grass, trying, since words have no sense, to convince her by violence that passion can still be revived. Slowly she yields, trying alike to recall a god that has deserted them and to re-create a communication that has long been impossible. The camera tracks obliquely away.

39. *La Notte*

One could still feel, at the end of *L'Avventura*, that a reconciliation was possible between Sandro and Claudia, that even though the first violent instinctive passion was dead, a certain 'mutual pity', as Antonioni himself defined the situation, would somehow carry them through. For Giovanni and Lidia no such hope is possible. One by one Antonioni dismisses the possible solutions and evasions of the problems. Another myth has fallen, he said apropos of *L'Avventura*, the myth that self-knowledge is sufficient. Lidia knows that Giovanni no longer loves her, perhaps never did, and by the end knows also that she no longer loves him. He for his part refuses to admit what he knows to be true. His dependence on her condemns them to years of living nominally together, dead from the neck up, and probably from the waist down as well. But both, independently, reject the alternative of separation and of the further choice it brings between solitude or hitching up with someone else, Giovanni perhaps to play the intellectual communication game with Valentina, Lidia to become the mistress of some nonentity. So long as the last thread holds they cannot leave each other.

The sculptural effect of the harsh lighting and of the montage, the accuracy of the detail and the pitiless objectivity of the style, give *La Notte* an impression of necessity even more rigorous than in Antonioni's other films. Giovanni and Lidia become a 'case', and seem (unlike Sandro and Claudia in *L'Avventura*) imprisoned in an implacable determinism, inexorably frozen into their impossible Italian Attitudes. But too much is in doubt throughout the film, too much is consciously ambiguous in the dialogue, the contingency of the situation too apparent, for us to treat the film as an essay in doctrinaire pessimism, an exposure of the bankruptcy of feelings in an alienated world. And the horrifying revelation, for the characters, that love does not exist, is true only for them; but for them in their situation it is true absolutely. This limited necessity within the artistic framework is the object of the art we call classical, and in this sense *La Notte* is a classical film. It is also classical in its refusal to admit any falsely emotional mystification. The absence of theme music; the sparing use of close-ups, and then only as part of a series of movements; Antonioni's autocratic direction of the actors; and above all the terrifying lucidity of the characters themselves, are all classical features whose effect is to stimulate the mind rather than play on the emotions. And yet as the film pushes deeper and deeper into the desperate ambiguities of human feeling, our emotions are none the less inevitably engaged. Intellectual convictions that it would be so much better if people were only sensible about sex, as much as sentimental feelings about the beauty of romantic love, are brushed roughly aside, and replaced by the *angoisse* of those to whom our various liberal and conservative solutions seem only evasions. But at the same time we know that, for their part, they too have been guilty of the same evasion, and we pity them for it, as we pity the heroes of Aristotelian tragedy.

After two thousand years we have made some progress from where Aristotle left off, and it should be said, in fairness to Antonioni, that the Aristotelian interpretation does not really fit. Compared with *L'Année Dernière* of Resnais, which presents reality as an infinite series of possibilities, all equally present and equally real, *La Notte*, in its attempt to make intelligible order out of chaos, seems excessively conventional; but this is an illusion. The order it presents so perfectly is not absolute. It is a provisional construct which requires perpetual re-creation; and in the contemporary cinema Antonioni seems the only person who can do this, both construct the edifice, and renew it constantly from film to film.

1962

The Front Page

Marilyn Monroe and James Dean, the two stars who seemed, more than anyone else, to sum up the Hollywood of a few years ago: both now dead. The circumstances of their dying—the overdose of sleeping tablets, the crash in a speeding Porsche—belong, with tragic appropriateness, to the B-movie script. Hollywood's own writers might have killed them so on the screen, just as their lives had become an inextricable tangle of public and private appearances, an exploitation of personality and at the same time a submerging of identity into whatever image of them the public wanted. Both had the quality of vulnerability: they looked as though they could easily be hurt. Both were rather more than stars and rather less than actors: on the screen, they could manage to strip away the top layer of personality, convincing us—rightly or wrongly—that we were seeing through to some essential quality of loneliness, some private happiness or despair. Unlike the great Hollywood indestructibles, the Joan Crawfords and Cary Grants born to an eternal stardom, they seemed to belong ineluctably to the uneasy, nervous Hollywood of the last few years.

Dean's death was followed by a wave of necrophiliac emotionalism: the audiences who had chosen to identify themselves with him went into extravagant mourning, making the most of every melancholy relic they could lay their hands on. But this doesn't seem likely to happen in the case of Marilyn Monroe. Rather, there has been a reaction of anger, frustrated pity, a sort of shared guilt summed up in Sir Laurence Olivier's graphic comment that she was 'exploited beyond anyone's means'. Part of Marilyn's appeal, consistently, was to the audience's protectiveness. Anyone who attended one of her press conferences in London, six years ago, can remember the extraordinary sympathy generated, so that when one reporter seemed to be trembling on the verge of an awkward question, you felt that he would be forcibly silenced if he persisted. The feeling survives. Not, of course, that the newspapers who have been accusing Hollywood, the star system, the exploitation of personality, of conniving to destroy her were not also the first to make capital out of her, in death as in life. Some of the funeral bake-meats have taken a good deal of swallowing.

'A sex symbol becomes a thing. I just hate to be a thing,' said Marilyn in the celebrated *Life* interview. Now the pitiful circumstances of her death have again made her a symbol. An era, we are told, is over, the stars have fallen, Hollywood no longer needs them and no longer makes them. We have, of course, been told all this before: assured that there are only four or five stars in the world big enough to sell a picture in their own right, and then informed, with no less conviction, that performers clearly of much lesser magnitude are in a position to hold the studios to ransom. Fox's much publicised decision to stop production on Marilyn's last picture, *Something's Got to Give*, was presented as a re-assertion of authority; although at the same time pictures are being sold, as they always have been, primarily on personality.

The truth, probably, is that star personality counts for not much less than it ever did, but that Hollywood has surrendered the old, solid confidence that it knew exactly what qualities the public was looking for, and could provide these to order. Efforts—and there were many—to construct a synthetic Monroe failed pitiably. That Marilyn did not know what to do with stardom, and that Hollywood did not know what to do with her, became increasingly and sadly obvious. But this applies to more than a single actress: it is a sign of the uncertain times.

In an interview published in this issue of *Sight and Sound*, John Houseman confesses his own increasing bewilderment about the nature of the modern cinema audience, the kind of public a film can be expected to reach and the way they are liable to react to it. This, really, is the problem for contemporary Hollywood and for the entertainment cinema in general; and the uncertainty about whether stars have too much power or too little, are running wild acting as their own producers or are necessary to hold a movie on its box-office course, is only a small part of a much wider anxiety.

The expressions of guilt following Marilyn's death reflect this failure of confidence. The public, as Pauline Kael pointed out in an article earlier this year, has been finding it all too easy to confuse the star on the screen with the star in private life: 'the new heroine of our films is the wretched star herself.' Exploitation has become so familiar, so desperate, that only a shock pulls everyone up with a jolt to realise that there are real people involved. And the industry, no longer seeing its own way clearly, more readily accepts the imputations of responsibility. If Marilyn Monroe's death symbolises anything, it is disenchantment: the slow fading of a dream, and one dreamt not only by the star ('It's nice to be included in people's fantasies,' she said, 'but you also like to be accepted for your own sake'), but also by the industry and the public which created her.

1962

Flavour of Green Tea over Rice

The two most obvious and unwavering characteristics of an Ozu film are familiar enough by now: in subject-matter, the rigid adherence to the *shomin-geki* genre, dealing with the lives and domestic problems of middle-class families; and in technique, the stationary camera fixed some three feet above the floor and gazing unwinkingly at the characters without benefit of such devices as fades or dissolves. Camera angles are rare, tracking shots even rarer, pans almost non-existent; often (*Good Morning, An Autumn Afternoon*), the camera never moves at all from one end of the film to the other.

Ozu is frequently described, with good cause, as the most Japanese of directors, and is at once the easiest and most difficult to write about. Phrases like Donald Richie's 'Ozu's world, its stillness, its nostalgia, its hopelessness, its serenity, its beauty . . .' tend to roll comfortably (even though accurately) off the pen of a critic faced with the task of conveying the hypnotic, deeply emotional quality of films which all seem much the same—same sets, same stories, same camera set-ups, same rhythm, same actors even—and which yet retain their power to absorb even when viewed one after another, or for a second or third time. It is a little like looking at those endless Picasso variations on the dove, where the simplicity of line would appear to leave little scope, and yet the subtle new perceptions keep on coming.

Exactly *how* Ozu does it will probably remain his secret, and the difficulty of analysing his work is increased by the fact that in the West we have only been able to see a pitiful handful of the fifty-four films which he has directed since his debut in 1927 with *Sword of Penitence* (*Zange no Yaiba*) up till last year's *An Autumn Afternoon* (*Samma no Aji*). To be precise, the recent National Film Theatre season brought the total of Ozu films seen in London to eight, and the London Festival will add one more—none of them shown commercially. Until the NFT season, in fact, trying to assess Ozu's work seemed to be rather like trying to analyse the work of a director like Ford on the basis of the post-war Westerns, without knowing that a few years earlier he had made films like *The Grapes of Wrath, The Long Voyage Home, Tobacco Road* and *They Were Expendable*. There are still huge gaps, of course, but on the evidence of the 1932 silent film, *I Was Born, But*

..., it appears that Ozu's development has been remarkably consistent, a process of refinement along a single track rather than a series of adventures down convergent paths.

His most recent, and to my mind most masterly film, *An Autumn Afternoon*, is worth fairly close analysis as it shows his method at its most completely formal. The story, as usual, is a simple one about a widower, Hirayama San, who realises that it is time his daughter, who keeps house for him, found a husband. The film keeps an even, witty keel as Hirayama goes composedly and purposefully about his matchmaking task, and the daughter is quite agreeable, especially when she discovers that her proposed husband is a young man she is already half in love with. A setback comes when they find that this young man is already bespoken, but another prospect is chosen, the daughter finds him acceptable, and the marriage takes place. The film closes on a strangely moving, almost cathartic note of mingled grief, resignation and tranquillity when Hirayama, alone at home after his self-sufficient younger son has gone to bed, breaks down and weeps quietly. Apart from one deeply poignant moment when the daughter realises she cannot marry the man she loves, the tone of the film has hitherto been mainly light, often humorous, occasionally ribald. Nothing, apparently, has prepared for the emotional depth of the last scene, yet it is a perfectly natural climax towards which the whole film has been imperceptibly moving through a mosaic of characters and incidents which interlock, sometimes obviously and sometimes obliquely, to illuminate the underlying theme of loneliness.

On the most obvious level, there is the character of 'The Gourd', an elderly teacher who is given a reunion dinner by his middle-aged ex-pupils after one of them has run into him by chance. At the dinner, the Gourd gets roaring drunk and has a whale of a time. Hirayama is detailed to see him home, only to discover that he no longer teaches, but runs a scruffy noodle-shop with his unmarried daughter. Later, the Gourd gets drunk again, and pours out his loneliness and his guilt about his daughter, who has become a sour spinster. In retrospect, the reunion dinner and the old man's enjoyment of it take on a new pathos; and Hirayama, through his pity, is brought face to face with the future.

Similar, but more subtle, is the role played by Hirayama's friend Kawei. We first meet him at the very beginning of the film when he plants the idea of marriage in Hirayama's mind. Very soon after we acquire two apparently unimportant pieces of information about him: he dislikes the Gourd, and refuses to attend the reunion (though he does); and when Hirayama asks him to go for a drink with another friend, Professor Horei, he refuses as he has tickets for a baseball game (in fact, he does go). Approximately an hour later in the film, there is a very brief scene at Kawei's house, when he and Professor Horei, in revenge for an earlier joke, hoax Hirayama into thinking that his marriage arrangements have fallen through. Kawei's wife overhears, and puts Hirayama out of his misery by telling him the truth. The scene is insignificant in itself, and could well have taken place in the saké shop where the earlier joke was perpetrated, but Ozu obviously chose this setting because he needed to introduce Kawei's wife at this point. We suddenly discover that Kawei has a charming wife and a very happy home life, and this fact illuminates the earlier behaviour of both men. Obviously Kawei's earlier refusal of the two invitations came because opportunities for conviviality and conversation mean little enough to him; and, by extension, his refusals point up Hirayama's eagerness to take up offers of companionship.

When, for example, he goes to the Gourd's noodle-shop for the second time, to deliver a gift of money, he is greeted by a repair-shop mechanic who says that he had served under Hirayama during the war. Although Hirayama obviously does not recognise him, he readily accepts an invitation to celebrate their meeting. They repair to a bar where the loneliness theme is furthered on two levels. Firstly, in the nostalgic talk and sing-song recalling wartime comradeship; and second, more importantly, in the woman behind the bar who, as the father later tells his children, looks like their dead mother. Later still the elder son goes with his father to the bar to examine the lady, and roundly declares that she doesn't look at all similar. 'No,' the father agrees dreamily and with unshaken confidence, 'not if you look too closely, but she does.' Treated lightly, and completely without emotional stress so that one is almost unaware of their role in the mosaic, these scenes yet add their grain to the weight that is building up. Then there is Professor Horei, also a widower, recently remarried to a young wife, and the object of a barrage of ribald jokes about virility pills and dropping dead from exhaustion—a painful question-mark about the future. And finally, at the centre of the film, but again apparently connected only in a loose 'family chronicle' sense, are the scenes involving Hirayama's married son and his wife. Most of the time we see them they are bickering about money which his father has given them for a new refrigerator. They finally come to an agreement where, if he spends some of it on golf clubs, she will buy a new handbag. Maliciously, though affectionately, Ozu records their reconciliation: they have, through all their squabbles, something which the father unconsciously but desperately seeks—the security and companionship of marriage.

It is difficult, without literally re-telling the entire film, to convey the manner in which each scene is dependent on every other scene for its meaning. Perhaps the most illuminating comparison is with music: each sequence comes like the entry of a new subject in a sonata, which is then developed and counterpointed with the other themes already intro-duced. Ozu, it is said, considers the preparation of the script to be the most important part of film-making, and will spend up to a year with his faithful collaborator, Kogo Noda, on the elaboration of a script. Even judging mainly by the subtitles, it is obvious that the dialogue is not only rich and probing but capitally important, but it would be a mistake to suggest that the script takes precedence over the *mise en scène*: they are, in the fullest sense of the word, complementary.

The action of *An Autumn Afternoon* takes place within a strictly limited number of settings: Hirayama's house and his office, the son's flat, Kawei's house and office, the noodle-shop, and four bars or restaurants (in addition there are two brief exteriors: a railway station, and a rooftop used for golf practice). Each scene is introduced by its own establishing shots. The film opens, for example, with two different shots of factory chimneys; a third shot through a window framing the chimneys; a fourth showing an empty corridor; a fifth showing the widower at his desk.

40. Transience: *An Autumn Afternoon*

41. *An Autumn Afternoon*

The sixth shows a secretary entering: Hirayama questions her about another girl who is away getting married, and jokingly says 'Your turn next'; her reply that she has to look after her father introduces the subject of the film.

Each time the film moves from one locale to another, the new scene is introduced by its establishing shots, so that at any point in the film one knows not only where one is but where one is going to be. These establishing shots are, of course, instantly recognisable, though they may contain minor variations, indicating time of day (for instance, one particular shot of the block of flats where the son lives shows washing hanging on every balcony). A more subtle use is made of the corridor which introduces Hirayama's home. Normally the camera has opened up on the empty corridor, and we watch the sliding door at the far end open to let someone enter. The last sequence, however, after the wedding, opens with the corridor shot, held; nobody enters; cut to the living-room where the two sons and daughter-in-law are awaiting Hirayama's return, and one of them says 'He's late'. There is no reason why anyone should have come through that door, but the fact that it does not open adds a note of foreboding to the words 'He's late', which lingers over the final sequence of Hirayama's grief.

But these shots seem to have another function over and above 'establishing'. They are always of inanimate objects—a corridor, a block of flats, chimneys, a pile of petrol drums, a neon sign—and the first shot in an establishing sequence never contains human figures (though subsequent shots may—someone passing across the far end of the corridor, for example). The idea of the transience of human life is basic to Buddhist thought: human existence is a mere drop in the ocean of time. And herein lies, perhaps, one of the secrets of the tranquillity, the deep reconciliation, which pervades Ozu's work. Each of his scenes is introduced by an object, durable and immovable; against it, his characters live out their lives, and long after their suffering has ended, the object will endure.

Some of Ozu's objects, obviously, will not endure in any strict sense, for a shop sign can be changed, a pile of petrol drums be dispersed or pulped. But each of his establishing shots (every shot, in fact) is composed with minute care, so that even a row of factory chimneys, or a corridor empty except for a tin of polish, has, in its immobility and beauty, the essential timelessness of a work of art. And love of beauty, in the Japanese, amounts to reverence, comparable to their deeply-rooted reverence for nature, which finds expression in such passionately observed activities as flower arrangement, or changing scroll paintings on walls to harmonise with the changing seasons, and which is probably a tradition surviving, in a very traditional people, from the pre-Buddhist animistic religion of Japan. It is this which lends to certain of Ozu's exterior scenes a reverberation far beyond the natural beauty of the photography or the grace of movement of his actors: the scene in *Early Autumn* when the two women kneel by the lake, for instance, or in *An Autumn Afternoon*, the oddly moving little scene when the daughter and the boy she loves lean against the fence on the railway platform as they wait for a train.

Another useful pointer to Ozu's work is the *haiku*. The *haiku*, as every good Zen Buddhist knows, is a strict poetic form composed of three lines, the first containing five syllables, the second seven, and the last, five again. For example, a *haiku* by the 17th century poet, Bashô:

Furuike ya	*An old pool*
Kawazu tobikomu	*A frog jumps in*
Mizu no oto	*The sound of water*

Professor Ernst analyses the poem as follows: 'A crude expansion of the immediate images of this *haiku* is that the old pool signifies permanence or perhaps the continuity of time, while the frog jumping into the pool implies the brief duration of life. The surface of the water is broken, the concentric ripples agitate it, but soon the motion dies. The brief movement of life has disappeared into the eternal unchanging. Even this general description of the "meaning" of the poem is a falsification, for its poetic effect lies not in a precise intellectual concept but in a terse statement of sensuous images, producing a sense of the fragmentary and the isolated.'

The application to Ozu's work is obvious, both in the relationship between establishing shot and subsequent scene, and in the relationship between the scenes themselves, which, like the images of the *haiku*, combine to create an interlinear meaning. At the same time, though, the *haiku* illustrates another facet of Japanese art which is particularly relevant to Ozu's method of *mise en scène*. To quote Professor Ernst again:

Although the Japanese schools of Buddhism show wide variations in theory, all are in general agreement about the nature of existence. Existence consists in the interplay of a plurality of elements whose true nature is indescribable and whose source is unknown. Combinations of these elements instantaneously flash into existence and instantaneously disappear, to be succeeded by new combinations of elements appearing in a strict causality . . . Time is an empty concept invented by the mind; the past has no existence because it has ceased to be, the future is unreal because it does not yet exist. The only concrete reality is the moment . . . Japanese art tends always, as it does in the *haiku*, toward the isolation of the single, significant, visual moment . . .

In *An Autumn Afternoon*, for instance, there is a breathtakingly beautiful moment which, in the context of a European film, might well be a cliché of virtuosity. The daughter has just been told that she cannot marry the man she loves; her father knows that she is upset, and goes to her room to beg her at least to meet the substitute, emphasising that she need not marry him if she dislikes him. Silently she nods agreement. Instead of photographing the two actors within a single frame as he often does, Ozu cuts from one to the other: the father standing, calm, kind, but imperturbably insistent; the daughter seen first from behind, then in front, inscrutably toying with a tape-measure as she agrees to meet the man. As the father leaves, a final shot observes the girl from behind, and after a moment she slowly raises a hand to tuck a stray lock of hair into place. The gesture, surely a 'significant visual moment', vividly captures the girl's grief and helpless isolation. More particularly, however, it is worth noting that because there is no dissolve or fade, there is no tapering or artificial prolongation of the emotion: it is complete in itself. Moreover, because there is no pan from one character to the other, the shot of each of them retains its purity: energy (i.e. emotional content) is not drained from one to feed the other. And the cut comes at the very last moment, with Ozu holding the shot of the father until one feels that he *must* cut to the girl; a dynamic relationship is thus created between the shots which allows the emotional content of each to remain quite separate, held suspended as it were, shot against shot, scene against scene, awaiting their place in the pattern of the whole.

Essentially, these techniques and this method of construction are at the basis of all Ozu's films, sometimes more and sometimes less successfully used, and obviously refined through the years to the present diamond-sharp precision (in particular, his use of establishing shots seems to have developed recently to an even greater formality). Ozu himself has said that he used dissolves only once, in the 1930 *Life of an Office Worker* (*Kaishain Seikatsu*), and that by 1932, with *I Was Born, But* . . .(*Umarete Wa Mita Keredo*), he had deliberately given up the use of the fade-in and fade-out. Certainly in this early but astonishingly fine film—a brother in minor key to Donskoi's Gorki trilogy—his technique is basically very much what it is today. The main difference is that *I Was Born, But* . . . is clearly a young man's film, and works in a slightly different way: it is *active* rather than contemplative. Compositionally, it rarely achieves the exquisite simplicity of the later films. One sequence, for instance, opens with a shot of the father taking the early morning air and exercising with chest expanders. He stands in the garden, framed by lines of washing hung up to dry; to the left, and in the background, the garden fence; behind the rear fence, a road; and behind the road, a railway line with a train passing. From the point of view of the later Ozu, this shot can be faulted on two grounds. Firstly, that it contains too complex a pattern of movement—the man using the chest expanders, the washing flapping, the train passing; and secondly, that it is too complex lineally—the two fences, the washing lines, the road, the railway track.

The scene, in fact, is active rather than passive, and the whole film follows suit. There is, comparatively speaking, a good deal of camera tracking, but more striking is Ozu's use of dynamic cutting (almost, shock cutting used for comic purposes). For instance, after the father has discovered that his sons have been playing truant, there is a sequence in which he escorts them to the school gates before departing for his own office; the boys peer in at the gates, see the bully waiting for them, and turn to run away. Ozu cuts sharply to reveal the father still standing and watching sternly, then cuts equally sharply back to the boys as they meekly wheel about and return to the school. This editing technique is used throughout the film, and lends it a rhythm which is unique in his work.

Twenty-seven years later, Ozu remade, or rather re-worked, the theme of *I Was Born, But . . .* in the 1959 *Good Morning (Ohayo)*. Comparison between the two films is particularly interesting, as the later one reveals a distinct change of emphasis. *I Was Born, But . . .* concentrates almost entirely on the two boys, their pains and joys as they discover society and the difficulties it presents. As with the Gorki films, we feel by the end that we have shared a difficult experience with the children, who are trying to understand why their father should have to bow obsequiously to his boss, while they rule the boss's son with a hand of iron; and the last sequence, when they solve their problem by admitting to the rich child that his father is better than theirs, while forcing him to admit that *they* are better than *he* is, is a charming and brilliantly perceptive insight into the growth of childish experience. The only characters of any importance in the film, apart from the boys and their schoolfellows, are the mother and father, and the boss.

In *Good Morning* the emphasis shifts from the boys to society in general. A whole host of characters is introduced—more parents, neighbours, a very ancient grandmother, a pedlar, a teacher—as well as certain episodes which have nothing to do with the boys at all (a good deal of catty speculation, for instance, caused by the disappearance of some Women's Club funds). The central situation still remains the same: in *I Was Born, But . . .* the boys rebel against their parents with a hunger strike because they cannot see why their father should kow-tow to anybody; in *Good Morning*, they rebel with a silence strike because they cannot see why they shouldn't have a television set like everybody else. But in *Good Morning* Ozu's concern is mainly satirical, and he uses the silence strike to spark off a series of malicious sketches about 'keeping up with the Joneses' and the backbiting of neighbours who feel sure the parents have instructed the boys not to speak to them for snob reasons. Here Ozu is so little interested in his original and central theme that the boys' problems, as well as everybody else's, are solved all too simply and impermanently when their parents are finally driven to buy a television set. *Good Morning* is extremely funny (perhaps Ozu's funniest film), and often brilliantly sharp in its satire, but it has no real centre.

Failure of a more serious kind is illustrated by *Early Spring (Soshun)*, made in 1956 and the only really unsatisfactory Ozu film I have seen. Alan Lovell has already pointed out the similarity between Ozu and Jane Austen, and although the comparison cannot be taken very far, it is a useful one. Like Jane Austen, Ozu usually keeps to his 'little bit of ivory': when he strayed from it in 1950 at his producers' request, to introduce a romantic love interest into *The Munakata Sisters*, the result, according to Donald Richie, was one of his few post-war flops. Although *Early Spring*

42. The last sequence of *Tokyo Story*

appears to be highly regarded in Japan, it seems to me to stray, heavily and uninspiringly.

The subject, slightly unusual for Ozu, deals with a married man, bored with his wife, who embarks on an unsatisfactory affair with a free-and-easy girl; disillusioned with her, he accepts a transfer to a provincial branch of his firm; there, away from the bustle of Tokyo, he ponders his life, and is eventually reconciled to a forgiving wife. The first image of the film is one of emptiness and boredom, as the husband and wife get up in the morning to start their day; and Ozu—probably because the lasting communion of marriage is to him self-evident—never bothers to *demonstrate* the value of their marriage. Consequently the final reconciliation, shot in characteristically exquisite style, seems completely arbitrary. Several other episodes which contribute to the husband's spiritual odyssey add their rather melodramatic weight to the feeling that the film is overloaded on a very slender base: the scene, reminiscent of some tormented Russian play, when he visits a young office friend who is dying, for instance; or when another friend talks despairingly to him about abortion because his wife is having a baby which he cannot afford.

Late Spring (*Banshun*, 1949) and *Late Autumn* (*Akibiyori*, 1961) again offer a useful contrast. *Late Spring* has a very similar theme to *An Autumn Afternoon*—a father's decision to marry off his only daughter—and is one of Ozu's most beautiful films. *Late Autumn* is a remake, considerably changed, in terms of a mother and daughter, and much less successful. As with *Good Morning*, many of the characters seem arbitrarily introduced merely to make a good scene: for example, the daughter's pert young office colleague who suddenly emerges to take a major role in the film, roundly telling off the matchmakers for their shady dealings, and rather unconvincingly becoming the mother's mainstay against loneliness by visiting her regularly after the daughter's marriage. In *Late Spring*, on the other hand, every character and every scene is perfectly integrated in the main theme (not a father's loneliness as in *Autumn Afternoon*, but rather a daughter's reconciliation to the idea of marriage), and the character of the daughter's friend is carefully established so that her final offer of friendship to the father is completely and convincingly in character.

The integration of character and incident is so exact throughout the film that it is one of his great masterpieces, and the sequence in which father and daughter make a last trip together to Kyoto before her marriage is probably one of the most perfect in Ozu's work. At the end of their visit, the daughter, realising that this is their last trip together, becomes afraid; he calms her, and they go to bed. As they talk peacefully in the dark, the father falls asleep, and the camera cuts from a close-up of the daughter's face, now tranquil, to a shot of a single vase framed in the window. The image is one of perfect elegiac beauty, carried over in the following sequence (the father and an elderly friend sitting next morning in the calm of a ruined temple yard, talking of the pain of raising children only to watch them grow away), to the scene back in Tokyo, preparing for the wedding, when the father sinks to his knees in wonder at the beauty of his daughter in her wedding-dress. By comparison, the *Late Autumn* remake gives short change indeed, with a rather perfunctory conversation between mother and daughter on their last trip, and then, quite simply, a conventional studio photograph of bride and groom in their wedding clothes. It is as though Ozu, because it was a remake of a subject he had already explored, used bits and pieces without ever becoming involved.

Late Autumn, in fact, like *Good Morning* and like *Early Spring*, has no true centre, and therefore no dynamic growth: the sum of its scenes adds up to no more than the sum of its scenes. In the great films, on the other hand—*Late Spring*, *Tokyo Story*, *An Autumn Afternoon*—there is a subtle

Ozu alchemy whereby the separate elements expand and coalesce to form a perfect whole. At the end of *Tokyo Story*, the old man mourning for his wife walks out on the terrace in the early morning. 'It was a beautiful sunrise,' he says quietly. 'I think we're going to have another hot day.' This is the point to which the entire film has been moving: it is a summation of experience.

1963

Pabst and Lulu

LOUISE BROOKS

Frank Wedekind's play *Pandora's Box* opens with a prologue. Out of a circus tent steps the Animal Tamer, carrying in his left hand a whip and in his right hand a loaded revolver. 'Walk in,' he says to the audience, 'walk into my menagerie!'

The finest job of casting G. W. Pabst ever did was casting himself as the director, the Animal Tamer of his film adaptation of Wedekind's 'tragedy of monsters'. Never a sentimental trick did this whip hand permit the actors assembled to play his beasts. The revolver he shot straight into the heart of the audience.

As Wedekind wrote and produced *Pandora's Box*, it had been detested, banned and condemned from the 1890s. It was declared to be 'immoral and inartistic'. If, at that time when the sacred pleasures of the ruling class were comparatively private, a play exposing them had called out its dogs of law and censorship feeding on the scraps under the banquet table, how much more savage would be the attack upon a film faithful to Wedekind's text made in 1928 in Berlin, where the ruling class publicly flaunted its pleasures as a symbol of wealth and power. And since nobody truly knows what a director is doing till he is done, nobody connected with the film dreamed that Pabst was risking commercial failure with the story of an 'immoral' prostitute who wasn't crazy about her work, surrounded by the 'inartistic' ugliness of raw bestiality.

Only five years earlier the famous Danish actress Asta Nielsen had condensed Wedekind's play into the moral prostitute film *Loulou*. There was no lesbianism, no incest. Loulou the man-eater devoured her sex victims—Dr Goll, Schwarz and Schoen—and then dropped dead in an acute attack of indigestion. This kind of film, with Pabst improvements, was what audiences were prepared for. Set upon making their disillusionment inescapable, hoping to avoid even my duplication of the straight bob and bangs Nielsen had worn as Loulou, Mr Pabst tested me with my hair curled. But after seeing the test he gave up this point and left me with my shiny black helmet, except for one curled sequence on the gambling ship.

Besides daring to film Wedekind's problem of abnormal psychology— 'this fatal destiny which is the subject of the tragedy'; besides daring to show the prostitute as the victim; Mr Pabst went on to the final damning immorality of making his Lulu as 'sweetly innocent' as the flowers which adorned her costumes and filled the scenes of the play. 'Lulu is not a real character,' Wedekind said, 'but the personification of primitive sexuality who inspires evil unaware. She plays a purely passive role.' In the middle of the prologue, dressed in her boy's costume of Pierrot, she is *carried* by a stage hand before the Animal Tamer, who tells her, '. . . Be unaffected, and not pieced out with distorted, artificial folly, even if the critics praise you for it less wholly. And mind—all foolery and making faces, the childish simpleness of vice disgraces.'

This was the Lulu, when the film was released, whom the critics praised not less wholly, but not at all. 'Louise Brooks cannot act. She does not suffer. She does nothing.' So far as they were concerned, Pabst had shot a blank. It was I who was struck down by my failure, although he had done everything possible to protect and strengthen me against this deadly blow. He never again allowed me to be publicly identified with the film after the night during production when we appeared as guests at the opening of an UFA film. Leaving the Gloria Palast, as he hurried me through a crowd of hostile fans, I heard a girl saying something loud and nasty. In the cab I began pounding his knee, insisting, 'What did she say? What did she say?' until he translated: 'That is the American girl who is playing our German Lulu!'

In the studio, with that special, ubiquitous sense penetrating minds and walls alike, Mr Pabst put down all overt acts of contempt. Although I never complained, he substituted another for the assistant who woke me out of my dressing-room naps, beating the door, bellowing, 'Fräulein Brooks! Come!' The subtler forms of my humiliation he assuaged with his own indifference to human regard. Using his strength I learned to block off painful impressions. Sitting on the set day after day, my darling maid Josephine, who had worked for Asta Nielsen and thought she was the greatest actress in the world, came to love me tenderly because I was the world's worst actress. For the same reason, the great actor Fritz Kortner never spoke to me at all. He, like everybody else on the production, thought I had cast some blinding spell over Mr Pabst which allowed me to walk through my part. To them it was a sorry outcome of Pabst's search for Lulu, about which one of his assistants, Paul Falkenberg, said in 1955: 'Preparation for *Pandora's Box* was quite a saga, because Pabst couldn't find a Lulu. He wasn't satisfied with any actress at hand and for months everybody connected with the production went around looking for a Lulu. I talked to girls on the street, on the subway, in railway stations—"Would you mind coming up to our office? I would like to present you to Mr Pabst." He looked all of them over dutifully and turned them all down. And eventually he picked Louise Brooks.'

How Pabst determined that I was his unaffected Lulu with the childish simpleness of vice was part of the mysterious alliance that seemed to exist between us even before we met. He knew nothing more of me than an unimportant part he saw me play in the Howard Hawks film *A Girl in Every Port*. I had never heard of him, and knew nothing of his unsuccessful negotiations to borrow me from Paramount until I was called to the front office on the option day of my contract. Ben Schulberg told me that I could stay on at my old salary or quit. It was the time of the switch-over to talkies and studios were cutting actors' salaries just for the hell of it. And, just for the hell of it, I quit. Then he told me about the Pabst offer, which I was now free to accept. I said I would accept it and he sent off a cable to Pabst. All this took about ten minutes and left Schulberg somewhat dazed by my composure and quick decision.

But if I had not acted at once I would have lost the part of Lulu. At that very hour in Berlin Marlene Dietrich was waiting with Pabst in his office. 'Dietrich was too old and too obvious—one sexy look and the picture would become a burlesque. But I gave her a deadline and the contract was about to be signed when Paramount cabled saying I could have Louise Brooks.' It must be remembered that Pabst was speaking about the pre-von Sternberg Dietrich. She was the Dietrich of *I Kiss Your Hand, Madame*, a film in which, caparisoned variously in beads, brocade, ostrich feathers, chiffon ruffles and white rabbit fur, she galloped from one lascivious stare to another. Years after another trick of fate had made her a top star—for Sternberg's biographer Herman Weinberg told me that it was only because Brigitte Helm was not available that he looked further and found Dietrich for *The Blue Angel*—to Travis Banton, the Paramount dress designer who transformed her spangles and feathers into glittering, shadowed beauty, she said: 'Imagine Pabst choosing Louise Brooks for Lulu when he could have had me!'

So it is that my playing of the tragic Lulu with no sense of sin remains generally unacceptable to this day. Three years ago, after seeing *Pandora's Box* at Eastman House, a priest said to me, 'How did you feel? playing—*that girl!*' 'Feel? I felt fine! It all seemed perfectly normal to me.' Seeing him start with distaste and disbelief, and unwilling to be mistaken for one of those women who like to shock priests with sensational confessions, I went on to prove the truth of Lulu's world by my own experience in the 1925 *Follies*, when my best friend was a lesbian and I knew two millionaire publishers, much like Schoen in the film, who backed shows to keep themselves well supplied with Lulus. But the priest rejected my reality exactly as Berlin had rejected its reality when we made *Lulu* and sex was the business of the town.

At the Eden Hotel where I lived the café bar was lined with the better priced trollops. The economy girls walked the street outside. On the corner stood the girls in boots advertising flagellation. Actors' agents pimped for the ladies in luxury apartments in the Bavarian Quarter. Racetrack touts at the Hoppegarten arranged orgies for groups of sportsmen. The night club Eldorado displayed an enticing line of homosexuals dressed as women. At the Maly there was a choice of feminine or collar-and-tie lesbians. Collective lust roared unashamed at the theatre. In the revue *Chocolate Kiddies*, when Josephine Baker appeared naked except for a girdle of bananas, it was precisely as Lulu's stage entrance was described. 'They rage there as in a menagerie when the meat appears at the cage.'

I revered Pabst for his truthful picture of this world of pleasure which let me play Lulu naturally. The rest of the cast were tempted to rebellion. And perhaps that was his most brilliant directorial achievement—getting a group of actors to play characters without 'sympathy', whose only motivation was sexual gratification. Fritz Kortner as Schoen wanted to be the victim. Franz Lederer as the incestuous son Alva Schoen wanted to be adorable. Carl Goetz wanted to get laughs playing the old pimp Schigolch. Alice Roberts, the Belgian actress who played the screen's first lesbian, the Countess Geschwitz, was prepared to go no farther than repression in mannish suits.

Her first day's work was in the wedding sequence. She came on the set looking chic in her Paris evening dress and aristocratically self-possessed. Then Mr Pabst began explaining the action of the scene in which she was to dance the tango with me. Suddenly she understood that she was to touch, to embrace, to make love to another woman. Her blue eyes bulged and her hands trembled. Anticipating the moment of explosion, Mr Pabst, who proscribed unscripted emotional outbursts, caught her arm and sped her away out of sight behind the set. A half hour later when they returned, he was hissing soothingly to her in French and she was smiling like the star of the picture . . . which she was in all her scenes with me. I was just there obstructing the view. In both two-shots and her close-ups photographed over my shoulder she cheated her look past me to Mr Pabst making love to her off camera. Out of the funny complexity of this design Mr Pabst extracted his tense portrait of sterile lesbian passion and Madame Roberts satisfactorily preserved her reputation. At the time, her conduct struck me as silly. The fact that the public could believe an actress's private life to be like one role in one film did not come home to me till last year when I was visited by a French boy. Explaining why the young people in Paris loved *Lulu*, he put an uneasy thought in my mind. 'You talk as if I were a lesbian in real life,' I said. 'But of course!' he answered in a way that made me laugh to realise I had been living in cinematic perversion for thirty-five years. ·

Pabst was a short man, broad shouldered and thick chested, looking heavy and wilful in repose. But in action his legs carried him on wings

43. Louise Brooks in the theatre sequence of *Pandora's Box*

which matched the swiftness of his mind. He always came to the set, fresh as a March wind, going directly to the camera to check the set-up, after which he turned to his cameraman Guenther Krampf, who was the only person on the film to whom he gave a complete account of the scene's action and meaning. Never conducting group discussions with his actors, he then took each separately to be told what he must know about the scene. To Pabst, the carry-over of the acting technique of the theatre, which froze in advance every word, every move, every emotion, was death to realism in films. He wanted the shocks of life which released unpredictable emotions. Proust wrote: 'Our life is at every moment before us like a stranger in the night, and which of us knows what point he will reach on the morrow?' To prevent actors from plotting every point they would make on the morrow, Pabst never quite shot the scenes they prepared for.

On the day we shot Lulu's murder of Schoen, Fritz Kortner came on the set with his death worked out to the last facial contortion; with even his blood, the chocolate syrup which would ooze from his mouth, carefully tested for sweetness lest it might surprise an unrehearsed reaction. Death scenes are dearer than life to the actor, and Kortner's, spectacularly coloured with years of theatrical dying, went unquestioned during rehearsal. Pabst left it to the mechanics of each shot to alter Kortner's performance. The smoke from the firing of the revolver became of first importance, or the exact moment when Kortner pulled my dress off my shoulder, or the photographic consistency of the chocolate syrup—all such technical irritations broke a series of prepared emotions into unhinged fragments of reality.

Dialogue was set by Pabst while he watched the actors during rehearsal. In an effort to be funny, old actors and directors have spread the false belief that any clownish thing coming to mind could be said in front of the camera in silent films. They forget the title writer had to match his work to the actors' speech. I remember late one night wandering into Ralph Spence's suite in the Beverly Wilshire, where he sat gloomily amidst cans of film, cartons of stale Chinese food and empty whisky bottles. He was trying to fix up an unfunny Beery and Hatton comedy and no comic line he invented would fit the lip action. Silent film fans were excellent lip readers and often complained at the box-office about the cowboy cussing furiously trying to mount his horse. Besides which, directors like Pabst used exact dialogue to isolate and intensify an emotion. When Lulu was looking down at the dead Schoen, he gave me the line, 'Das Blut!' Not the murder of my husband but the sight of the blood determined the expression on my face.

That I was a dancer, and Pabst essentially a choreographer in his direction, came as a wonderful surprise to both of us on the first day of shooting *Pandora's Box*. The expensive English translation of the script which I had thrown unopened on the floor by my chair, had already been retrieved by an outraged assistant and banished with Mr Pabst's laughter. Consequently I did not know that Lulu was a professional dancer trained in Paris—'Gypsy, oriental, skirt dance', or that dancing was her mode of expression—'In my despair I dance the Can-Can!' On the afternoon of that first day Pabst said to me, 'In this scene Schigolch rehearses you in a dance number.' After marking out a small space and giving me a fast tempo, he looked at me curiously. 'You can make up some little steps here—can't you?' I nodded yes and he walked away. It was a typical instance of his care in protecting actors against the blight of failure. If I had been able to do nothing more than the skippity-hops of Asta Nielsen his curious look would never have been amplified to regret, although the intensity of his concern was revealed by his delight when the scene was finished. As I was leaving the set he caught me in his arms, shaking me and laughing as if I had played a joke on him. 'But you are a professional dancer!' It was the moment when he realised all his intuitions about me were right. He felt as if he had created me. I was his Lulu! The bouquet of roses he gave me on my arrival at the Station am Zoo was my first and last experience of the deference he applied to the other actors. From that moment I was firmly put through my tricks with no fish thrown in for a good performance.

Four days later I was less wonderfully surprised when he also subjected my private life to his direction. His delight in Lulu's character belonged exclusively to the film. Off the screen my dancing days came to an end when a friend of mine from Washington, with whom I had been investigating Berlin's night life till three every morning, left for Paris. On the set the next day I had just accepted an invitation to an 'Artists' Ball—Wow!' when Mr Pabst's quiet, penetrating voice sounded behind me. 'Pretzfelder! Loueees does not go out any more at night.' Pretzfelder melted away as I began to howl in protest. 'But Mr Pabst, I have always

44. *Pandora's Box* (Louise Brooks, Franz Lederer)

gone out at night when I worked! I can catch up on my sleep between scenes here at the studio. I always have!' He didn't hear me because he was busy laying down the law to Josephine, who thereafter, when the day's work was done, returned his Eve to the Eden where I was bathed, fed and put to bed till called for next morning at seven. Cross and restless, I was left to fall asleep listening to the complaints of the other poor caged beasts across Stresemann-Strasse in the Zoologischer Garten.

In the matter of my costumes for the picture I put up a better fight, although I never won a decision. My best punches fanned the air because Pabst had always slipped into another position. Arriving in Berlin on Sunday and starting the picture on the following Wednesday, I found he had selected my first costume, leaving me nothing to do but stand still for a final fitting. This I let pass as an expedient, never suspecting it would be the same with everything else I put on or took off, from an ermine coat to my girdle. Not only was it unheard of to allow an actress no part in choosing her clothes, but I had also been disgustingly spoiled by my directors at Paramount. I had played a manicurist in 500 dollar beaded evening dresses; a salesgirl in 300 dollar black satin afternoon dresses; and a schoolgirl in 250 dollar tailored suits. (It tickles me today when people see these old pictures and wonder why I look so well and the other girls such frumps.)

With this gross over-confidence in my rights and power, I defied Mr Pabst at first with arrogance. The morning of the sequence in which I was to go from my bath into a love scene with Franz Lederer, I came on the set wrapped in a gorgeous negligée of painted yellow silk. Carrying the peignoir I refused to wear, Josephine approached Mr Pabst to receive the lash. Hers was the responsibility for seeing that I obeyed his orders, and he answered her excuses with a stern rebuke. Then he turned to me. 'Loueees, you must wear the peignoir!' 'Why? I hate that big old woolly white bathrobe!' 'Because,' he said, 'the audience must know you are naked beneath it.' Stunned by such a reasonable argument, without another word I retired with Josephine to the bathroom set and changed into the peignoir.

Not to be trapped in this manner again, when I objected to the train of my wedding dress being 'tied on like an apron' and he explained that it had to be so easily discarded because I could not play a long, frantic sequence tripping over my train, I answered that I did not give a damn, tore off the train and went into an elaborate tantrum. The worst audience I ever had, Mr Pabst instructed the dress designer to have the pieces sewn together again and left the fitting room. My final defeat, crying real tears, came at the end of the picture when he went through my trunks to select a dress to be 'aged' for Lulu's murder as a streetwalker in the arms of Jack the Ripper. With his instinctive understanding of my tastes, he decided on the blouse and skirt of my very favourite suit. I was anguished. 'Why can't you *buy* some cheap little dress to be ruined? Why does it have to be *my* dress?' To these questions I got no answer till the next morning, when my once lovely clothes were returned to me in the studio dressing-room. They were torn and foul with grease stains. Not some indifferent rags from the wardrobe department, but my own suit which only last Sunday I had worn to lunch at the Adlon! Josephine hooked up my skirt, I slipped the blouse over my head and went on the set feeling as hopelessly defiled as my clothes.

Dancing for two years with Ruth St Denis and Ted Shawn had taught me much about the magic worked with authentic costuming. Their most popular duet, *Tillers of the Soil*, was costumed in potato sacking. In her *Flower Arrangement*, Miss Ruth's magnificent Japanese robes did most of the dancing. But the next three years of uncontrolled extravagance in films had so corrupted my judgment that I did not realise until I saw *Pandora's Box* in 1956 how marvellously Mr Pabst's perfect costume sense symbolised Lulu's character and her destruction. There is not a single spot of blood on the pure white bridal satin in which she kills her husband. Making love to her wearing the clean white peignoir, Alva asks, 'Do you love me, Lulu?' 'I? Never a soul!' It is in the worn and filthy garments of the streetwalker that she feels passion for the first time—comes to life so that she may die. When she picks up Jack the Ripper on the foggy London street and he tells her he has no money to pay her, she says, 'Never mind, I like you.' It is Christmas Eve and she is about to receive the gift which has been her dream since childhood. Death by a sexual maniac.

1965

Preston Sturges

PENELOPE HOUSTON

At long last, the films of Preston Sturges are out of cold storage. BBC Television has acquired most of the best (though not, for some reason, the matchlessly insouciant *Miracle of Morgan's Creek*). Through the cooperation of the BBC and the copyright owners, the National Film Theatre mounted a Sturges season earlier this year. It would be an exaggeration to say that nobody came. Towards the end, word of mouth had done its usual work, and the audiences were at least respectable. One realised, however, that for all sorts of people Sturges had simply ceased to be one of the names that count. He died in 1959; he had directed only twelve films, eight of them during five intensely active years between 1940 and 1944. Yet the idea that his films should be in any need of rediscovery seems quite ludicrous: they are so dazzlingly, unequivocally there.

Seeing the films again was like resuming a conversation broken off a decade or more ago. They hadn't dated at all, except for the clothes, and they hadn't acquired any of the classic's patina of respectability. The years had done nothing to make them more suitable for the textbooks. They were still just as proudly rumbustious, noisy, casual, bursting with intelligence and energy, as though their creator hadn't died six years ago but had just strolled out of the projection room for a few minutes, to think up a new situation in which Franklin Pangborn could register the agonised despair of a shopwalker surrounded by kleptomaniacs, or William Demarest the growing mania of the one sane man who realises that all the rest are mad.

Sturges was one of those perversely talented people (John Huston is perhaps another) who achieve a kind of total professionalism, while at the same time contriving to suggest that their films have been tossed off more or less between drinks. He wrote some fifteen scripts during the Thirties, and finally persuaded Paramount to let him direct one of them (*The Great McGinty*, 1940) by offering it to the studio for a nominal ten dollars provided he could make it himself. He won an Oscar for it, and Paramount soon realised that they had a phenomenon on their hands and were producing awed and slightly nervous studio handouts about the man who 'writes everything he directs'. During the five productive years at Paramount he could do no wrong; which may be slightly more of a tribute than it seemed at the time to the solidarity of a major studio in its heyday. After 1944, certainly, nothing was quite the same. A partnership with Howard Hughes produced *Mad Wednesday*, with Harold Lloyd. He directed *Unfaithfully Yours*, a comedy which was nearly brilliant but not quite Sturges; then the less exhilarating *The Beautiful Blonde from Bashful Bend*. There was a long silence, and then in 1955 came *The Diaries of Major Thompson*, with Jack Buchanan as an Englishman in Paris. It was Sturges' last film, and it was sadly, defiantly unfunny, as though somewhere along the line the mainspring of that perfect comedy timing had snapped.

He must be one of the few film-makers ever to have been publicly psychoanalysed by a critic. The critic was James Agee, who wrote of Sturges with a kind of nagging, apprehensive affection, generous towards his talent but continually disturbed by his apparent lack of conscience. Sturges had had a quite extraordinary childhood, with a mother who sent him to school in Chicago dressed in a Greek tunic, and later dragged him on resolutely cultural jaunts around Europe. When Preston was sixteen, she installed him as manager of the Deauville branch of her cosmetics business. Sturges, a passionate gadgeteer who is also credited with inventions ranging from a library filing system to a vertical flight aircraft, is said to have rewarded her by devising the first kiss-proof lipstick. The much-married mother (Sturges took the surname of one of his stepfathers, an amiable Chicago businessman) liked to claim descent from the d'Estes and started her business, the Maison Desti, to market a face cream which reached her by way of another husband, the son of the Turkish court doctor. None of it sounds probable; apparently it all happened. Rather later in her career, she lent Isadora Duncan the scarf which, wound too casually, got caught up in a car wheel and snapped back to break the dancer's neck.

Agee's theory was that out of all this Sturges developed 'a permanently incurable loathing for anything that stank of "culture"' and 'an all but desperate respect and hunger for success which ... again assumed the dimensions of a complex'. Of the films Agee wrote: 'They seem to me wonderfully, uncontrollably, almost proudly corrupt, vengeful, fearful of intactness and self-commitment ... their mastering object, aside from success, seems to be to sail as steep into the wind as possible without for an instant incurring the disaster of becoming seriously, wholly acceptable as art. They seem ... the elaborately counterpointed image of a neurosis.' This was in *The Nation*. Writing less analytically in *Time*, Agee risked one of the more idiotic speculations that can ever have been made by a great critic: 'It remains to be seen what Sturges might do with really major material, such as *Seven Against Thebes* or the Oberammergau Players.'

Happily, we never found out. This extraordinary suggestion apart, however, it isn't too difficult to understand the nature of Agee's concern.

Part of Sturges' wayward brilliance lay in an eel-like ability to wriggle out of any tight corner ever set him by a picture. He appears to have allowed a plot to handcuff him and tie him down; he appears to have reached the moment when he must reward Agee by turning serious. And then there's a great convulsion, and Houdini/Sturges is free again. Like Hitchcock, the other great showman, he seems to have felt total confidence in his ability to manipulate an audience, together with a small, genial contempt for the people who allowed him to run such rings round them.

The last reels of Sturges' pictures add up to a whole series of spectacular volte-faces, always designed to reward the characters on their own terms. *Palm Beach Story*, for instance, is a romantic comedy about a wife (Claudette Colbert) on the run from her loving husband. On the train to Florida, she encounters, by stepping firmly on his face, one of the most engaging characters Sturges ever invented. This is Hackensacker III (Rudy Vallee), a wistful, melancholy multi-millionaire, whose generous impulses are always being curbed by some vestigial family instinct for keeping a watch on his small change. His days are spent in recording (but not adding up: that would be pointless) his tips and taxi-fares in a little notebook. While Miss Colbert looks greedily on, he gravely weighs up the merits of the 50 cent or the 75 cent breakfast. Peering out from behind the towering barricades of his money, he sadly notes 'One of the tragedies of this life: that the men who are most in need of a beating are always enormous.' Sturges uses him cruelly. Hackensacker's serenading of the heroine, with full orchestra stationed in the garden, is the occasion for her romantic reconciliation with her husband. But the last sequence relents. Wife and husband produce an identical twin sister and brother (one for Hackensacker; one for his sister, Mary Astor), so that everyone gets what they think they want.

What so exasperated Agee was Sturges' extension of this gay opportunism into more serious areas. The supremely equivocal ending of *Hail the Conquering Hero* is a case in point. Here, at the height of the war, Sturges had the temerity to question such things as mother love, the US Marines, and the nervous respect paid by civilians to the returning combat veteran. The leading character is Woodrow Truesmith, son of a first war hero, and brought up to venerate the Marines above all else. When he is discharged from the Corps because of hay fever, he is so scared of telling his mother that he takes a job in a shipyard and pretends to be on overseas service. Six Marines, one of them suffering from the most pronounced mother complex on record, befriend Woodrow and take him home. Hideously, they find that the town has laid on a hero's welcome, with Franklin Pangborn in distracted command of four competing bands. Worse still, the solid citizens insist on drafting Woodrow as their candidate for mayor. His final embarrassed confession brings the town down on his heels like a lynch mob. But they only *look* like

45. *Hail the Conquering Hero*

a lynch mob: in fact they love him more than ever, and deliriously acclaim their truthful mayor.

This ending has been interpreted as a really catastrophic sell-out, with Mother and the Marines triumphant, simple honesty vindicated, and hardly a dry eye in the house. Or, equally validly, since the scenes are shot both with and against the grain of their content, it has been seen as an expression of a basic contempt. There is no pretence that a town which would elect poor, blundering Woodrow is anything but out of its mind; and consequently this is only a happy ending if you think it is. Woodrow certainly thinks so, and Sturges enjoys rewarding his heroes far beyond their just deserts, but up to the level of their dreams. His films fade out into a series of Cheshire cat grins: not the expression on the face of the work 'wholly acceptable as art'.

Agee thought that Sturges' childhood had a lot to answer for. But if one feels like following him in this risky attempt to explain an artist in terms of his upbringing, one might find other and more sympathetic clues. Sturges was born in 1898, and he got all this European education, and the detested museum tours, between about 1906 and 1914. It becomes tempting, in the light of these dates, to see it all as one of those great

Jamesian expeditions, with the innocents setting sail from Chicago to bring home the cultural loot of the old world. Take it a little further back in time, and you have the perfect image: Preston in his Greek tunic matched against the bored little boy in *Daisy Miller* who says so crossly, 'My father ain't in Europe; he's in a better place than Europe'—Schenectady, not Heaven.

In any case, several things do seem to stand out from Sturges' films. Although only two of them (those starring Eddie Bracken) are actually set in the classic American small town, one's overriding impression is of this genial, comfortable, more than slightly ridiculous small town world. In *Sullivan's Travels*, he even made Hollywood look conspicuously more run down and homely than one usually sees it. Partly this may be due to his company of small part actors, who all seem to know each other so well, and to make such allowances for each others' quirks, that they travel from film to film like a collection of indulgent, gossiping neighbours. But the Sturges town itself belongs to some period much earlier than the 1940s: it is like some childhood recollection brought hazily to life on the Paramount lot, as though in his ideas of America Sturges had somehow skipped a generation.

Paradoxically, it is this time-lag, this feeling that Griffith's idyllic Americana has somehow got cluttered up with jukeboxes, lunch-counters, Forties hair styles and the US Marines, that makes Sturges' films seem so dateless now. Eddie Bracken, the tormented innocent of *Hail the Conquering Hero* and *Miracle of Morgan's Creek*, is more naïve than any Forties character had any conceivable right to be; but he is, in his wistful determination to do the right thing, very like someone out of a silent comedy. Even Sturges' language, with its mixture of slang, repetitions, gibbering hesitations, and entirely formal turns of speech, is quite timeless. Above all the racket of a Sturges film voices can be heard talking in the relaxed, balanced aphorisms of the classic English stage comedy. 'Let us be crooked but never common,' is the motto of the con man in *The Lady Eve*. 'Chivalry is not only dead; it is decomposed,' laments Hackensacker III. 'Rich people, and theorists are usually rich people, think of poverty only in the negative,' says the Wildean butler of *Sullivan's Travels*. 'The poor know all about poverty, and only the morbid rich would find it glamorous.'

It is this timelessness which seems to me to give his films their free-wheeling assurance and their conjuror's freedom of action. The links with reality are deliberately kept tenuous. Take, for instance, *The Miracle of Morgan's Creek*. The film's heroine, Gertrude Kockenlocker (Betty Hutton), is the volatile daughter of the local policeman, who contrives during one night to meet, marry, become pregnant by, and irrevocably mislay a soldier about whom she remembers only that his name may be something like Ratsky-Watsky. (Only in a Sturges film could one find a family named Kockenlocker gravely debating whether someone else could possibly be called Ratsky-Watsky.) Norval Jones (Eddie Bracken), already pining for the military glory that eludes him in *Hail the Conquering Hero*, is summoned to the rescue. Dressed in a borrowed 1914 uniform, like some lunatic fugitive from *Shoulder Arms*, he gallantly sets out to provide Trudy with a marriage licence in the name of Ratsky-Watsky. Arrest; wild confusion; wonderfully funny mock jail-break, with constable Kockenlocker (William Demarest) doing everything but order Norval out of his jail, Norval refusing to see that he is being invited to escape, and the two Kockenlocker daughters arriving with their own rescue equipment, in the form of ropes and spades. Then comes one of Sturges' sentimental interludes, with Kockenlocker banging crossly away at a Christmas tree star but pausing to remind Trudy, very seriously, of the stable in Bethlehem. And then the pandemonium of the ending, with Trudy producing sextuplets, bedlam let loose in the hospital, and headlines ('Canada Protests', 'Hitler Demands Recount') flashing on and off.

The 'miracle' makes everyone happy: it is frantic, absurd and rather touching, and it allows Sturges to play his favourite trick of flinging a film into such total chaos, as though all the characters were being swept off their feet by a tidal wave, that he can get away with practically anything. In *Miracle of Morgan's Creek* he employs most, if not quite all, his range of moods; and each of them remains valid for precisely as long as it lasts on the screen. Scenes between Norval and Trudy, mostly played out in wistful or irate dialogues as they walk through the classic small town streets, with the neighbours perched watchfully on their porches, have a genuine tenderness. The wedding sequence, with the justice of the peace (Porter Hall) roused from sleep to stumble peevishly through the ceremony, while his beaming wife stands by in her dressing-gown, is sad and foolish, toppling over into absurdity when Porter Hall whips out an ancient blunderbuss. In the middle of all this is the rock-solid figure of William Demarest, a gallant Puritan who doesn't see why his daughter should want to go out with soldiers, and who insists on standing no nonsense until nonsense overwhelms him.

By the end, nobody on or off screen is encouraged to remember that Norval is not the father of the sextuplets, and that this final masquerade is the most painfully ludicrous of any he has been asked to endure. This, too, is characteristic: if there is one consistent element running through Sturges' films, it is a view of life as some gigantic game of false pretences. In his first film, *The Great McGinty* (originally written seven years before he filmed it), the hero is a tramp (Brian Donlevy) who ingratiates himself with the boss of a political machine by voting some forty times, at two dollars a time, in a local election. Under the boss's patronage he finally achieves the Governor's mansion. Marriage to a charming prig, however, has undermined him, and it is the rogue's attempt to play the honest man that brings about his downfall. In *Christmas in July* (also 1940), a young clerk is tricked into believing that he has won $25,000 in a coffee company's slogan competition. (His terrible slogan—'If you can't sleep, it isn't the coffee, it's the bunk'—is repeated so insistently, and in so many contexts, that it acquires all the maddening force of an incantation.) This supposed success changes his life: he becomes the sort of man who wins $25,000. And the Sturges twist, after the trick has been revealed and he is left in the debris of his imaginary fortune, is that he wins the contest after all.

Right you are if *they* think you are: that is the fairly explicit point of all these masquerades. A tramp becomes state governor; a booby is elected mayor; a clerk emerges from anonymity to an office with his name on the door; a girl's life changes (in *Easy Living*, one of the Thirties scripts) when she acquires a fur coat and finds everyone expecting her to live up to it. Likeable buffoons are whirled into fantastic impostures, go through them in a state of quaking terror, and usually come out on top. But Sturges, unlike Capra, never uses his barnstorming finales as a means of suggesting that guileless virtue may defeat entrenched corruption. In his films, the victory is more likely to go to plain human silliness and gullibility; and that presumably is what a good liberal like James Agee couldn't stand. In one biting comment he called Sturges a coward, a snob and a cynic. But you can't accuse a man of lacking the courage of his convictions, when his main conviction would seem to have been that in this game of deception anyone can win.

In the best critical article I know on Sturges (*Film Culture*, Fall 1962) Manny Farber and W. S. Poster comment that: 'The first impression one gets from a Sturges movie is that of the inside of a Ford assembly line smashed together and operating during a total war crisis.' This very American comparison comes in the context of an article which sees Sturges' work as 'an extreme embodiment of the American success dream' and analyses his suspect cynicism as 'the highly self-conscious philosophy of the hack'. It makes a useful antidote to Agee's reproaches, and a more sophisticated approach to the problem of coping with Sturges' equivocations. As for the speed and confusion that make up the surface of a Sturges film, I would choose a more European comparison. To me the impression is rather of an old-fashioned coach business adapting itself in a flurry of urgent incompetence to the demands of the motor car, while a collection of cross-grained Dickensian minor characters stand grumbling in corners, convinced that no good will come of anything if they haven't personally approved it.

Never less than middle-aged, sometimes seeming almost dangerously advanced into senility, the members of the Sturges stock company show a marvellous capacity to stand the pace, like so many Edwardian grandfathers dancing their juniors into the ground. There is Raymond Walburn, the proud embodiment of inane gravity, forever rehearsing his acceptance speech as mayor, or realising with horror that he has just given away $25,000 to a total stranger; little Jimmy Conlin, the tiny, spectacled old man, usually bouncing between two larger figures, like a highland terrier warding off two Alsatians; Robert Greig, the butler frozen in eternal disapproval of his delinquent employers; Franklin Pangborn, of the despairing gestures and the prim manner; Torben Meyer, glittering of eye and wild of accent; Georgia Caine, beaming mother or flirtatious widow.

Many of them turn up among the members of the Ale and Quail Club, that immortal group of ageing sportsmen encountered by Claudette Colbert in *Palm Beach Story*. With timid gallantry, and a proper show of

46. *Palm Beach Story*: the Ale and Quail Club

decorum on both sides, they buy Miss Colbert's train ticket. But the excitement of the occasion overcomes them. Soon the sporting guns are out, the howling dogs are released from the luggage van, and the Negro barman, with an ice bucket over his head and the white towel of surrender in his hand, waves feebly over the top of his bar as the millionaire huntsmen take pot shots through the train window. Chaos rages up and down the train; a posse of Pullman attendants moves in with cries of 'Misdemeanour'; and the great American clubmen, still shooting up the night, are abandoned in a railway siding.

Sturges' affection for these rich, battered relics, cast up on the further shores of middle age, is extended to almost all his minor characters. They are old and odd, spry and bumbling, firmly entrenched in their own concerns and—when not reduced to baffled, helpless speechlessness—given to a fierce articulacy. They form an American chorus, standing by while the hero falls over his own feet, gets tangled up in political intrigue, or learns the full horror of the wiles practised on him by the girl he loves.

A press handout for *The Lady Eve* describes in gloating detail what Sturges could do to one of his innocent young men. Henry Fonda in this film 'twice trips over Miss Stanwyck's trim legs and knocks down a tray-bearing waiter; falls over a sofa and lands in a platter of hors d'oeuvres; trips and drags box portières (curtains) crashing down on his head; gets a huge hunk of roast beef and gravy dropped into his lap; is drenched with hot coffee; sits down in a mud puddle during a rainstorm; is conked on the head by a falling hatbox; is nuzzled and licked on the neck by a horse . . .' All these things certainly happen, and it wouldn't surprise me if the handout had forgotten one or two more. There are moments when Sturges seems to feel that the only thing funnier than a man falling flat on his face is a man dragging the curtains down with him. Bracken falls; Joel McCrea falls; and Fonda, whose placid love affair with a snake is interrupted by the appearance of Barbara Stanwyck, a cool card-sharper of the Transatlantic liners, falls most often of all. He seems to be forever retreating sadly to change his clothes, while Miss Stanwyck, masquerading as Lady Eve Sidwich ('I've been English before,' she says crossly when asked if she can manage the accent), looks remorselessly on.

If such basic slapstick needs justification, it finds it in the speed of the films. 'A Capra, Wilder or Wellman takes half a movie to get a plot to the point where the audience accepts it and it comes to cinematic life. Sturges often accomplished as much in the first two minutes,' wrote Manny Farber in the article already quoted. He could even achieve it before the movie starts at all, as in the action that goes on behind the credit titles of *Palm Beach Story*. Here bride and groom hurtle in fantastic disarray towards the altar; a maid keeps fainting dead away at the telephone; and the effect is of action that could sustain the average comedy for a good half-hour compressed into two absurd, lightning minutes. Sturges wasn't

47. *The Lady Eve* (Henry Fonda, Barbara Stanwyck)

a particularly inventive film-maker: he liked to keep a scene in medium two-shot, moving into close-up on key dialogue; his settings did their job, but they seldom strike the eye. But he knew everything about comic timing, and how to play a scene so that the impression is of unfaltering action, a steady flow of bustling, breathless movement which seems to be held just on the point where it threatens to break out of the frame.

The essence of such a film-maker is that he should never be seen to be exerting himself. Lines flash by, half-heard; satirical comment must be caught on the wing; nothing is made too coherent or consistent, so that a heartless charmer like Barbara Stanwyck's Lady Eve can inflict atrocious wounds without the audience quite realising what she is doing or losing their regard for her. There is one film, however, in which Sturges very nearly came out into the open: *Sullivan's Travels*.

It opens, in Sturges' most allusive and involving style, with a fight between two men on the roof of a speeding train. Almost immediately, up comes an end title. We are in a Hollywood viewing theatre, watching the latest film of a comedy director making a more or less desperate effort to go straight; and the fight, as he angrily explains, is symbolic of Capital versus Labour. Sullivan (Joel McCrea) wants to film a novel called 'Brother, Where Art Thou?', while the studio bosses want only a repetition of 'Hey, Hey in the Hayloft' or 'Ants in Their Pants of 1939'. Goaded by their insistence that he doesn't know the meaning of poverty, Sullivan borrows a tramp outfit from the wardrobe department and takes to the road to find out. Behind him, at a barely discreet distance, creeps a vast studio bus, with doctor, chef, secretary, bodyguard and publicity men, all under orders to watch over the great director.

It is a wonderfully succinct opening, as fast and economical as anything Sturges ever achieved, and it leads into a series of absurd adventures, as Sullivan tries vainly to break with Hollywood. Running away from two over-kindly ladies whose liking for having a man about the house verges on the alarming, he gets a lift straight back to his starting point. Here he picks up Veronica Lake, coolest and quietest of the Sturges heroines, as a failed actress who can think of no greater present than an introduction to Lubitsch. 'There's nothing like a deep-dish movie for driving you out into the open,' she insists, when Sullivan tries to tell her that in a suffering world a director ought not to be making 'Ants in Their Pants of 1941'. Together they set off to sample poverty, first getting the butler to check with the booking-office where a tramp might properly be expected to board a freight train.

Slowly, Sturges begins to modulate the film's tone. The rich boy's search for the poor no longer seems quite so ludicrous; and it becomes something entirely different when Sullivan is robbed in a freight yard, attacks a railway policeman, and winds up in a Southern chain gang. Again, the point is one of identity—of who other people think you are. Once Sullivan is recognised, he could have hit ten policemen and no one would keep him locked up. In the meantime, however, Sturges has put everything he knows (and a curious everything it is) into the theatrical, fanciful, maddening and effective staging of his key scene. As a treat, the convicts are taken to a film show in a Negro church hall, where the minister instructs his tattered congregation on their welcome to those 'less fortunate than we are'. Through the mists around the hall, the men advance to a rhythm of clanking chains. Inside, they and the Negroes join in wild laughter at a Disney cartoon. Back in Hollywood, Sullivan confounds his bosses and dismisses 'Brother, Where Art Thou?': he now knows that he wants to make people laugh.

As a comedy director's apologia this is notably unconvincing—for the reason that any director who went into comedy with a sense of mission would probably make some terrible movies. And even at its face value, the scene of the laughing convicts has a kind of hysteria, a strained convulsive agony of mirth. Was Sturges here showing us the heart Agee suspected he hadn't got? Or was he simply playing with an idea, and barnstorming it through when it got too hot to handle? Because Sturges was the great equivocator, we never quite trust him. He has trained us to keep up our guard against his own seriousness.

In all its details, *Sullivan's Travels* is beautifully organised. The gossiping studio staff, boxed up in their absurd bus; Sullivan's two butlers, so deeply distrustful of the whole adventure; Veronica Lake, chirping cool jokes from behind that wave of hair; Sullivan's terrible wife, laying flowers on his supposed grave with a gesture of frozen boredom; Jimmy Conlin, the trusty in the labour camp determined to get the recalcitrant Sullivan to the picture show—these are all among Sturges' best inventions. And the feeling of movement, of freight trains trundling through the night, makes this a very specifically American adventure.

When it came to the point, however, Sturges didn't know what to do with the poor. He sentimentalises them, as Sullivan and the girl wander among the down-and-outs, and at the same time he is scared of them. He doesn't want to get too close; and so he falls back on mist, distance and romantic music, with only the publicity cameraman, busily recording Sullivan's progress from a vantage point in a tree, to hold the film in contact with its satiric intention. Faced with something extremely simple to put across—the real thing, as opposed to Sullivan's hopelessly romantic view of it—his machinery of expression simply collapsed under him.

It is a very interesting collapse, because it reveals Sturges face to face with his own limitations. His defences were built up in depth; his favourite approach was the oblique and glancing one, with all the retreats into burlesque left open. His films give the impression of running on sheer, undiluted nervous energy rather than on thought. Confronted with an idea to be followed straight through, Sturges brought his elaborate defence mechanisms into play. Yet for a man who is supposed to have thought only of success, he was extraordinarily preoccupied with the byways of failure, with age and decay, and that wistful realisation of their own uselessness that suddenly hits his most sympathetic characters. His films are sometimes nearly serious, and always wildly funny. Perhaps the key scene in a Sturges movie is really an earlier one in *Sullivan's Travels*, when the director goes to another rural film show. There are the howling babies, the popcorn-chewing children, the snoring farmers, the tired, apathetic, misty faces—and among them the Hollywood aristocrat, dressed in a borrowed suit of clothes, confronting the ultimate object and purpose of it all: the audience.

1965

Keaton at Venice

JOHN GILLETT and JAMES BLUE

Saturday, 4 September 1965 was Buster Keaton day at the Venice Festival. At the Press Conference after the preview of *Film* (in which Keaton interprets a Beckett script), the appearance of the familiar stocky figure determinedly stumping on to the platform was the signal for a standing ovation of wild affection from the press. 'Caro Buster . . .' said somebody happily, after a long pause while Keaton blandly seated himself among a line of fussing officials, and went on to ask what he thought of the Beckett film. 'I don't know what it was all about,' the hoarsely grating voice promptly replied, 'perhaps you can tell me.' A hand waved expressively in the air: 'The camera was *behind* me all the time. I ain't used to that.'

What was he doing in Italy? He was making a comedy called *Two Marines and a General*—'I'm the General'. Loud cheers made it clear that the audience agreed, and an attempt by the young lady valiantly struggling with three languages to translate this as 'Il Maresciallo' was drowned by roars of protest.

Keaton was obviously warming to his task. He stood up and started talking without waiting for questions, and spoke of the new Dick Lester film he was shortly joining in Spain. 'I've had several other offers, but couldn't take 'em. No time to spare'—and there was a certain satisfaction in the way he said these last words, as if his present activity made up a little for the waste and neglect of the last twenty years. One notes that, unlike certain comedians, Keaton does not need to keep up a stream of wisecracks. Buster himself had taken over the Palazzo, in full command of his audience once again.

At the evening gala show, more unexpectedly, the smart Venetian audience also rose to their feet with delighted applause as the celebrities took their places. Somebody in the next seat poked Keaton. He looked surprised. 'For me?' one could almost hear that dead-pan eyebrow exclaim; and he got up and bowed, beautifully.

Next day, we were able to interview Keaton at the Excelsior Hotel. Several other papers and television networks also had the same idea, and we had to wait a little while. Eventually we saw him peering through a door off the main foyer, apparently wiping down the glass panel with his handkerchief for the benefit of a lady admirer. It was only when he put his head through the space and started cleaning the 'glass' from the other side that we realised that it was a beautiful Buster gag.

Keaton started talking almost before we got our equipment ready, and insisted on giving us the most comfortable chairs. He sat bolt upright on the other side of the table, large eyes staring straight ahead, with the Great Stone Face set throughout in expressive immobility except for one charming moment duly noted in the interview. Our questions triggered off an immediate response, precise down to the last little detail, almost as if his films were parading before him as he talked. And in his mind, Keaton the director seemed quite inseparable from Buster the actor.

Buster Keaton: I ought to do something about the new release print of *The General* that was shown in London. When the film was to be revived in Europe we brought over as many old prints as we could find, in order to pick out the best reels—to find the ones that hadn't faded, or been chewed up by the machine. We gave them to the outfit in Munich who were handling the film, and they made a duped negative. They did a beautiful job of it. The first thing they wanted to do, as an experiment, was to translate all the English titles into German so that they could release the film in Germany. It did a beautiful business there, so immediately they made some more prints with French titles for release in France. Now they must have lost the original list of English titles, so they put them back again into English from their own German translation.

I happened to see a print of this new English version in Rome last week—the same version you had in London—and the titles are misleading. For instance, when I'm trying to enlist and I'm asked 'What is your occupation?' I say 'bartender'. Well, that type of man gets drafted into the army immediately. In the new version the title reads 'barkeep'—that means you own the place. And it doesn't sound as funny anyway in English: it might in German, I don't know. Then they put 'sir' on to the ends of sentences because I'm talking to an officer, but there's no 'sirring' at all in our titles. Some of the explanatory titles were changed or dropped as well. Do you remember, for instance, the scene where we all got off the train and while we were away the engine was stolen? We actually stopped off there for lunch: the conductor comes into the car and says 'This is Marietta: one hour for lunch.' But they left that title off, and without it you'd think the train had emptied out because it was the end of the run. In which case there's no reason to steal the engine then: they could have waited until everyone had gone and the place was deserted.

J.G.: *Apart from the comedy values, the most impressive thing about all the features you made during the Twenties is their distinctive visual style. They all have a kind of look which one associates with a Keaton film. How did you work with your various co-directors to achieve this? Who actually did what?*

Number one, I was practically my own producer on all those silent pictures. I used a co-director on some of them, but the majority I did alone. And I cut them all myself: I cut all my own pictures.

J.G.: What exactly would the co-director do?

Co-direct with me, that's all. He would be out there looking through the camera, and I'd ask him what he thought. He would maybe say 'That scene looks a little slow'; and then I'd do it again and speed it up. As a rule, when I'm working alone, the cameraman, the prop man, the electrician, these are my eyes out there. I'd ask, 'Did that work the way I wanted it to?' and they'd say yes or no. They knew what they were talking about.

J.G.: You would choose the actual camera set-ups yourself?

Always, when it was important for the scene I was going to do. If I had an incidental scene—someone runs in, say, and says 'here, you've got to go and do this'—the background wasn't important. Then I generally just told the cameraman that I had these two characters in the scene, two full-length figures, and asked him to pick a good-looking background. He would go by the sun. He'd say, 'I like that back crosslight coming in through the trees. There are clouds over there right now, so if we hurry up we can still get them before they disappear.' So I would say 'Swell,' and go and direct the scene in front of the cameraman's set-up. We took pains to get good-looking scenery whenever we possibly could, no matter what we were shooting.

J.G.: What about the visual idea of the films? Take, for instance, a picture like Our Hospitality, *which has a beautiful period feeling.*

We were very conscious of our stories. We learned in a hurry that we couldn't make a feature-length picture the way we had done the two-reelers; we couldn't use impossible gags, like the kind of things that happen to cartoon characters. We had to eliminate all these things because we had to tell a logical story that an audience would accept. So story construction became a very strong point with us.

On *Our Hospitality* we had this one idea of an old-fashioned Southern feud. But it looks as though this must have died down in the years it took me to grow up from being a baby, so our best period for that was to go back something like eighty years. 'All right,' we say. 'We go back that far. And now when I go South, am I travelling in a covered wagon, or what? Let's look up the records and see when the first railroad train was invented.' Well, we find out: we've got the Stephenson Rocket for England and the De Witt Clinton for the United States. And we chose the Rocket engine because it's funnier looking. The passenger coaches were stage coaches with flanged wheels put on them. So we built that entire train and that set our period for us: 1825 was the actual year of the invention of the railroad. Now we dress our people to that period. And that was fine because we liked the costumes: you've got away there from

48. *Our Hospitality*: 'They pumped out my ears and drained me'

the George Washington short pants and into the more picturesque Johnny Walker type of costume.

J.G.: *One of the best gags in the film is the moment when you swing out by a rope from the river-bank and catch the girl almost in mid-air as she goes over the big waterfall. How did you stage this very tricky shot?*

We had to build that dam: we built it in order to fit that trick. The set was built over a swimming pool, and we actually put up four eight-inch water pipes, with big pumps and motors to run them, to carry the water up from the pool to create our waterfall. That fall was about six inches deep. A couple of times I swung out underneath there and dropped upside down when I caught her. I had to go down to the doctor right there and then. They pumped out my ears and nostrils and drained me, because when a full volume of water like that comes down and hits you and you're upside down—then you really get it.

J.G.: *How long did it take to shoot the scene? How many takes were there?*

I think I got it on the third take. I missed the first two, but the third one I got it ... And it's hard to realise that it was shot in 1923. It sounds like going back into ancient history.

J.B.: *But it still works. Two weeks ago in Paris I saw* The Three Ages, *which is also forty-two years old, and the audience were rolling in the aisles. Presumably you did this as a take-off on films like* Intolerance?

I was thinking of *Intolerance* when I made it. I told the three separate stories the same as Griffith did; and of course in that film I did take liberties, because it was more of a travesty than a burlesque. That's why I used a wristwatch that was a sun-dial, and why I used my helmet the way I did. Fords at that time had a safety device to stop people from stealing the cars: a thing with a big spike which you locked on the back wheel and which looked just like my Roman helmet. So I unlocked my Roman helmet off me and locked it on to the wheel of my chariot. At that time the audience all compared it with the safety gadget for a Ford.

J.B.: *This seems to lead to the question of how you find your gags. Do you get them from the set, things in the decor . . .?*

Yes, props, and characters, and everything, and then look for the simplest things to go wrong. And that leads to bigger things. But there is nothing worse with us than a misplaced gag. Someone may suggest a good gag, or even an excellent one, but if it doesn't fit the story I'm doing and I try to drag it in, then it looks dragged in on the screen. So it's much better to save it, until some time when it does fit what I'm doing.

J.B.: *Quite often you start off a film rather slowly, and the camera movement increases as the action builds up.*

Deliberately. I always do that. I use the simplest little things in the world, and I never look for big gags to start a picture. I don't want them in the first reel, because if I ever get a big laughing sequence in the first reel, then I'm going to have trouble following it later. The idea that I had to have a gag or get a laugh in every scene . . . I lost that a long time ago. It makes you strive to be funny and you go out of your way trying. It's not a natural thing.

J.G.: *In the short films it was different, of course, because you had to make it funny all the way.* Playhouse—*the one about the theatre in which you play almost every part—is absolutely packed with jokes. Was it in some ways easier to think up these separate gags for the short films, or did you prefer to have time to work out a story?*

We didn't rush. When we thought we had what we wanted, we went ahead and ordered the sets built. But I made one very bad mistake with that picture *The Playhouse*. I could have made the whole two-reeler just by myself, without any trouble. But we were a little scared to do it, because it might have looked as though we were trying to show how versatile I was—that I could make a whole half-hour picture all alone, without another soul in the cast. That's the reason why we brought other people into the second reel, and that was a mistake.

J.B.: *By the time you came to the features, the action was no longer just the basis for the gags but thoroughly integrated with them. Do you consistently look for a gag that will help to advance the action?*

Take one from a picture that I am about to re-release, *The Seven Chances.* I am running away from a batch of women who are chasing me. A friend has put it in the paper that I'll marry anybody so long as I can be married by five o'clock—it has to do with inheriting an estate or whatever. So all the women in the world show up to get married. They chase me out of the church, and so on. I went down to the dunes just off the Pacific Ocean out at Los Angeles, and I accidentally dislodged a boulder in coming down. All I had set up for the scene was a camera panning with me as I came over the skyline and was chased down into the valley. But I dislodged this rock, and it in turn dislodged two others, and they chased me down the hill.

That's all there was: just three rocks. But the audience at the preview sat up in their seats and expected more. So we went right back and ordered 1,500 rocks built, from bowling alley size up to boulders eight feet in diameter. Then we went out to the Ridge Route, which is in the High Sierras, to a burnt mountain steeper than a forty-five degree angle. A

49. *Seven Chances*

couple of truckloads of men took those rocks up and planted them; and then I went up to the top, and came down with the rocks. That gag gave me the whole final chase, and it was an accident in the first place.

J.G.: *The great thing about that chase is that a lot of it is shot from a long way away, so that you get the effect of the tiny figure with the rocks all round. You often seem to prefer to work within a rather large shot, rather than using a lot of close-ups.*

When I've got a gag that spreads out, I hate to jump a camera into close-ups. So I do everything in the world I can to hold it in that long-shot and keep the action rolling. When I do use cuts I still won't go right into a close-up: I'll just go in maybe to a full figure, but that's about as close as I'll come. Close-ups are too jarring on the screen, and this type of cut can stop an audience from laughing.

If I were going to show you this hotel lobby where we are now, for instance, I'd go back and show you the whole lobby on that first shot, and then move in closer. But the main thing is that I want you to be familiar with the atmosphere, so that you know what my location is and where I am. From then on I never have to go back to the long shot again unless I get into action where I am going to cover space in a hurry.

J.G.: *Could you tell us something about* Steamboat Bill Jr.*, with the big cyclone at the end when you get the impression that the whole set is being systematically destroyed? It must have been one of the most elaborate of all your films to stage.*

The original story I had was about the Mississippi, but we actually used the Sacramento River in California, some six hundred miles north of Los Angeles. We went up there and built that street front, three blocks of it, and built the piers and so on. We found the river boats right there in Sacramento: one was brand new, and we were able to age the other one up to make it look as though it was ready to fall apart. My original situation in that film was a flood. But my so-called producer on that film was Joe Schenck, who at that time was producing Norma Talmadge, Constance Talmadge and myself, and who later became president of United Artists. Then later on 20th Century-Fox was Joe Schenck, and his brother Nicholas Schenck was head man of Metro-Goldwyn-Mayer. Schenck was supposed to be my producer but he never knew when or what I was shooting. He just turned me loose.

Well, the publicity man on *Steamboat Bill* goes to Schenck and he says: 'He can't do a flood sequence because we have floods every year and too many people are lost. It's too painful to get laughs with.' So Schenck told me, 'You can't do a flood.' I said, 'That's funny, since it seems to me that Chaplin during World War One made a picture called *Shoulder Arms*, which was the biggest money-maker he'd made at that time. You can't get a bigger disaster than that, and yet he made his biggest laughing picture out of it.' He said, 'Oh, that's different.' I don't know why it was different. I asked if it was all right to make it a cyclone, and he agreed that was

50. *Steamboat Bill Jr.*: the cyclone

better. Now he didn't know it, but there are four times more people killed
in the United States by hurricanes and cyclones than by floods. But it was
all right as long as he didn't find that out, and so I went ahead with my
technical man and did the cyclone.

J.G.: *How about the technical side? The marvellous shot, for instance, of the front
of the building falling on you, so that you are standing in the window as it hits the
ground. What were the problems in staging that scene?*

First I had them build the framework of this building and make sure
that the hinges were all firm and solid. It was a building with a tall
V-shaped roof, so that we could make this window up in the roof
exceptionally high. An average second storey window would be about 12

feet, but we're up about 18 feet. Then you lay this framework down on the ground, and build the window round me. We built the window so that I had a clearance of two inches on each shoulder, and the top missed my head by two inches and the bottom my heels by two inches. We mark that ground out and drive big nails where my two heels are going to be. Then you put that house back up in position while they finish building it. They put the front on, painted it, and made the jagged edge where it tore away from the main building; and then we went in and fixed the interiors so that you're looking at a house that the front has blown off. Then we put up our wind machines with the big Liberty motors. We had six of them and they are pretty powerful: they could lift a truck right off the road. Now we had to make sure that we were getting our foreground and background wind effect, but that no current ever hit the front of that building when it started to fall, because if the wind warps her she's not going to fall where we want her, and I'm standing right out in front. But it's a one-take scene and we got it that way. You don't do those things twice.

J.B.: *Your usual method was to start with a story and then look for the gags. Where did you begin with a film like* The General?

I took that first page out of the history book. Disney did it about nine years ago and called it by its original name—*The Great Locomotive Chase*, with Fess Parker. But he made a mistake and told it from a Northerner's standpoint. And you can always make villains out of the Northerners, but you cannot make a villain out of the South. That was the first mistake he made.

In *The General* I took that page of history and I stuck to it in all detail. I staged it exactly the way it happened. The Union agents intended to enter from the State of Kentucky, which was neutral territory, pretending that they were coming down to fight for the Southern cause. That was an excuse to get on that train which takes them up to an army camp. Their leader took seven men with him, including two locomotive engineers and a telegraph operator; and he told them that if anything went wrong they were to scatter individually, stick to their stories that they were Kentuckians down to enlist in the Southern army, and then watch for the first opportunity to desert and get back over the line to the North. As soon as they stole that engine, they wanted to pull out of there, to disconnect the telegraph and burn bridges and destroy enough track to cripple the Southern army supply route. That was what they intended to do. And I staged the chase exactly the way it happened. Then I rounded out the story of stealing my engine back. When my picture ended the South was winning, which was all right with me.

J.B.: *How did the plot develop apart from the historical story line—the involvement with the girl and so on?*

Well, the moment you give me a locomotive and things like that to play with, as a rule I find some way of getting laughs with it. But the original

51. *The General* (Keaton, Marian Mack)

locomotive chase ended when I found myself in Northern territory and had to desert. From then on it was my invention, in order to get a complete plot. It had nothing to do with the Civil War.

J.G.: *What many of us like about your films is the treatment of the women. These poor ladies, like Marian Mack in* The General, *are subjected to all kinds of humiliations and yet they battle on. They get pulled and pushed around, but they always stand by you. Did they mind at all?*

No, no. They didn't mind at all. Oh God, that girl in *The General* had more fun with that picture than any film she'd made in her life. (*At this point Keaton's face, hitherto frozen as usual, eased into a wide, knowing smile.*) I guess it's because so many leading ladies in those days looked as though they had just walked out of a beauty parlour. They always kept them looking that way—even in covered wagons, they kept their leading ladies looking beautiful at all times. We said to thunder with that, we'll dirty ours up a bit and let them have some rough treatment.

J.B.: *There is a moment of almost pathetic beauty, which is a gag at the same time, when you are both sitting on the steering rod of the wheel and the train starts to move. Not at the very end, but towards the middle of the film.*

I was alone on it when it moved. We were afraid to put her on it, or I would have moved it at the finish.

J.B.: *Can you remember how that gag came to you, out of the film's situation?*

Well, the situation of the picture at that point is that she says 'never speak to me again until you're in uniform.' So the bottom has dropped out of everything, and I've got nothing to do but sit down on my engine and think. I don't know why they rejected me: they didn't tell me it was because they didn't want to take a locomotive engineer off his duty. My fireman wants to put the engine away in the round-house and doesn't know that I'm sitting on the cross bar, and starts to take it in.

I was running that engine myself all through the picture: I could handle that thing so well I was stopping it on a dime. But when it came to this shot I asked the engineer whether we could do it. He said: 'There's only one danger. A fraction too much steam with these old-fashioned engines and the wheel spins. And if it spins it will kill you right then and there.' We

52. Keaton and cat in *Film* (1965), scripted by Samuel Beckett

tried it out four or five times, and in the end the engineer was satisfied that he could handle it. So we went ahead and did it. I wanted a fade-out laugh for that sequence: although it's not a big gag it's cute and funny enough to get me a nice laugh.

J.G.: *It's also beautiful: it has another quality than just a laugh. On this question of emotion, there is the difference between your films and those of Chaplin, who sometimes seems to go into a sequence with the intention of milking it for all the emotion it can stand. You are rarely deliberately pathetic. In* Go West, *however, there is a slight element of conscious pathos. Did you feel you needed something more emotional there than in the other films?*

I was going to do everything I possibly could to keep that cow from being sent to the slaughter-house: I only had that one thing in mind. And I ran into one disappointment on that film. One of the most famous Western shows ever seen in the United States was called 'The Heart of Maryland,' in which these two guys are playing cards, and one guy calls the other a name, and he takes out his six-shooter and lays it down on the table, pointing right at this fellow's middle, and says, 'When you call me that, smile . . .' Well, because I'm known as frozen face, blank pan, we thought that if you did that to me an audience would say, 'Oh my God, he can't smile: he's gone; he's dead.' But it didn't strike an audience as funny at all: they just felt sorry for me. We didn't find that out until the preview, and it put a hole in my scene right there and then. Of course I got out of it the best way I could, but we run into these lulls every now and then.

J.B.: *And you look for a gag to get yourself out of a situation: the pole-vault gag with the spear for instance in* The Three Ages. *There you were in a situation where you had to get the girl out of the hands of Wallace Beery. How did you work your way to the spear vault from that?*

I couldn't just run over a batch of rocks or something to get to her: I had to invent something, find something unexpected, and pole-vaulting with a spear seemed to be it.

J.G.: *You very often use gags which couldn't be managed except in films. For instance the scene in* Sherlock Jr. *where you are dreaming yourself into the picture, and the scenery keeps changing. How did you get the idea of this scene?*

That was the reason for making the whole picture. Just that one situation: that a motion picture projectionist in a theatre goes to sleep and visualises himself getting mixed up with the characters on the screen. All right, then my job was to transform those characters on the screen into my (the projectionist's) characters at home, and then I've got my plot. Now to make it work was another thing; and after that picture was made every cameraman in Hollywood spent more than one night watching it and trying to figure out just how we got some of those scenes.

J.G.: *How did you actually do the sequence where you are near a tree, and then you are on a rock in the middle of the ocean. Was it some kind of back projection?*

No, that hadn't been invented then. We call it processing, but back projection is correct. But it hadn't been invented. We used measuring instruments for that sequence. When I stood on that rock I was going to jump into the ocean, but as I jumped the sea changed to something else. As I looked down I held still for a moment, and we ended that scene. Then we brought out tape-measures, put a cross-bar in front of the camera to square it off, and measured me from two angles. That made sure that I was in exactly the same spot as far as the camera was concerned. We also used surveyor's instruments to get me the same height, so that when we changed the scene and I went back on the set I was in exactly the same place as in the first shot. Then the cameraman just starts to crank and I jump; and when I jump I hit something else. I don't remember what I hit, but I hit something. This was all done just by changing the sets. But I on the screen never changed.

1966

Minimal Cinema:
The Chronicle of Anna Magdalena Bach

RICHARD ROUD

Minimal art is much in the news this year, and the recent Knokke Festival Grand Prix winner, *Wavelength*, was, theoretically, an excellent example. Forty minutes (not however without cuts, as most people would have it, and not without certain . . . minimal changes of angle) moving slowly down a room to the window wall. Then in London in April, we finally saw one of Warhol's minimal films. Not the 12-hour *Empire*, but *Harlot*, a seventy-minute film which consists only—or as nearly as 16 mm. film magazines will let it—of one shot. Amusingly, Warhol plays with the idea by including a rather rambunctious cat who is the only uncontrolled element in the shot; his (or her) constant efforts to escape out of frame did indeed provide a certain tension, a certain playful attitude towards the problems of minimal cinema.

But it seems to me that Warhol with his aleatory cat will go down in history as the Marcel Duchamp of the post-war period: an artist who has thrown out a steady stream of ideas, who has changed our way of looking at things without being able—or willing—to realise them fully. It is not an unenviable position. However, the important thing about minimal cinema, it seems to me, is that it must be meaningfully minimal. 'Less is more,' Mies van der Rohe told us, but less implies less of *something*. Stripped-down cinema, as in Bresson, implies both that there was something to be stripped down in the first place and, even more important, that when the stripping has to stop, something—however minimal—is left.

So when I say that Jean-Marie Straub's new film (actually it was co-directed with his wife Danièle Straub-Huillet), *The Chronicle of Anna Magdalena Bach*, lasts ninety minutes and contains scarcely more than a hundred shots (instead of the usual eight hundred to a thousand); that all movement, whether of camera or within the frame, is held to a minimum; and that what one sees consists almost entirely of period-costumed musicians executing selections from the works of J. S. Bach, I do not mean that these facts in themselves suffice to make the film an important

53. Diagonals: *Chronicle of Anna Magdalena Bach*

achievement.[1] If such were the case, then I would have to call *Harlot* a masterpiece. For all its ground-breaking, it isn't. But Straub's film, I think, is.

To be sure, readers of *Sight and Sound* will know that I have always had a weakness for the film that extends one's idea of the cinema, of what it can do, and what, in fact, it can get away with. But apart from the excitement of cliff-hanging, if one does not believe that there is any such thing as a definable, 'essential' cinema, that rather it is in a perpetual state of becoming, then it is only natural that one should prize those films which go out on a limb. Like, for example, *Gertrud*. Those who judged it by received standards found it talky and slow; it never moved, and certainly, they added self-confidently, the one sure thing about movies is that they must *move*.

True enough, but there is movement and movement. Whole sequences of *Gertrud* consisted of a single shot of two characters sitting on a divan, talking. But in such scenes Dreyer was able to achieve with a smile, a turning of the head, that same exhilaration of movement which other

[1]cf. Alain Resnais: 'I won't admit that the image counts most; why not the other way around? It all depends on the subject, but a film which consisted entirely of a sound-track with nothing in the frame would still be a film as long as the rhythm of the splices was in harmony with the rhythm of the words or the music.'

directors can only get from a whole army crossing the Super Panavision Alps. True, one was constantly holding one's breath: would the scene, like Warhol's cat, suddenly slip away from us into boredom? (And this was not the least exciting element of such sequences: let the psychiatrists explain why.)

But Dreyer at least had a story. Those who saw Straub's first film, *Nicht Versöhnt* (*Unreconciled*) will remember his diabolical skill in taking a straightforward, if complex, novel and reducing it—abstracting it—into an unchronological series of extremely brief Brechtian/Bressonian tableaux; of bafflingly elliptical moments. *The Chronicle of Anna Magdalena Bach* works the other way round: Straub starts with the tableaux in the first place. In a sense, the construction of the film is very much like that of Bach's *St Matthew Passion*. The story, as it were, is almost entirely confined to the recitative of the Evangelist. But for the most part it is the arias and choruses, the set-pieces, which really provide the drama. Simply and straightforwardly, we are given the information in order to clear the decks

54. *Chronicle of Anna Magdalena Bach*

for expression of the emotional significance both of what we have been told, and of what we have not.

The St Matthew role of narrator is taken by Anna Magdalena, so the film only covers Bach's last years, from his second marriage in 1721 to his death in 1748. Throughout, performances of music are linked by Anna Magdalena's calm, non-expressive narration, or occasionally by the words of Bach himself. The film begins, for example, in the Music Room of the Prince of Anhalt-Cöthen: Bars 154 to 227 of the Allegro of the 5th Brandenburg Concerto are performed. Then, we cut to 'A Wall and a Clavichord' and Anna Magdalena begins her tale: 'He was a chapel-master, director of the chamber music at the court of Anhalt-Cöthen. My father was a trumpeter at the court . . . His wife had died a year before; and from their marriage three sons and a daughter survived . . . For Friedemann, his father had started a little clavier book . . .' And then we hear the 6th Prelude from Wilhelm Friedemann Bach's Clavier Book.

In this section, the music has been chosen, at least partly, to illustrate the text. At other times, the music is only very tenuously related to the text. Or rather, the other way round. Because the film is not really about Bach, but about the *music* of Bach. Just as it could be said that *Diary of a Country Priest* was not a film about religion, but a film *of* religion, so this film *is* music. Not musical: music. Except in a very special sense, it does not attempt to express the music; rather it lets it express itself. This may sound pleonastically futile; the same was said about Bresson when he had his actor read out loud what we could all see written on the screen.

In somewhat the same way, Straub lets the music speak for itself, and yet the final result is much greater than the music alone could achieve. For just as his cantata-like form achieves drama without plot—through the music—so he has managed to find a way of filming music without 'copying' it, and of achieving action without movement.

On the one hand, the film is shot in an extremely simple manner—any attempt to compete with Bach's architectonics would be doomed to failure. Instead, Straub intensifies the dynamics of the music by positively limiting the visual effects, and this contrast throws into brilliant perspective the complexity of the music. However, the apparent simplicity of his style should not fool us. Each of his thirty-two scenes is cunningly composed; many of them find a kind of imaginative equivalent to the baroque quality of the music by employing certain of the principles of baroque painting—notably what we might call the oppressive diagonal. Many of the sequences make effective use of the baroque practice of 'dissolving the logic of the plane and giving to space a troubled directional energy, a compulsive and oblique drive.'[1] Thus the diagonal

[1] Wylie Sypher, *Four Stages of Renaissance Style*.

gives its own impression of movement to an essentially static scene. Furthermore, Straub's compositions are often heavily weighted, alternately to the left and to the right, so that when he cuts from one diagonal to another, he achieves a strangely effective sense of motion. Oftentimes within one of the sequences, the camera at a certain point in the tableau will make a kind of lazy arabesque starting from the right and circling down and then up to the left. On other occasions it tracks in, making a new diagonal in opposition to the original set-up.

At Knokke, much was talked about the triumph of the contemplative cinema, of which *Wavelength* was the prime example. And it was true that after staring at that damned room for forty minutes, some rather startling effects occurred. But these effects were almost purely retinal. Straub's film is also a kind of contemplative cinema, but infinitely more important, and certainly more rewarding in that the contemplation is on a far more profound level and results in that sense of exaltation which is after all the surest sign of the presence of great art. 'Music,' wrote Lévy-Strauss, 'is the middle way between logical thought and aesthetic perception . . . We know that music is a language, since we understand what it is saying, but its absolute orginality, what distinguishes it from articulated language, is that it is untranslatable.' This could also be said about *The Chronicle of Anna Magdalena Bach*.

1968

The Confrontation

ROBERT VAS

'Hey, our banners are unfurling in the joyful wind ...' The original Hungarian title of *The Confrontation* comes from this rallying song of the Communist youth movement in Hungary in the mid-1940s. '... written on it, hey, stands Long Live Freedom!' There they stand, a group of young boys and girls, with their newly acquired freedom, pressing their flushed faces against the old-fashioned wrought-iron gate of a church school, convinced about their own truth, holding a piece of red cloth which stands for the flag, their eyes shining, singing with fervour: 'Tomorrow we'll turn the whole world upside down!' The picture expresses what we all felt in those days, twenty to twenty-five years ago: not only were we happy to be young, but to our exuberant youth we were given, without having to work out something for ourselves, a view of life, an ideology to believe in. 'In the history of the world,' says one of the boys who stage the confrontation, 'this is the first power that is honourable.' So we felt; and they too: the group that climbs over the fence to go to convince the pupils of the church school about the righteousness of their cause.

They could be the great-grandchildren of the condemned outlaws of *The Round-Up*; the grandchildren of the dispersed Red Army soldiers of *The Red and the White*. They got ready-made what their elders were fighting for and gave their lives for. Even their rallying songs they inherited. 'Rise, you Red proletariat, you star-spangled soldiers!' It is perhaps significant that the original Hungarian title of *The Red and the White* ('Star-spangled Soldiers') is also a quote from a fiery, romantic song of the Movement: 'Great tasks are awaiting you: the palaces are still standing!' And when the remnants of Sándor's band are given the news that the Emperor has granted a reprieve to their leader, spontaneously they break into a song: 'Long live the Freedom of Hungary!'

Whereby they finally betray their identity and, blindfolded, are dragged away. Those star-spangled soldiers of the song massacre each other long before they can embark on the 'great tasks'. And their young successors in *The Confrontation*, who would like to turn the whole world upside down, will soon see their romantic ideals crumble to pieces. The real confrontation is not with the pupils of the church college (and the action of the film centres on the various stages of this confrontation, from peaceful persuasion to active terror) but with their own idealism, which is ultimately incompatible with the very nature, the totalitarian ideals, of the regime which gave them their songs and their right to sing them. They will soon have to adapt themselves to the rules of the game ('How? Everyone will have to decide that for himself') if they want to survive both morally and physically.

Again, the subject is the gulf between ideals, and the way they fail to materialise. The crowd that unfurls flags, knocks down palaces and dances with arms held tightly together as if a chain, never to come apart, the crowd consists of *people*. When their arms do, finally, come apart they turn into individuals who have the equal potential of becoming both oppressors and oppressed, victims or victimisers, and if requested change roles without difficulty. And the gradual disintegration of the group, the way these young, defenceless, genuine believers, proudly upholding their newly gained freedom, become the potential cogwheels in an enormous bureaucratic machinery—this process disturbs and hurts perhaps even more than the senseless, casual massacres in the other two films. We can observe step by step, and with the inevitability of the process as only Jancsó can express it, the way a genuine belief that could, perhaps, really have accomplished those 'great tasks', is harnessed and deflated by the regime and forced to sink into the grey anonymity of the political everyday.

The way such ideals turned into bitter disillusionment led to the revolt of 1956. But Jancsó's film is necessarily sceptical even about this great, seemingly immaculate historic moment; causes, even *such* causes, can gobble up their own creatures and achievements. His film ends on exactly the same frame with which it began: you could splice it together into a vicious circle, the same story repeats itself again and again under different circumstances. For it is relatively easy to link arms, to sing songs and even to capture barricades—but it is practically impossible to maintain power in a way that is worthy of the ideals. 'The terror reacts upon those who exercise it.' 'What is the role of the individual in history?'—the young Communists pose the question to their supposed opponents at the church school, but soon they'll have to ask themselves for an answer in a regime which pretends to be their very own ('I am a policeman and I represent your State').

In an atmosphere like this you cannot just dump a pile of old religious books in the courtyard and stop there; in the end there'll always be someone prepared to throw a burning match to it. If a doctrine happens to fail there is always a group in fresh white shirts and well-creased trousers coming forward with another doctrine. An enemy will have to be produced artificially to stir up the people from their apathy of 'sly fascism'—and a traditional rallying song is immediately at their disposal:

'To strangle us, to ruin us—that's the plan of the wicked rascals!' The process is endless. It is inevitable. And it is practised to the accompaniment of rhythmic applause, to singing and dancing.

Such singing and dancing dominate the film, keep it in a constant movement like the wind waves a flag, and remind us of the way in which complicated life-and-death issues that concern us all are brought down all the time to the level of captivating, deceptive simplification, turning us into onlookers instead of protagonists. The young people in the film march in with songs, convince their opponents with songs, frighten and

55. *The Confrontation*

humiliate them with songs, fight against their own mounting doubts by singing songs; and when they finally betray their ideals, there's a song ready for that purpose, too. These songs express the quality of the ideals and their cocky readiness to fight for them, and at the same time have a threatening, potentially destructive and—in the songs about the old Jew and in 'Come on then, stab and slaughter!'—an even overtly fascist power. They transform the film into a kind of ritual; as exuberant (though, at least to me, never really genuinely jolly) as it is frightening.

At the same time it is through this incessant singing and dancing that Jancsó achieves a rich stylised texture for the film. It acts as an alienating device. Everything here is given in signs, in appearances rather than in depth. Flags, songs, shirts red, grey and white; the stone cross and the red cloth over it; the ecclesiastic habits; the policemen's jeep; the text of the official regulation whereby Jews had to wear the yellow star: these are the expressive means of a morality play, a parable or a mime-play or even a *tableau vivant*. It is a cold film and it is not easy to come to terms with it after a single viewing. Once again, the camera is rowing up and down, following and recording the action seemingly impassively, symbolising our own helplessness to take part in the happenings and reducing us to onlookers.

Everything that happens in the frame is potentially suspect and dangerous; that jeep, for instance, that now enters in the distance as a tiny, harmless dot, brings out the goose-pimples on your back: what is it coming for? That heap of books in the courtyard that the camera now brings into frame slowly, dispassionately: is it possible that they are going to burn them? And the drama of a sharp confrontation of ideals acted out by aggressive young people is photographed in a tired, yellow, late afternoon sunshine (with Jancsó's favourite icy wind blowing again in the distance): disillusionment is imminent and inevitable.

All this adds up to a fascinating, remarkable film; an attempt by an artist, in a political climate where this may be more than difficult, to remain true to himself and talk with honesty and integrity about the true problems of his people. But can this be possible? Can he 'get away with it'? *The Confrontation* shows us an apparatus in which decisions are made behind the scenes and the individual has to fall in, obey and not ask questions. How can the artist invite us then for a truly courageous dialogue? If the police inspector is watching over how people should act and feel, how can Jancsó and his film be an exception? And even be shown at international film festivals? Can the regime afford such a bargaining? Or does Jancsó himself fall victim to the very process he puts on to the screen, telling us not the truth but only a useful truth—and in this case how can we trust him? 'It is easy to be a revolutionary now,' says the Jewish boy to the protagonist in the red shirt, 'with the Russian tanks backing you up.'

And yet, the *way* Jancsó tells his stories, the obstinacy with which he tells them again and again, the constant invitation to dialogue in which, perhaps, one single sentence of genuine insight will illuminate the whole unspoken truth—they make his search, his repeated challenge to his people to face up to themselves as they really are, an act of authentic courage. Somewhere between the romantic songs we used to sing and the curt, ruthless orders of the policemen there is the voice of hard, caring intellect: the voice of Jancsó and his fellow artists.

1970

Performance

PHILIP FRENCH

With its hallucinogenic mushrooms, its direct equation of the underworld with respectable society, its obtrusively restless visual style, *Performance* runs the gamut from Henry Livings' *Eh?* to Costa-Gavras' *Z* by way of Fritz Lang's *M*. There is the noticeable influence of such contemporary sages as R. D. Laing (*The Politics of Experience and the Bird of Paradise*), Norman O. Brown (*Life Against Death*) and Erving Goffman (most especially the chapter on 'Performances' in his *The Presentation of Self in Everyday Life*), an elaborate score that combines rock numbers by Mick Jagger and Indian-style music by Jack Nitzsche (no kin, as *Time* would say, to Germany's famed philosopher Friedrich Nietzsche), rib-nudging references to painters like Magritte, Peter Blake, Richard Hamilton and Francis Bacon, the looming presence throughout of Jorge Luis Borges, and lurking beneath it all the ethos of the so-called underground and its cinema.

Coupled with the much publicised troubles that the makers have had with their distributors, and to a lesser extent with the censors, it's not surprising therefore that the film has been acclaimed as an urgent mind-blowing revelation or dismissed as a trendily mindless confection. There is certainly ample evidence to support both views. Yet for all its faults I found it a most engaging movie, and I have yet to meet anyone (though some there must surely be) prepared to deny its manifest technical merits—and for this credit must go individually to Nicolas Roeg for his virtuoso camerawork and to Donald Cammell for an inventive, often very funny script; and to Roeg and Cammell jointly as co-directors for the remarkable acting (or should one say performances?) they've elicited from their oddly assorted cast.

Fundamentally *Performance* is a crime movie (which may or may not explain why Warner Brothers initially took such exception to it), didactic in immediate aim, metaphysical in ultimate ambition (or pretension—for the jokey surface conceals an underlying portentousness), and intermittently surrealist in character. What appears on the screen is often elliptical and deliberately ambiguous, and I do not pretend to understand (or really worry about) certain aspects. For instance, the opening frames which seem to be documentary material from some Cape Kennedy space-shot may or may not be intended as some latterday equivalent of the eye-slashing that prefaces *Un Chien Andalou*; several people I've spoken to can't recall having seen them. If I saw what I thought I saw, the implication is of some sort of trip out of this world that, as an analogy to Buñuel's razor, might be related to the high decibel music and absorption in technological equipment by which the underground attempts, in contradictory fashion, to dissociate itself from mundane reality. But as I say I could be wrong.

Reduced to its bare narrative bones, the film is that old Hollywood stand-by, the confrontation between the criminal-on-the-run and the inhabitants of his place of temporary refuge. Traditionally in these circumstances the crook will gain a new sense of humanity and the occupied household will achieve a fresh solidarity from the experience. One could make up a whole NFT season from these films. For there are alternatives that propose more interesting interchanges, as in the hollowly pretentious *Petrified Forest* where the washed-out Eliot-quoting intellectual (Leslie Howard) gets the gangster to kill him, or *49th Parallel* where the etiolated, Mann-quoting intellectual (Howard again) abandons his cherished pacifism when faced by two Nazi fugitives. Then there's the glib situation in *The Dark Past* in which a mentally disturbed criminal is swiftly psychoanalysed and rehabilitated by a smug psychiatrist whose home he enters; and in terms of black comedy we have Roman Polanski's *Cul-de-Sac*, with the simple-minded crook becoming the victim of his deeply disturbed hosts.

Performance has something in common with all these films, with the initial difference that the fugitive criminal Chas Devlin (James Fox) is the apparently well-adjusted member of square society and that his place of refuge is the home of the self-elected social outcast, a former pop star called Turner (Mick Jagger) who has lost his 'demon'. Chas is a strong-arm man who has threatened the respectable front of his employer, the homosexual London racketeer Harry Flowers, by committing a murder. On the run from the law and from his former associates, Chas takes the basement room in the Notting Hill retreat of the hermit-like former pop performer by passing himself off as a nightclub juggler.

In the belief that he is having his photograph taken for a forged passport, Chas submits to letting Turner and his two bi-sexual female companions, the well-built Pherber (Anita Pallenberg) and the boyish (to Chas 'skinny') Lucy (Michèle Breton) play with his identity even further, until under the influence of covertly administered drugs he is completely disoriented and drawn into their private world. The phlegmatic Pherber's interest in Chas is seemingly disinterested, almost therapeutic, while Turner's is more personal, possibly demonic. He seems to recognise in the unhappy criminal a guinea-pig that in the controlled environment of

56. *Performance*: Mick Jagger

his flat he can play with—much as Prospero worked on the
castaways—and so examine the violence he once generated in the
audiences from which he has fled. Eventually Flowers' henchmen come
to take Chas away for a fatal drive in the country, but before going the
intruder—virtually at the singer's request—shoots Turner dead. Or at
least he appears to do so, for there is the same calculated confusion
between fantasy and reality, and even as to whom we are watching, that
Bergman achieved in *Persona*, one of the many movies (another obvious
one would be John Boorman's *Point Blank*) that have influenced
Performance.

As a crime picture the film works very well. The first half-hour in which
we see Chas going diligently about his work is perhaps the best and (from
what one has read of the Richardsons and Krays) the most authentic
account the cinema has given us of organised crime in Britain. There is a
brooding menace to which no one is invulnerable, brilliantly etched
portraits of crooks (especially Johnny Shannon as the slimy, ingratiating
Flowers, but he's only one in a whole gallery), dialogue that sounds like
taped conversations edited by Pinter.

Unfortunately, Cammell and Roeg do not restrict themselves entirely to subtle suggestions in establishing Chas' ostensible self-assurance and neatly organised life, or in making their other point that legitimate business and organised crime share a similar language and morality. They sometimes resort to sledgehammer blows as blatant as party slogans lowered from the flies in a Brecht play; as for instance in cross-cutting between a commercial fraud case at the Old Bailey and Chas going about his work of intimidation to further Flowers' business 'mergers'. One gathers, however, that the elliptical style and overemphasis of the underworld sequences was partly due to a considerable condensation of the opening section demanded by the American distributors, who were anxious for their star property, Mick Jagger, to make an earlier appearance.

I have spoken of the film's didactic aims, metaphysical aspirations and surrealistic mode, and it is perhaps most easy to look at these elements through the picture's formal strategy—a series of mirror images, antitheses, puns, visual associations and mystical connections that vary from the crass to the relatively profound. At a didactic level we have a confrontation between love and hate, male and female, underworld and underground, between two drop-outs, one with a sure sense of his masculine identity, the other experimenting with new life-styles. As drop-outs, fugitives from their assigned or elective roles, Chas has fallen through enjoying his work too much, not appreciating that he is a cog in a wheel; Turner has withdrawn, more obscurely, as a result of questioning

57. Mirrors: Anita Pallenberg, James Fox, Mick Jagger

58. Role-playing: James Fox

his function and the uncontrollable forces it released. Chas' underworld, however, is part of society, dependent upon it, offering no threat; Turner's underground, in its naïvely idealised aspect, is a genuine revolutionary alternative. In the first part of the film, characters are always looking into mirrors narcissistically, their sexual aberrations are viewed as departures from a prescribed norm, they are plagued with guilt, if only of a kind imposed upon them by Cammell and Roeg. In the second part, Turner and his androgynous seraglio use mirrors and cameras to probe beyond, to question the surface of reality; they have abandoned the notion of fixed sexual and social roles.

Both Chas and Turner are 'performers'; Turner in the more usually understood sense, Chas in the terms of underworld argot for his kind of dramatic, stylish thuggery. But Turner and Pherber introduce Chas to the notion that everyone engaged in social activity is a performer, playing a variety of roles either consciously (Chas pretending to be a juggler) or unconsciously (Chas believing himself to be a tough he-man). In this way the film is making a rather obvious assault upon the complacency of square society in the name of an open, honest, uninhibited, self-interrogating alternative society. The rituals and games played around the nature of performing and performances, the vulnerability of identity and so on, are sophisticated and dramatically valid. They are not less so for my feeling that the polemical points made through them have the glibness and over-simplification one has come to expect from underground philosophers when they make large statements about the fundamental shortcomings of the square world, and what form a revolutionary life-style to replace it might take.

Of course, there is more to *Performance* than this; and whether it contributes ultimately to a greater depth or is merely the piling up of rhetorical impasto on the film's already overloaded surface is a matter of personal taste and judgment. Rising above, or lurking beneath, the psychological, sociological and political statements that constitute the movie's central drift, is a mystical or metaphysical thrust that seeks to translate us to another plane of speculation. This is partly connected with the shared violence of the two 'performers' and the similarities rather than the contrasts between their two worlds. In Chas' drugged fantasy, Turner takes over from Harry Flowers as gang boss and leads his henchmen in a wild debauch that resembles one of Francis Bacon's sado-masochistic homosexual paintings of the Sixties. This is a less benign variation on an earlier motif, that poses a relationship between the gymnasium atmosphere of Flowers' world, with its male physique magazines and studied pugilistic portraits that adorn the gang boss's walls, and Peter Blake's coyly elegant paintings of all-in wrestlers that are pinned up among the pop posters of Chas' basement hideout.

Rather less dramatically, Turner reads a resonant passage from some early account (possibly Marco Polo's) of the mediaeval, middle-eastern assassin cult led by the Old Man of the Mountains, and his dedicated, drug-crazed followers with their dream of paradise. And he infers significant parallels between that vexatious, controversial cult and, on the one hand, Harry Flowers' gang, and on the other (perhaps prophetically), the hash-smoking underground of today with their search for a new ecstatic order.

Even more striking than this is the use made of the septuagenarian Argentinian author Jorge Luis Borges, in whose stories the gangster figures as a kind of tragic or epic hero. In view of the importance that Roeg and Cammell so obviously attach to his work I find it odd that no reviewers have thought it necessary to comment on it—even in a quizzical or querulous way. Borges' writings are certainly more flaunted in *Performance* than Céline's *Death on the Instalment Plan* in *Une Femme Mariée* or Hermann Broch's *The Sleepwalkers* in *La Notte*.

The first intimation of Borges' illuminating presence appears in the first half-hour when—rather oddly one might feel—the cool gangster

Rosebloom (Stanley Meadows in excellent form) is sitting in a car reading Borges' *Personal Anthology*, while Chas puts 'the frighteners' on a blue-movie exhibitor—a foreigner incidentally whom our gangster views with predictable xenophobic disdain and who in turn appeals ironically to some vague notion of 'British justice'. Borges surfaces again when Turner begins to perceive the use he might make of Chas, and in a wild peroration invokes Borges' *Tlön Uqbar and Orbis Tertius*, a strange tale that proceeds from the discovery of a single copy of a pirated encyclopaedia containing the description of a non-existent middle-eastern country, to the further revelation that a 300-year-old conspiracy of idealist intellectuals has been working on the invention of a new and totally consistent planet. In Borges' world dreams can become reality and reality become a dream, systems of rational speculation can lead to a nightmare demonstration that life is like a labyrinth, both carefully ordered and meaningless.

Next Turner switches to a tale that represents another, complementary side of Borges and quotes from the penultimate paragraph of *The South*, a tale of cool, existential horror, about a different kind of epiphanous experience, in which a German Argentinian recovers his identity in the act of taking on a challenge—as arbitrary as it is inexorable—to join a knife fight that will end in his own death. The film refers twice more to Borges. We see a copy of *Personal Anthology* again in the cut between Rosebloom's discovery of Chas' hiding place and a scene confirming that the fugitive has become part of the Turner ménage. The final one comes when Borges' portrait briefly fills the screen following a close-up of the bullet from Chas' pistol entering Turner's head.

To what extent this latter gesture is a mere act of homage one cannot be sure. Maybe the two stories quoted—which are incidentally the first and last pieces in the English edition of *Ficciones*—are intended to define and enlarge the relationship between Chas and Turner and to take us spiralling away from the singer's Notting Hill pad. And the portrait following the murder is thus intended to suggest that in the moment of decision and death Chas and Turner have become one in the Borgesian universe. Whether this comes off is another matter. In following up these references the critic might profitably recall another Borges story, *Death and the Compass*, where a master detective is lured to his death by a master criminal, who lays a trail of wild clues in the correct belief that only his hated quarry, the detective, could make a meaningful pattern out of them, and thus arrive at the prescribed place at the right moment in time to be executed.

1971

Bertolucci and the Dance of Danger

MARSHA KINDER and BEVERLE HOUSTON

Last Tango in Paris is a disturbing film that causes a lot of arguments. Fury at the disgruntled vulgarians who came to see a *Deep Throat* and want everyone around them to know 'they didn't get their money's worth'. Disagreement with companions who see Brando only as a sexist pig or romantic ideal. Our own confusion when we see the film again and respond to everything differently. These encounters release the powerful emotions evoked by the film, but they also grow out of its richness. Bertolucci's confrontation of the issues is profound; the performances (particularly Brando's) are amazingly authentic; and our own needs and fantasies concerning sex, love and death pull us very strongly into private visions of the film. One way of understanding the film itself is to see it in the context of Bertolucci's earlier works. The central conflicts in *Last Tango* bear close similarities with those in *The Conformist* (1970), *The Spider's Stratagem* (1969), and *Before the Revolution* (1964). In all these films, one of the central characters is a young person trying to escape from his social class and family background, but who inevitably lives out the values from his past. Unconventionality is always associated with left-wing politics. In *Before the Revolution*, Fabrizio joins the Communist Party but ultimately rejects it for its imperfections and returns to his bourgeois family. The young hero of *The Spider's Stratagem* is unwillingly drawn into the mystery surrounding the death of his father, who was supposedly assassinated by the Fascists. In trying to avenge the murder, the son's identity almost merges with that of his father. In *The Conformist*, Marcello Clerici tries to escape his father's insanity and his mother's eccentric decadence. In order to appear 'normal', he joins the Fascist Party; but when Mussolini falls, he renounces the Fascists and retreats into madness like his father. In *Last Tango*, Jeanne, daughter of a French army colonel, delights in shocking her conventional mother with her liberated life style. But later she destroys her outrageous lover and chooses a conventional marriage. In all these cases, the gap between conventionality and rebellion, between outward appearance and inner emotional reality, makes the person frightened and dangerous, particularly to those who love him.

In *Revolution*, *Conformist* and *Last Tango*, each of these characters chooses between a conventional marriage and a dangerous love affair associated with childhood. In rejecting the romantic lover (who is neurotic or deviant by society's norms), and entering the marriage, each destroys the potential for growth and, as if to ensure that the decision is final, each destroys the loved one. In *Revolution*, Clelia was destined from childhood to be Fabrizio's bride. He temporarily abandons her for a stormy, incestuous relationship with his aunt Gina, who is neurotic and promiscuous, dislikes adults and tries to remain a child. She is the one who leaves first, but Fabrizio makes the break permanent when he marries. The film ends with the wedding; as the bride and groom drive off, Gina is sobbing and smothering Fabrizio's younger brother with kisses. In *The Conformist*, Marcello marries Julia, a sensuous but shallow member of the middle class, who offers him a superficial respectability. But he really loves Anna, the wife of the liberal professor whom he is trying to assassinate. Marcello visits Anna at her dancing school where she is instructing little girls in ballet, associating her with children. In their final scene, he, like Fabrizio, sits inside a car with the windows rolled up

59. *Before the Revolution*

as Anna sobs hysterically outside; Marcello not only rejects her as a lover, but also abandons her to the assassins.

In *Last Tango*, Jeanne must choose between her fiancé Tom, whose passion is focused on directing a film about her and her family, and Paul, a stranger, who insists on knowing nothing about her background or outside life. She meets Paul in an empty room where they play like children and explore the extremes of sexual fantasy. With Tom she can have a 'pop marriage' where the smiling youths, dressed in overalls, work on their relationship as if it were an automobile. But Jeanne acknowledges that love is not pop. For love, 'The workmen go to a secret place, take off their overalls, and become men and women again.' This is what she has experienced with Paul, but when he tries to bring their love outside their secret room, she flees in terror.

Each of the characters has a parallel conflict about a male authority figure—an idealistic father surrogate who arouses ambivalent feelings and is ultimately rejected. This theme is central in *Spider's Stratagem*, where the son tries to discover whether his father was really a traitor or a hero. In *Revolution*, Fabrizio ignores his bourgeois father and idolises Cesare, his childhood teacher. Unlike Fabrizio, Cesare combines his communist ideology with humanity and realism. When Fabrizio abandons the Party and his youthful idealism to marry Clelia, the wedding scene is intercut with shots of Cesare reading from *Moby Dick* to a class of small children. It is the passage describing Ahab's obsessive pursuit of the white whale—the kind of mad but courageous journey on which the Brando character is embarked. But Cesare is an Ishmael, not an Ahab.

In *The Conformist*, Cesare is transformed into Quadri, the idealistic left-wing philosophy professor who has fled Fascist Italy and settled in Paris. Marcello had been one of his best students, doing his thesis on Plato's allegory of the cave. But he has rejected Quadri and adopted as his new guide Montanari, a Fascist whose physical blindness reinforces Quadri's interpretation that the Italians now see only shadows instead of the truth. On his way to the assassination, Marcello describes a dream in which, after having his eyesight restored by the professor, Marcello runs off with Quadri's wife (a reversal of the plot of *Oedipus*). Relating to Quadri as a father implies that Marcello's relationship with Anna is incestuous (as was the relationship between Fabrizio and Gina in *Revolution* and the potential sex between the son and his father's mistress in *Spider's Stratagem*). Instead of enacting this dream, Marcello watches Quadri and his wife being murdered, explicitly linking the rejections of the true love and idealistic father (only implicit in *Revolution*).

In *Last Tango*, the lover and surrogate father become the same person. Paul is old enough to be Jeanne's father; in the secret room she returns to her childhood where she can live out her incestuous desires. When she says of her father: 'The Colonel—I loved him like a God', Paul shouts, 'What a steaming pile of bullshit. All uniforms are bullshit. Everything outside this room is bullshit.' But later, when he chases her to her parents' apartment, he puts on her father's military cap (simultaneously mocking his memory and embodying him) and clowningly says: 'How do you like your hero? Over easy or sunny side up?' She responds by killing him with her father's army pistol. Earlier, when she tried on the same cap and looked like Shirley Temple in *The Littlest Rebel*, she had said: 'How heavy it was when father taught me how to shoot it.' It is doubly heavy when she finally puts the gun to use.

In all the films the sexual and political conflict is expressed in a brilliant dance sequence where romantic joy and conventional sterility are polarised. In *Before the Revolution* Gina and Fabrizio, who have just become lovers, are celebrating Easter Sunday in the bosom of their bourgeois family. The lovers begin to dance, and finally kiss. The extraordinary eroticism of the scene is achieved by drawing us into their intense feelings, expressed in the music and the subtle detail of their faces, revealed through the lingering close-up. The excitement is heightened by the unseeing presence of the family, who have overeaten and are easing into somnolence. The father looks up briefly from his newspaper, momentarily aware, but lapses back into unconcern; the grandmother naps, her mouth agape. When Fabrizio's younger brother enters, his childish face registers awareness of the atmosphere generated by the lovers; Gina brings him into the dance, foreshadowing the film's ending. *Spider's Stratagem* presents a dance sequence which is the setting for one of the key flashbacks. The father, at his most heroically romantic moment, mocks the Fascists with his bold moves on the dance floor. In *The Conformist* the contrast is between the tight, controlled machinations of Marcello and his Fascist accomplice and the open, sweeping enchantment of the dance created by the two beautifully clad women. Even the bourgeois Julia is transformed, shouting 'This is Paris . . . I'm a New Woman.' But in *Last Tango* the forces of sterility are represented by the tango dancers, as they snap into ritualised postures and stylised grimaces to compete for a prize dispensed by the bourgeois establishment. It is in this context that Paul offers Jeanne a commitment of an older style, but his behaviour clearly shows that whatever he shares with the past, it is not the deadness. Although she is rejecting him, he succeeds in drawing her into the dance, which is their last fling of childlike, playful spontaneity. He carries her piggy-back and wiggles his ass defiantly at the outraged lady judge, who tells him, 'It's a contest. Where does love fit in? Go to the movies to see love!'

While all the films share an elaborately textured style, they also imply that style must express the politics of society and emotion in order to transcend an empty formalism. In *Revolution*, this point is made explicitly.

When his friend Agostino is in the grips of suicidal despair, Fabrizio urges him to see *Red River*, as if a good movie were all he needed. Later, when he is suffering as a result of Gina's infidelity, Fabrizio goes to see Godard's *Une Femme est une Femme*, and encounters a film buff who insists that Nicholas Ray's 360 degree pan is a 'moral fact', and that it is 'impossible to live without Rossellini'. The weakness that results from Fabrizio's bloodless idealism is contrasted with the boldness of Bertolucci's own style.

Only 23 when he made this film, Bertolucci was able to integrate influences from Rossellini, Antonioni, and especially Godard, into a personal style marked by experimentation. Sometimes the results are gimmicky, as in the shift to colour in the *camera obscura* sequence, and the looped embrace between Fabrizio and Gina. But usually the innovations are effective vehicles for important ideas and feelings. In the lyric sequence at the riverside, the sweeping camera movement, greyed tones and romantic music powerfully express the sadness and beauty of Puck's feelings, which Fabrizio so callously discounts. The brilliant opera sequence, juxtaposed with the workers' parade, begins in a kind of satiric *cinéma vérité* with the arrival of the socialites. Inside the auditorium, the characters are seated according to social class. The music starts to build, preparing us for the powerful emotions soon to be experienced. When Gina's eyes meet Fabrizio's, the camera suddenly zooms back and pans round the opera house, dizzying us with the impact of her feelings. The opera house is also the location for the assassination and its re-enactment in *Spider's Stratagem*. But in the surrealistic scene where the townspeople sit in the square listening raptly to the opera being piped out to them, the aesthetic passion of these art lovers contrasts ironically with the cowardice and treachery that marked their behaviour under Mussolini.

In *The Conformist* the dazzling compositions and visual effects seem to comment on the concern for surface beauty; which parallels Marcello's desire for the appearance of normalcy. Thus Bertolucci uses empty visuals in order to mock empty visuals, ironically making them meaningful after all. In many scenes, the drama is played out against a background that is fascinating to watch, but which has little inherent relationship to what is going on. When Marcello gives Manganiello information for planning Quadri's assassination, they are standing in the busy kitchen of a Chinese restaurant. And if that weren't enough to distract our attention, a bright light swings back and forth on the left side of the screen. In the sequence where Julia and Marcello make love, the landscapes flash by, tinted blue and gold like a romantic backdrop; dreamlike, the reflected images are superimposed on their bodies. But ironically, all this romance decorates a vicarious eroticism that results from Julia telling how she was seduced by the fat lawyer Perpuzzio; further, Marcello does not love her, but has chosen her coldly, to enhance

60. *The Conformist*: self-mocking visuals

his apparent normality. Perhaps most bitterly ironic is the contrast between the bloody assassination and the romantic, hazy, snow-covered landscape in which it takes place. The film abounds with these self-mocking, dazzling visuals.

Although *Last Tango* also has a highly controlled visual surface and many of the same images as *The Conformist*—the elevated train, the frosted glass, the Hotel d'Orsay, the façades of Paris buildings, and images flashing through the windows of a moving train—the style is less self-consciously dazzling. The visuals enhance the romantic tone surrounding Jeanne and Paul rather than deflate or distract from its emotional impact. The stylistic parody is located primarily in the character of Tom the film-maker, played by Jean-Pierre Léaud, the actor used by Truffaut for autobiographical roles and by Godard in *La Chinoise* for the pseudo-revolutionary leader of the Rosa Luxemburg theatrical cell, who act out their political fantasies within the confines of an apartment. (Tom tells Jeanne he wants to name their daughter Rose for Rosa Luxemburg.)

Linked to the film buff in *Before the Revolution*, Tom is constantly translating real life into aesthetic principle. In contrast to the Brando character, Tom is aroused to passion and violence only when Jeanne threatens to withdraw from his movie. Pretending to himself that he is doing *cinéma vérité*, he actually needs to stage and control every movement and speech. He cannot conduct his romance without the help of film allusions. When he proposes to Jeanne, a life preserver marked

L'Atalante (the name of the Vigo film in which marriage is seen as a trap) is knocked into the water, and promptly sinks. As she models her wedding gown, he rhapsodises as he dances into the rain: 'You're better than Rita Hayworth and Kim Novak . . . than Ava Gardner when she loved Mickey Rooney.' Meanwhile, he has failed to notice that Jeanne has disappeared. As part of Paul's playfulness, he also alludes to movies. When Jeanne is about to reject him, he quips, 'Quo vadis, baby,' and later does a Cagney imitation. In their final encounter, he echoes the cliché line, 'It's the title shot, baby, we're going all the way.' Unlike Tom, who gets so caught up in the films that he loses touch with what is going on around him, Paul always transforms the allusion to a personal statement that expresses the dynamics of the specific context.

At worst, Tom offers a modern counterpart to the grotesque tango—a denial of love and spontaneity in the service of a sterile and ritualised art. At best, he offers a possibility for Jeanne that focuses on herself. Though he manipulates her into remembering her past, he gives her the gift of genuine recollections from her childhood. He rejects the apartment because it is too old and sad, the same reasons she uses in rejecting the tango ballroom. He wants to become adult, but in a creative way, saying that they must 'invent gestures and words'. He mocks his own inadequacies by defining adulthood: 'Adults are serious, logical, circumspect, hairy; they face problems,' and by admitting that his film has failed to fulfil his vision. Though his own pompous style and limitations make him ridiculous in comparison to Paul, Tom has not systematically denied the identity and needs of Jeanne as a whole human being. Yet in the Métro fight she accuses him of the very same things of which Paul is eminently guilty: 'You make me do things I've never done, you take advantage of me, you steal my time, you make me do what you want, I'm tired of having my mind raped, the film is over.'

Bertolucci develops this contrast early in the film. After Jeanne has totally abandoned herself to Paul at their first encounter, she runs to meet Tom at the station. Outraged at the presence of the film crew and his announcement that he is shooting a film for TV, she snaps: 'You should have asked my permission.' Jeanne is able to deny Tom's control because it is concerned largely with his art. But with Paul, her whole being is tyrannised in a way that activates her deepest fantasies. Thus the pop battle in the subway provides a kind of comic rehearsal for the deadly earnest showdown in the apartment.

Despite its close similarities to the other films, *Last Tango in Paris* is a unique artefact—significant in its aesthetic innovation, and almost overwhelming in its emotional intensity. Perhaps the most important reason for this heightened power is the conception and development of the Brando character. Whereas the other films centred on the young men who had to choose between the romantic and the conventional, this film focuses on the exotic, dangerous lover (this time a man). In *Last Tango*, the opening shot confronts us with Brando at the moment of peak intensity, reeling with despair after the bloody suicide of his wife. Drawn to him like a magnet, the camera zooms in for a tight close-up of his face. This strange, intense figure also arouses the curiosity of the young girl passing by. Thus the opening shots establish that in this film Bertolucci will explore the extraordinary pull inherent in the romantic fantasy, far stronger in Paul than in Gina or Anna.

The power of the dream embodied in Brando results partly from the depth of experience and passion in both the character and the performance, giving Paul the symbolic resonance of an archetypal figure. Paul is old. His forty-five years have brought him full measure of suffering and humiliation; his hair is thinning and his waistline growing thick. Jeanne is young and naive; in the opening scene, she telephones her mother to report that she is about to rent her first apartment. When she tries to get the key, the black concierge warns her: 'The key has disappeared. Many strange things happen ... I'm afraid of the rats.' Laughing wickedly, she says: 'You're very young, right?' Like a prophet, the black woman knows the truth, but tells it with a touch of madness. Jeanne hears the madness, but denies the truth.

The age difference is mirrored in the choice of players. Brando is the veteran actor in the middle of a comeback; Maria Schneider is making her film debut and holding her own. Within the film, the great difference in their experience is expressed in two recollections of childhood. Though Jeanne is charmed by her early essay on cows, it is merely a dictionary exercise, like those concerning 'menstruation' and 'penis'. Paul recounts the time his father forced him to milk the cows before taking a girl to a basketball game; in the car, he suffers from exquisite humiliation when he finds that his shoes smell from cowshit.

Jeanne, like Tom, has grown up in the conventional, fairly rigid class structure of French society. Their superficial rebellion is modelled after American pop culture. But Paul goes back to an earlier American tradition of rebellious individualism. Like Ahab, he has travelled the world, pursuing his vision in the face of repeated defeat and disaster. This pattern of dangerous self-fulfilment is loved by Americans even in cartoons, where creatures are dismembered or exploded, only to get right up and begin again. Perhaps this is the American comic vision of Sisyphus; since we must continue struggling, we might as well glorify the effort. In the bathtub scene, when Jeanne tells Paul that she has fallen in love, he makes a speech that is at the centre of this vision.

PAUL: Is this man going to love you, build a fortress to protect you so you don't ever have to be afraid, lonely, or empty? Well, you'll never make it. . . . It won't be long before he wants *you* to make a fortress of your tits and your smile and the way you smell till he feels secure enough and can worship in front of the altar of his own prick. You're alone, you're all alone, and you won't be free of that feeling until you look death in the face . . . you have to go up the ass-hole of death, into the womb of fear. You won't be able to find him until you do that.

JEANNE: But I've found him—it's you. You're that man.

PAUL: Get me the scissors . . . I want you to put your fingers up my ass.

Although Paul begins by cynically denying love, he ends up affirming that it is possible—but only if one goes to the extremes of experience. Jeanne is understandably frightened by this vision, but at the same time she is drawn into the fantasy of total commitment. Through this ritual act, Paul engages Jeanne in his pursuit, as Ahab initiated his crew (the very passage read by Cesare in *Revolution*). Paul becomes her Moby Dick, but she is finally able to destroy her demon and escape from his power, allying herself to Tom, the Ishmael figure who records the story but can't get it all told.

Paul is a protean hero who undergoes many transformations on his quest. Originally Bertolucci sought Jean-Louis Trintignant for the role; though he is a fine actor, he could not have brought the richness of implication evolving out of Brando's past performances. We learn that Paul has been a boxer, like Brando in *On the Waterfront* where he laments: 'I could've been a contender'; in *Last Tango*, even though he loses, he makes it to the 'title shot'. Paul has also been a revolutionary in South America, evoking Brando's role as Zapata; Paul then went to an island in the Pacific and later was a journalist in Japan, reminding us of Brando's adventures in making *Mutiny on the Bounty*, and his roles in *Teahouse of the August Moon* and *Sayonara*. Paul has also been a bongo player and actor, linking him with Brando's personal life. Finally, Paul went to France where he married a Frenchwoman and lived on her money, the fictional situation unique to this film.

At the last Academy Awards, in a brief homage to the movie hero, the film clips moved from Valentino, the master of the tango, to Brando as Stanley (in *A Streetcar Named Desire*) and as Zapata, combining the heroic forces of sexuality and rebelliousness which are central to his role in *Last Tango*. Ironically, Brando was offered the Oscar for his portrayal of corrupt power in *The Godfather*. Perhaps his refusal was 'cutting through the bullshit' in the spirit of the hero he has come to represent in some of his finest performances—*The Wild One, On the Waterfront, Viva Zapata!, Streetcar, One-Eyed Jacks* and *Last Tango*. In this way, then, Paul's character and Brando's performance epitomise the American dream of romantic heroism developed through the history of our cinema, and reiterated in Brando's own career.

Bertolucci strengthens the elemental appeal of the Brando character through the style of the film. In contrast to the earlier movies, *Last Tango* is developed through a relatively simple linear narrative, alternating between scenes of Paul and Jeanne in their secret space and shots of their lives in the complex city outside. An element of circularity helps to intensify the experience. Between Jeanne's discovery that Paul has abandoned the apartment and the tango sequence, many scenes from the opening encounter are repeated, but in reversed order: Jeanne alone in the room, her encounter with the black concierge, Jeanne walking outside the building, Jeanne phoning Tom from the booth where she earlier called her mother, her meeting in the room with Tom (whom she tries to substitute for Paul) and her reunion with Paul under the bridge where they first met. In the apartment, Tom tells her that his film is finished. 'I don't like things to finish. You should start something else right away.' In the next scene on the bridge when she tells Paul their relationship is over, he insists: 'It's over and then it begins again.'

This circular view of experience, in which new relationships merely repeat earlier encounters, is reinforced when we learn that Jeanne's first love was also named Paul, when Paul calls her Rose as she flees from the ballroom, and when Tom suggests to Jeanne that they name their daughter Rose. Perhaps Jeanne fears that Rosa's fate prophesies her own future: both women are trying to escape the stifling influence of a bourgeois mother; both are drawn into intense sexuality with strangers in the confines of a secret room; both are loved by two men; both help to destroy Paul who loves them. In the brilliant scene where Paul visits Marcel, his wife's lover, he discovers that Rosa had bought them the same bathrobes, and realises that she was trying to recreate another version of their relationship.

The fast movement and richly textured surface of the earlier films give way to other visual values. Nearly half of *Last Tango* takes place in the almost empty space of the apartment, which heightens the significance and intensity of what we are allowed to see. Within the apartment, the screen is filled with enormous close-ups of Jeanne and Paul, often bathed in golden light. Like the Francis Bacon paintings in the titles, the characters frequently appear alone in the empty space.

While Brando recounts the painful memories of his childhood, the camera remains fixed on an enormous close-up of his face, relying entirely on the emotional play of his features. Nothing changes except the light values as Jeanne moves between him and the window; the static camera affirms his humanity as a rich source of visual value. In one of the scenes where their playfulness and intimacy are most appealing, the camera cuts to an extreme close-up of their heads and shoulders as they embrace and look at each other tenderly. When Paul says, 'Now let's just look at each other,' the camera obeys, gradually drawing back to reveal their naked

61. *Last Tango in Paris*: Marlon Brando

bodies, entwined as they face each other. When Paul carries Jeanne through the apartment in her rain-soaked wedding dress, the shadows of the rain on the walls create subtle, flickering changes in the light. The light continues to shimmer as it reflects off the water in the bathtub scene a few minutes later. This soft, glowing light enhances the romantic quality of their relationship, but contrasts ironically with the ugly, bitter realities that he forces her to face throughout this sequence.

Outside the apartment, the camera is equally capable of conveying emotional intensity. In the first encounter between Paul and his mother-in-law, the subtle camerawork reveals the fluid movement between extremes of hostile distance and emotional sympathy. The sequence opens with the image of a pile of sheets, then cuts to unidentified hands rummaging through shelves filled with objects and then to a huge silhouette of Brando's profile. When the two figures are finally seen in the same frame, they are separated by a wide space. The camera moves in for a tighter shot of the empty space, eliminating both figures and focusing on the 'Privé' sign on the door. The woman is first to enter the frame; then Brando steps into the image and embraces her. After this contact, we see a close-up of his fingers tapping on the table, then a huge close-up of his face, revealing that he has withdrawn once more into emotional distance; the next cut reveals the woman alone in the frame. Before any dialogue can identify this woman as his dead wife's mother, searching for a clue to the suicide, the emotional dynamics have already been expressed through the visuals.

The camera's handling of space to reveal states of being is also effective in the extraordinary scene between Brando and his wife's corpse. It opens with Paul entering the darkened room; while we can just see flowers on the left side of the screen, the camera stays on the right, concealing the room's other occupant. As he spurts out his anger ('You look ridiculous in that make-up, like a caricature of a whore!') the camera begins to move to the left, revealing more of the flowers, hinting at the bed's occupant. Only as his anger changes to grief does the camera arrive at the face of Rosa. Unlike those of the earlier films, these subtle camera techniques do not call attention to themselves, heightening our emotional response without creating an aesthetic distance that would be inappropriate in the scenes involving Paul.

Outside the apartment, cars, people and trains rush by, from all directions and at many levels; lighting is naturalistic or harsh, emphasising the fantasy quality of the interior scenes. Moving trains are always associated with extreme action and danger. In the opening scene Brando's despairing scream merges into the sound of the train passing overhead. After their first frantic sexual encounter Paul and Jeanne return to the street like strangers, going their separate ways, as the train again passes over them. Later, when Paul buggers her and makes her repeat an obscene litany, her cries merge with the sound of a train, as the camera cuts outside briefly to the rushing elevated (the only time in the film that the outside world intrudes into their secret room). In the Métro, through the windows of the passing subway cars, we see Tom and Jeanne fighting, just as in the final desperate chase we see, through the windows of passing automobiles, Paul pursuing Jeanne. The chase takes on symbolic dimensions as we are reminded of the opening shots of *Before the Revolution*, where Fabrizio is running madly through the streets of Parma to see a woman.

The camerawork and situation also evoke films from the French New Wave, especially the last scene of *Breathless*, where Belmondo is betrayed by the woman he loves (an American) and is gunned down as he runs through the Paris streets. This fast-paced style is close to that used by Tom's film crew. Bertolucci parodies their efforts to capture exuberance and spontaneity as a crewman spins around wildly, trying to point the camera at Jeanne's old nurse, who has just made an inconsequential remark; instead, his camera lights on a beribboned portrait of de Gaulle. In the tango sequence, the fast cutting also creates a sense of mockery by emphasising the mechanical movements of the dancers.

Certain recurring images unite the worlds within and outside the apartment. Throughout the film, doors are opening into new experience or slamming shut in anger. Bertolucci is fascinated by frosted glass, which he uses to soften and romanticise, to distort, and to separate characters and settings. At key moments Jeanne must ride in a cage-like elevator. When she first looks at the apartment, the mood is ominous and the elevator gothic as it ascends out of camera range. When she tells her mother she is going to marry Tom, she mischievously escapes in the elevator as her mother and the camera look down with curiosity. After fleeing from Tom, Jeanne hides behind the elevator to wait for Paul, who tap-dances his way into the cage. In the final scene the desperate chase ends with the dizzying movements of a hand-held camera tracking Paul as he runs up the spiral staircase after Jeanne, who is fleeing from him in the elevator. The great variety of angles and tones makes it difficult to identify which is the real trap—the marriage with Tom or the love affair with Paul. This ambiguity is also visually expressed in the recurring image of the mysterious draped form in the smaller room of the apartment. After Paul has moved out, Jeanne vents her anger by pulling off the drape, discovering that what lies beneath is only a pile of junk.

The music also has a unifying function. Unlike the earlier films, which combined jazz, pop, classical and opera, *Last Tango* relies primarily on jazz saxophone music, composed and played by Gato Barbieri. The jazz is identified with Paul's values. Like the black concierge, the musicians are in touch with the kind of intense pain and suffering that Paul has experienced. An amateur at bongos and harmonica, Paul gets along with the musicians who stay in his hotel, but his bourgeois mother-in-law is threatened by their music and wants to make it stop. Like the close-ups and the film's simple structure, the unified music allows for an intense exploration within a very specific area of experience. When a shift in the music does occur, the contrast is all the more emphatic; as in the tango sequence, which presents a world from another era.

Another source of the film's intensity is the extraordinary handling of sex and death. Inside the room, sex is not merely the repetition of well-known steps (like the tango), but a genuine exploration, probing into every secret corner of mind and body. But at another level, the sex is not free, at least for Jeanne, because Paul is always in control. Though she has the power to come to the room when she chooses, once there, she seems always ready for sex; but it is Paul who dictates when and how. As their game confirms, she's Little Red Riding Hood and he's the Big Bad Wolf waiting to gobble her up. He orders her about: 'Get the butter,' 'Get the scissors,' and finally: 'I'm going to have a pig fuck you and vomit in your face, and you're going to swallow the vomit. Are you going to do that for me?' She submits adoringly: 'Yes, and more than that.'

He's the one who lays down the rules; then he wants to change them. When they first meet in the apartment and the phone rings, she asks: 'Do I answer it or not?', establishing that she expects him to take over. This sado-masochistic sexuality reflects a dominant pattern in male-female relationships throughout the culture. The film explores a woman's attempt to escape it when her own pull toward it is very strong. Even though he can't relinquish his aggressive dominance, Paul tries to transcend the machismo of his 'whorefucker, barfighter, super-masculine' father and combine sex with love. Sex has been a survival technique for Paul (as it was with Gina), combating his despair and death wish; but it moves him towards a fuller commitment.

Last Tango is as much about death as about sex, linking these two forces at the centre of human behaviour. In *Revolution*, Gina, like Jeanne, has lost her father; Agostino's suicide is parallel to Rosa's, but death was never central in the earlier film. In *Spider's Stratagem*, the main question is whether the father's death was suicide or murder. Suicide is also an ambiguous possibility for Anna in *The Conformist*, who decides to travel with her husband, and for Paul, who promises his wife's corpse that he, too, can find a way to death. In *The Conformist*, Marcello, like Jeanne, strikes a pose with a gun. These playful killers mock our naive image of the gun, learned from movie gangsters, cowboys and aristocratic duellists. In both films, death is dealt by someone who has sought identity from the outside, who does not have an autonomous centre. But in *Last Tango*, Paul is offering the vision that in order to live and love, one must look directly into the face of death.

When the movie's over, two questions haunt us. Why does he try to move their love outside the room? And, why does she shoot him? Paul's offer of love can be seen in a variety of ways. He is a sadistic chauvinist who wants to extend his control over her in order to possess her entirely. He is a crazy masochist with a record of humiliations who wants to fail again. In pursuing her for the first time, he actually gives up control, perhaps in search of a way to die. He is a romantic dreamer who has bought the fantasy of ecstatic oneness, despite all the evidence of his past experience and acknowledgment to Rosa's corpse that: 'Even if a husband lives two hundred fucking years, he's never going to understand his wife's nature.' He is a courageous idealist, always willing to try again, no matter how many times he's failed, because love is the only thing that makes life meaningful. He is willing to take any risk, because it's the only way of growing. Each identity is true; each is partial. But his vision of love must be lived out with a woman like Jeanne, whose limitations preclude the success of the brave dream.

The final question remains: why does she shoot him? In courageous self-defence, or cowardly evasion? As Jeanne well knows, Paul's preoccupation has been with himself. After the intimate scene in which they trade memories of their childhood, he turns away from her to play distractedly with his harmonica. She accuses him: 'Why don't you listen to me? You know it's like talking to the wall. Your solitude weighs on me. Your silence isn't indulgent or generous. You're an egoist . . . I can be by myself too, you know.' While he withdraws further into his private grief, Jeanne lies face down on the mattress and masturbates, then crouches, rocking like a child. Just a few moments before, she had romantically described her childhood experience with her cousin Paul, when the two of them masturbated together; but now this defiant attempt to retain her autonomy is sad and lonely. She also hates her helplessness in the face of his control. When Paul abandons the apartment, she grieves at the loss, but is angry because he has the power to end things and she does not. Earlier, when she came to him in her wedding dress, she humbly confessed: 'Forgive me. I wanted to leave you, and I couldn't. Do you still want me?' Finally, her intuition tells her that Paul is a woman-hater. She's righter than she knows, because his interactions with his mother-in-law, the hotel maid and the prostitute, as well as the fact of his wife's suicide, lend supporting evidence. Because her fantasies are not bound up with Tom's, she can resist his foolish attempts at control. But with Paul, like a trapped animal, she must kill her way out for survival and autonomy.

62. 'I don't know who he is': Maria Schneider in *Last Tango in Paris*

Her final act can also be seen as fear of risk-taking and involvement, a cowardice that Paul has recognised all along. When he first dictates the rules for their meetings in the room, he asks, 'Are you scared?' and she lies: 'No.' Later he tells her: 'You're always afraid.' When she describes the man she loves, she stresses his mystery and potency, but once outside the room, Paul becomes a vulnerable middle-aged man with a broken-down hotel, instead of a glamorous American sitting on the floor in the middle of a fantasy. She is afraid of the pain and humiliation that have brought him to this point; she's too young to take it on. So, she rejects him, despite her promises to endure anything for his sake. When she sees the reality that he is now presenting, she no longer knows him. Thus, in the end, as she stands bewildered, gun in hand, rehearsing her explanation for the police, the strange phrases that she utters are both true and false: 'I don't know who he is. He followed me on the street. He tried to rape me ... He's a madman ... I don't know his name. I don't know ... I don't know who he is.'

All these interpretations of the final acts have validity in the work of art, combining forces that generate its richness and emotional intensity. But as the film's dark vision implies, they are not equally fruitful in life. Trapped in the conventions and fantasies of their culture, Tom is ridiculous, Paul is dead, and Jeanne is a killer.

1973

Cries and Whispers

PHILIP STRICK

The first voices to be heard in *Cries and Whispers* are those of an army of clocks, muttering and chiming in a litany of comment at the uncontrollable passage of time. Surmounted by baroque helmets of golden cherubs, their faces stare at us in impassive accusation, as though confirming that to encase life in a mantelpiece ornament is one of mankind's more ludicrous ways of externalising his mortality. There is a close-up of the second-hand, chopping down like a scythe, and then, in an instant of heart failure, a clock has stopped. It is as if a miraculous suspension of nature lets us slip through into an uncertain period beyond, where a woman sleeps, clumsy and inadvertent, in a chair, while another struggles through a crisis of agony on her sickbed, rises feebly, and sets the clock to rights again. She'll last a little longer—long enough for us to explore whether her existence has been worth the struggle. 'It's early Monday morning,' writes Agnes in her diary, a Brontë sister striving to come to terms with the intolerable, 'and I'm in pain.'

It's a superb opening, rich, elaborate, familiar. The images are fresh, yet *Wild Strawberries* (for example), with its eager coffin and uncommunicative timepieces, began in much the same way fifteen years ago. Bergman has no right to expect us to join his game again, but one responds gratefully to the pattern as to an immaculate, freshly set-up chessboard, the symbols losing nothing in potency for their reappearance. Time always seems to have been running out for Bergman's characters, deported as they are from a clouded past to a baleful future through the insubstantial landscape of the present. The journey allows them a few questions, some inarticulate gestures of love and hatred, and nothing more. They endure a lifetime of sleepless mornings, and an entire inquisition of doubts and pains.

For Agnes in *Cries and Whispers* the pain is that of terminal cancer; she is dying among the blood-red furnishings of the family home, attended by her two sisters Karin and Maria, and by the devoted, motherly servant Anna. Despite its theatrical resonances, the situation assumes the usual Bergman complexity by the simplest of means—the flashback which we can believe or not as we please. Since the ambiguities of *Persona* and *Hour of the Wolf*, Bergman's sudden interpolations have not been the most precise means of following the narrative, but *Cries and Whispers* appears to provide genuine, if startling, recollections, heralded and concluded by floods of crimson across the screen.

Agnes (Harriet Andersson), who has never married, has passed the years in memory of the mother who largely ignored her except for a single sorrowful gaze. The others have suffered more eventfully. Maria (Liv Ullmann) has had an affair with the local doctor, leading her despairing husband to attempt suicide, while Karin (Ingrid Thulin) is imprisoned in marriage with a man she loathes so much that on one occasion she mutilated herself to avoid his clutches in the bedroom. These two operatic

63. *Cries and Whispers* (Harriet Andersson)

sequences—Maria's husband staggering about with a paper-knife in his chest and Karin hacking between her legs with a piece of glass and smearing the blood across her mouth—are punctuated by the hideous spasms of Agnes as she dies. Take it all seriously? Well, no. But the melodrama has prepared the way for the film's most extraordinary sequence, in which Anna the maid dreams, imagines, or remembers (it's not too important which) the resurrection of Agnes and the cries of her shrouded body for the embraces of her sisters. Their disgust and terror outweigh their affection for Agnes, and it is left to Anna to provide for any physical comforts that the living corpse may need.

Bergman's final images are tranquil, a symphony of white dresses and late summer colours; it is a day recorded by Agnes' diary as her happiest, spent in the company of her devoted sisters. Like Björnstrand's speech at the end of *Through a Glass Darkly*, it needs to be treated with suspicion, not least for the sentimentality with which Bergman infuses it. The joyful Agnes, whose feet never were too firmly on the ground, depended for her perfect day on the façade presented by the impulsive Maria and the unresponsive Karin, whose incompatibility (however much exaggerated by Anna's fantasy) has been illustrated by their parting conversation. Betrayal is more in their nature than love. So Agnes may be able to conquer pain with love, but it leaves her no better off than the rest of them—even the maid is a mother substitute and treats Agnes as a replacement for the child she lost. Yet Bergman's clocks keep ticking; since the duration of our lives is so brief, he seems to say, why not settle for an illusion or two? It's an unusually mellow conclusion, and he'll need to reach it several times in a row before we can believe he means it.

In all other respects, *Cries and Whispers* is a well-thumbed catalogue of disillusionments. As in *Hour of the Wolf*, Bergman has assembled characters from all stages of his previous work— the scornful lover from *Sawdust and Tinsel*, the tortured cleric from *Winter Light*, the rapacious sensualist and the brooding intellectual from *The Silence*, the below-stairs realist from *Smiles of a Summer Night*. All the old conclusions are there: marriage is a tissue of lies, men are weak, brutal and repulsive, sex is degrading, faith is inaccessible unless you have it already, in which case it's inexplicable. At times, *Cries and Whispers* looks like self-plagiarism, particularly when Anders Ek, voice atremble, tells us straight to camera that Agnes had a stronger faith than his, or when Erland Josephson and Liv Ullmann take each other's wrinkles to task in close-up. Occasionally there's even a narrator, chipping in abruptly to tide us over a bit of explanation the easy way, his contributions too arbitrary to appear much more than second thoughts. 'It's the same old film every time,' Bergman said while shooting it, 'the same actors, the same scenes, the same problems. The only thing that makes it different is that we're older . . .'

Nevertheless, the other differences are there. For a start, *Cries and Whispers* is a stunning Bergman experiment in the uses of red and white, its rooms upholstered with membranous scarlet, its occupants like brilliantly costumed ghosts. The elemental colours give a magnificent force to the anguish of the characters; if nothing else, they *look* too good to be disregarded. And striking in on them from the delicious, neglected world outside, like brief illuminations of their dark lives, come geometric slabs of sunlight, warming a face here, a smile there, until the breakthrough comes at last with the final open-air exuberance. Bergman and Nykvist have been achieving miracles with light for years, but *Cries and Whispers* is unquestionably their greatest collaboration.

Two other continuing dialogues in the film support Bergman's familiar contest between darkness and light: first, a whole subplot is revealed through the language of hands, caressing, clutching, tearing, breaking, at their most eloquent during the otherwise silent caresses between Karin and Maria, their most terrifying when the talons of Agnes rasp slowly down the edge of her bed. Second, there are the cries and whispers themselves, inarticulate murmurs at the fringes of the long night, somehow combining gossip with guilt, fear and anger, as each of the four women explores her own conscience. With the end title, with Agnes' apparent victory, they at last die away as if they were no more than the ill-formed vocabulary of darkness. But like the clocks, it's unimaginable that they have gone for good.

1973

Stolen Privacy: Coppola's *The Conversation*

When Francis Ford Coppola insisted that he made *The Godfather* for the freedom big money would bring him to work on his own personal projects, many people jeered at what they took to be the guilty old Hollywood bull, the promise so often made, so often not delivered. Well, Coppola has delivered and the cynics stand mute. *The Conversation* is remarkably ambitious and serious—a Hitchcockian thriller, a first-rate psychological portrait of a distinctive modern villain (a professional eavesdropper) and a bitter attack on American business values, all in one movie. I feel that Coppola has partially botched the thriller, but the film is a triumph none the less—gritty, complex, idiosyncratic, a rare case of freedom used rather than squandered.

People have also said that Coppola is congenitally lucky. *The Godfather*'s release coincided with a grisly Mafia carnival in New York (bodies stuffed into auto trunks or thrown into rivers—that sort of thing), and now *The Conversation*, which is about a man rather like Watergate bugger James McCord, profits from the great American national uproar over privacy and illegal surveillance. But Coppola claims that he began writing the screenplay for *The Conversation* in 1966, years before such things became national issues, so let us call his timeliness prescient rather than lucky. Timeliness isn't necessarily a sign of triviality in an artist; it may be a sign of good instinct, an ability to connect personal concern with national obsession. I think Coppola may become this sort of non-exploitative 'public' artist, a kind of cinematic Dickens (all proportions kept).

There's no doubt that he develops his protagonist, Harry Caul (Gene Hackman), with a Dickensian richness of eccentricity, an extension of spiritual condition into physical metaphor. The conception is audacious and aggressively paradoxical. Harry is a wiretapper, an eavesdropper, a man who listens through walls and across open spaces—in all, 'the best bugger on the West Coast'. He steals privacy for a living. At the same time he is obsessed with his own privacy, or what he takes to be privacy. We soon realise that Harry suffers from an extreme desolation of the spirit, a nearly pathological loneliness and guilt; his insistence on 'privacy' is just a way of keeping people at a distance. Repressed, awkward, terrified of his own powers and feelings, he cannot bear the demands people make on him, *any* demands. Yet he is immensely skilled, and the machines provide a refuge. At work in his fenced-off, prison-like corner of an immense warehouse loft, he thrusts the tape-recorder between himself and experience, and he feels in control.

The man who knows that any secret can be stolen protects his own 'secrets' by the simple expedient of living as little as possible. He pretends that he doesn't have a telephone (keeping it in a drawer) so people can't reach him, and in the modern world, that is a way of denying that one exists. Even the connection with *things* is kept to a minimum; possessions may also be a drain on 'privacy' ('I care about my *keys*,' he tells a friendly landlady who worries about his furniture in case of fire and has had the temerity to duplicate his keys). Coppola's paradox grows in power and wit as its logic becomes clear. Poor Harry is so fearful, so given over to obsession, that he begins spying on himself. Before entering his mistress's door he hides outside, 'casing' the apartment; since it's clear that she has not been unfaithful, who is he casing but himself, a man caught red-handed in the act of visiting his mistress? When the rumpled, affectionate woman grows restive, he agrees to end the connection, but still there's no possible safety; *Harry* knows about Harry, and that's dangerous enough. (In a dream that expresses both fear and longing, Harry tells his secrets, but never in life.)

His agonised diffidence, which invariably is misunderstood and gives pain, results from a self-loathing so extreme that no one can relieve it. Such a condition of spirit cannot be 'explained', and Coppola really doesn't try. It's enough to embody it. Gene Hackman, who has been physically imposing in some of his recent commercial pictures, here alters his carriage and stance, and his burly strength seems undistinguished, graceless, mere irrelevant weight. Repressed characters can be a trap for actors; they tend to overdo the fumbling mannerisms and show us too much acting, as if to distance themselves personally from the men they are playing. But Hackman, who has always demonstrated a rare talent for 'ordinary' men and non-actorish readings, here conveys a human being all locked up inside without nagging us with small points—the performance is *clean*.

Harry has blood on his hands, and as a congenitally guilty Catholic, it's killing him. We know that in the past his eavesdropping has led to three murders. Therefore when a mysterious corporate magnate (Robert Duvall) hires him to spy on his faithless young wife (Cindy Williams) and her lover (Frederic Forrest), Harry hesitates before turning in a tape of the lovers' conversation. On tape the two have made an assignation at a hotel. If the husband should take vengeance, wouldn't Harry be responsible? When a treacherous prostitute steals the tapes and turns

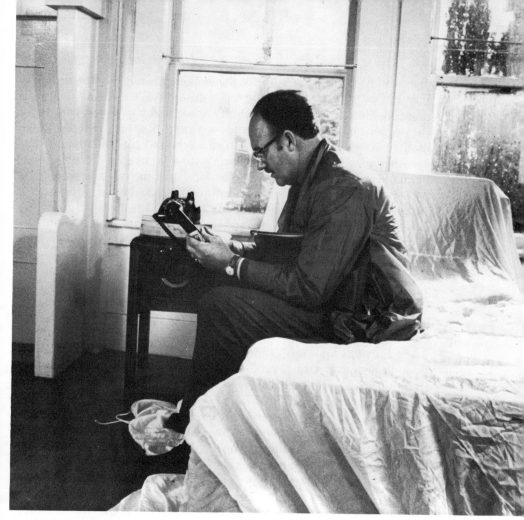

64. The invasion of privacy: Gene Hackman in *The Conversation*

them over to the husband, he is forced to confront his nightmare. In a scene of nearly unbearable moral tension, Harry's terror of involvement does epic battle against his agonising fear for the young couple, but he cannot resolve the crisis; with the screams for help literally coming through the wall, he falls down in a swoon. Coppola stays with Harry throughout this scene, and it's only later that we find out what happened. Someone gets killed, but in the emotional and moral terms of the movie the catastrophe is Harry's; he suffers a spiritual and moral death from which there is no possible resurrection.

There only remains the final working out of his fate, which is intricately and ironically just. Against his will, Harry has become part of a murder plot; when he discovers that his own apartment has been bugged by the plotters, he rips it to pieces, tearing up the walls, the floor, the furniture in a fruitless search for the microphone. The insane logic of Harry's obsession has thus been fulfilled: the bugger gets bugged, the man with only his privacy to protect destroys his possessions and winds up guarding literally nothing—an empty space, a cavity sealed with locks. The American mania for 'home security' here reaches its comic apotheosis. Our last view of Harry is very sad: he sits alone in the wreckage playing a saxophone along with a jazz record—halfway into life, halfway out. We're left with little doubt that the stasis is permanent.

Privacy, as we know, is a modern middle-class notion, a product of relative economic well-being and city living and respect for individual selves. Yet the same modern society which creates the demand for privacy also creates the technology which makes its elimination a fairly simple matter. Privacy can be bought, sold, or stolen, like any possession or commodity. Indeed, Harry Caul would like to operate as efficiently and impersonally as any other professional. He would like to think of his victims as anonymous 'targets', to lose himself in the delightful technical intricacies of robbing them without regard for what he is stealing or what they might feel about it.

The movie is an angry, funny attack on this sort of thinking, which Coppola sees as a natural product of American business values and our eternal boyish enthusiasm for technology as an end in itself. Stealing privacy has become part of the American way of life, and to make the point clear Coppola sends Harry to a San Francisco convention of security experts and equipment manufacturers, at which evil, destructive but undeniably ingenious little spying gadgets are hawked and sold like kitchen appliances or motorboats. To the businessmen-spies, it's just an ordinary convention, a professional meeting place; to us the ordinariness of such an event is perhaps the most peculiar thing about it. In *The Godfather*, also, the most extreme and fantastic behaviour was shown to emerge from a setting of normality—family life. Coppola seems to relish the more bizarre American contradictions, the clash between context and substance, between the style of an act (banal) and its meaning (horrifying).

Although he is drawn to extreme behaviour, Coppola's style of representation remains straightforwardly realistic. That's why his films may not at first appear to be the work of an artist. His attitudes and personality emerge not so much from the camera style as from the behaviour on screen. For instance, he has a genius for shallow, noisy, self-propelling types—the American as untrammelled egotist, powerful and infantile at the same time. He appears to love their theatrical energy and flash, and his sense of how such people reveal themselves in social situations is so accurate that he can do very funny, outrageous scenes without a trace of caricature. (Much of *The Godfather*, of course, was extremely funny.)

In *The Conversation*, Coppola has a savagely good time with Harry's surveillance colleagues. Boastful, frenetic, absurdly aggressive, these American go-getters can't stop competing for a moment, not even at a party, and so they begin showing off and playing dirty tricks on one another. Their viciousness while 'relaxing', more revealing than any amount of overt skulduggery, suggests that they are successful precisely because they don't give a damn who they hurt or how much. The code of 'professionalism' provides an apparent morality, a blinding justification for any act; they have no idea, not even a suspicion, that they are evil men. The surveillance experts are hideously funny and also tragic; looking at them it's hard for an American not to think of soldiers testing weapons in Vietnam and other examples of professionals run amuck. By immersing himself in a particular, idiosyncratic corner, accurately perceived, Coppola has made contact with a major strain in American life, a malaise that persists through generations. His unresolved love-hate relationship with the characters makes the bitterness of his criticism acceptable; if he entirely hated them, the film would have collapsed into diatribe, and we would have rejected his attitudes out of hand.

In a long, fascinating sequence, Harry reconstructs on tape the lovers' conversation as they walk slowly around a crowded San Francisco square. Some of the meandering talk has been recorded close-up by one of Harry's bugs, some of it from hundreds of yards away by long-distance microphones. As Harry mixes the separate tracks together, perfecting the aural image, we actually see the conversation; and it occurs to us that Harry is reconstructing and perfecting life—or at least a simulacrum of it. Of course film-making is also a reconstruction of life, and it's tempting to view *The Conversation*'s attack on irresponsible professionalism as also an implied attack on certain kinds of irresponsible film-making—empty, technically perfect work in which beautiful images are the director's only achievement; art without feeling or bite. Coppola's own sense of responsibility, I would say, requires him to give each of his characters as much dramatic and personal stature as he can muster. *The Godfather* was so pleasing, in part, because Coppola seemed to envelop all the characters in the warmth of his own appreciation. Everyone was 'on', and so we rejoiced in their entrances and bloody exits as if they were guests at a particularly brilliant and hilarious party. Most of *The Conversation* is sombre, even melancholy, in tone, but the principle of responsibility remains the same.

Did Coppola intend *The Conversation* as a critical commentary on *Blow-Up*, a way of showing how that kind of story could be done? (He started work on the screenplay the year *Blow-Up* was completed.) The similarity is suggestive; both films centre on technological voyeurism and irresponsibility, and Harry's work with the tape parallels the famous sequence in which the fashion photographer discovers a murder by repeatedly cropping and blowing up a photograph. At the very least, I

65. *The Conversation*: 'a nearly pathological loneliness'

feel I can say that the emotional thrust of *The Conversation* reminds me of what was wrong with *Blow-Up*. Now, more than ever, the inhuman chic of Antonioni's manner seems to invalidate his attack on non-involvement. Except for semi-prurient curiosity and vague disgust, Antonioni's own attitudes remained obscure and hidden; and so his people, stranded in an arbitrarily arranged and decorated vacuum, became mere inert portents of disconnection and alienation. They felt no pain, and neither did anyone watching *Blow-Up*. Since everybody in the film was dead, and reality was elusive and unknowable anyway, the photographer's criminal indifference never registered as an emotional fact.

Coppola has rescued the story from 'art'. He places his alienated man in a recognisable American business/social world, and the details and mood seem intuitively right, making emotional contact in a way that Antonioni's awkward, vaguely metaphorical use of swinging London commonplaces did not. Moreover, Coppola is far too *interested* in Harry to allow this sad technological wizard to become an example of modern man's inability to feel or communicate or any rot like that. Contradictory, stubbornly eccentric, intensively imagined as a particular kind of human futility, Harry could never inspire any such banal interpretation. As Gene Hackman plays him, he is anything but emotionally dead (that cliché of 'advanced' film-making)—he's inarticulate because he feels too much and too incoherently, immobile because every possible road of conduct becomes an imagined disaster. Participating in life is an agony for such a man; therefore whether he acts or fails to act, we are drawn to him emotionally.

I have tried to emphasise the solid benefits Coppola has derived from a relative aesthetic conservatism; yet I fear that because *The Conversation* holds to a framework of realism and is concerned with something so old-fashioned as spiritual anguish it will be dismissed as 'humanistic' in some quarters.

The Conversation is one of those movies (the classic example is *Rear Window*) which are told almost entirely from the restricted viewpoint of a single character, deriving their power and excitement from this apparent limitation. Of course Harry isn't immobilised in a single room like James Stewart's photographer; his immobilisation is spiritual and moral. Nevertheless, as there are only four major settings in *The Conversation*, feelings of claustrophobia and paranoia become a psychological factor in our response to Coppola's movie, too. The viewer chafes and frets as each man is drawn into a mystery by fragments—a clue here, a portent there. For the viewer, as for the central characters, the experience is one of reluctant passage from ignorance to knowledge, from a frightened surmise to a horrifying certainty.

These restricted viewpoint strategies direct our responses more coercively than 'open' constructions. The opening shot of *The Conversation*, which should become famous, closes off the big world, delivers us over to that segment that Coppola wants to explore; it's a continuous zoom which starts at an immense distance above Union Square and slowly moves closer, discarding irrelevancies and distractions from our view, until we finally discover Harry in the crowd, eavesdropping on the young couple. From thereafter we see nothing that Harry doesn't see or fantasise himself. Normally we like the characters we are forced to identify with; Coppola makes a more ambivalent and troublesome demand on us. We don't like Harry very much, but Coppola's narrative method holds us in tension, frustrating our moral bloodlust, our desire to see Harry destroyed; he's contemptible, pathetic, yet we are baffled and dismayed by the same things as he. The climax of *The Conversation*, when the murdered man's blood wells up out of the toilet and spills at Harry's feet, strikes us as a hideous moment of self-knowledge for Harry, the truth behind a lifetime of denial and evasion. It is one of the most grimly satisfying scenes in recent movies, a true horror epiphany. And at that moment our feelings are finally resolved into outright sympathy: Harry has been punished enough.

Unfortunately, after all the suspense build-up, the repeated playing of the tape, etc., Coppola never satisfies our curiosity about the mystery itself. Limited to what Harry knows, we never quite understand what is going on, and some of this confusion could have been avoided with a little extra exposition. For instance, I assume that Cindy Williams is Robert Duvall's young wife, although for all we know she could be his daughter; it's hard to understand how the prostitute who steals the tape knew she was going to be invited to Harry's workshop, and so on. Murder mysteries are often full of such loopholes, but we generally don't notice them—the pacing is too fast. *The Conversation*'s slow, repetitive, accumulative method forces us to review what we know, like a detective building a case, and the narrative sloppiness becomes irritating. Worst of all, the surprise denouement, in which the victims and murderers get reversed and Harry realises that he has been used even more viciously than he had thought, occurs so quickly and casually that we can hardly take it in. I sympathise with Coppola's dilemma. A confrontation between Harry and the young couple might have straightened things out easily enough, but by presenting Harry with an actual physical threat (as Hitchcock did to his voyeur in *Rear Window*) Coppola would have turned *The Conversation* into a more conventional melodrama. He sticks to the internal and psychological threat, thereby losing a part of his audience at the end—an honourable failure.

Some other details are not so honourable. The whole 'sinister' atmosphere of the corporate office, with its shadowy Mr Big and his ominous, cryptic young assistant, comes very close to the style of a TV movie. It's hard to say whether Coppola's imagination simply faltered or whether he felt a little TV trashiness was needed to get the film financed and widely attended. Like *Klute* a few years ago, *The Conversation* hangs a first-rate characterisation and an accurately perceived social milieu on to an implausible, badly resolved thriller plot. Still, Coppola is a most stirring example of a man purified by success. I have the feeling that after earning another $7 million or so on *Godfather II* he'll make some movies even more difficult and uncompromising than *The Conversation*, and among them will be a work of art satisfying in all its details.

1974

Nashville

JONATHAN ROSENBAUM

'A dialectic collage of unreality,' remarked pop singer Brenda Lee, emerging from the *Nashville* première in August. After a summer full of humourless rhetoric in the American press about 'the true lesson of Watergate', 'the failure of our civilisation', 'the long nauseating terror of a fall through the existential void', and equally grave matters—most of it implying that a movie has to be about 'everything' (i.e., the State of the Union) before it can be about anything—it was refreshing to discover that someone, at long last, had finally got it right. Even if Lee's comment was intended as a slam, it deserves to be resurrected as a tribute. For if *Nashville* is conceivably the most exciting commercial American movie in years, this is first of all because of what it constructs, not what it exposes.

From the moment we begin with an ad for the film itself—a blaring overload of multi-media confusion—and pass to a political campaign van spouting banalities, then to a recording studio where country music star Haven Hamilton (Henry Gibson) is cutting a hilariously glib Bicentennial anthem, *Nashville* registers as a double-fisted satire of its chosen terrain, and it would be wrong to suggest that its targets of derision are beside the point, even if the angle of vision subsequently widens to take in more than just foolishness. But a rich 'dialectic collage' of contradictory attitudes and diverse realities is what brings the film so vibrantly to life, and to launch moralistic rockets on such a shifting base is to miss its achievement entirely. In point of fact, the film celebrates as much as it ridicules—often doing both at the same time—while giving both its brilliant cast and its audience too much elbow room to allow for any overriding thesis.

Robert Altman and his collaborators have built a narrative out of many superimposed parts, and it is worth looking at some of their procedures. Joan Tewkesbury wrote her blueprint-script after spending only five days in the Tennessee capital, apparently guided mainly by Altman's request that its country music milieu be linked comparatively to politics, and that an assassination figure at the end. Actors were given the choice of following her dialogue or substituting their own, and many were invited to compose their own songs (usually with Richard Baskin) under the assumption that country music, like politics, is potentially anyone's game. Similarly, Thomas Hal Phillips was given the job of launching a presidential primary campaign—the film is set in 1976, the year of the US Bicentennial—for an invisible fictional candidate named Hal Phillips Walker, complete with local headquarters and a Replacement Party platform to be heard from a van, prowling the streets ignored like a ghostly proxy. Finally, the sound system inaugurated on *California Split*—a set-up using many on and off-screen microphones whose volume levels can be altered during the sound-mixing stage—enabled Altman to extend his principles of improvisation further, beyond the parameters of the camera's range.

A great deal was shot—two hours of rushes were reportedly screened every day—and at one stage Altman considered releasing two mammoth films, each of which would cover the same time span while concentrating on twelve different characters. That he settled on a more conventional solution, and concludes the film with a veritable surplus of Significance after over 150 minutes of open sailing, is of course commensurate with the querulous sociological responses. But prior to this capitulation he engenders his most adventurous structure to date, deftly juggling his cast of two dozen characters with the assurance of a master storyteller while simultaneously demanding (and rewarding) an unusual amount of alertness and participation from the spectator.

Quite simply *because* he has reinvented Nashville rather than discovered it, even the most spontaneous and wayward elements in his s-f fantasy remain firmly within his grasp. Starting with the campaign van, Hamilton with his mistress (Barbara Baxley) and son (Dave Peel) and musicians, an English groupie-interviewer named Opal (Geraldine Chaplin), a black gospel group with white lead singer Linnea (Lily Tomlin)—and leaving it partially up to the viewer to decide on the relative importance of each, to discriminate between characters and extras (a task not unlike that faced by most of the film's inhabitants)—Altman proceeds to shuffle these mini-plots while casually adding fourteen characters more, as everyone but Opal and Linnea appears or reappears at the airport; then deals them out in orderly succession as they leave the parking lot, finally assuming a recognisable narrative shape; and scrambles most of them again when they become caught in a freakish highway pile-up, to be joined by Linnea, Opal and others.

One proceeds through this constant play between organisation and chaos as though in a mystery, picking out threads that may be either loose ends or clues to future events—an aspect that makes *Nashville* well worth repeated visits. Cutting between the fatuous affirmations of Hamilton's song ('We must be doin' somethin' right to last 200 years') and the more unbridled ones of the gospel group establishes one kind of contrast, but when Opal starts prattling over the sound of the latter about 'darkest Africa' and 'naked frenzied bodies', our attention and response become

66. *Nashville* (Ronee Blakley, Henry Gibson)

further subdivided. Similarly, when she is holding forth about American violence during the traffic jam, what's funny isn't merely the delivery of her hysterical clichés in medium shot and screen centre, but the relationship between that and the sheer irrelevancy of a little boy outside the car in left foreground, simultaneously consuming an ice-cream cone like a detail out of Tati or Brueghel.

With the recurring juxtapositions of performers with spectators, insiders (Timothy Brown, Allan Nicholls, Cristina Raines) with outsiders (Robert Doqui, David Hayward, Bert Remsen), contrasts between public and private behaviour frequently come to the fore—epitomised by Connie White (Karen Black) trying on a variety of smiles while waiting to appear on the Opryland stage—and deceptions involving telephones become a minor leitmotif. If Barbara Jean (Ronee Blakley) is the only character who seems incapable of such duplicity, this may not be unrelated to her climactic 'breakdown' during a concert, which hinges on a lack of separation between private and public identities. Clearly the most professional of the singers, whose songs are least mediated by any sort of irony in their presentation, she is also the one who abandons herself most nakedly in her performances.

That she turns out to be the assassin's target seems to square with Altman's sense of cosmic injustice—formerly evidenced by the death of the hero in *McCabe and Mrs Miller*, the Coke bottle victim in *The Long Goodbye*, and equally present here in the sudden irrelevant speech of Pfc Kelly (Scott Glenn) to Mr Green (Keenan Wynn) just after the latter has learned of his wife's death. Cruelly twisting the screw, Altman cuts from his strangled sobs to the laughter of Opal and Triplette (Michael Murphy) in another scene, as if to underline the isolation of his grief. And to compound the sense of absurdity, it is Green's angry departure from his wife's funeral in search of his groupie niece (Shelley Duvall) that indirectly causes the assassination to take place.

Some characters—Duvall, David Arkin's chauffeur, Jeff Goldblum's magician—are static figures to be brought on like running gags; Opal and Tom (Keith Carradine) are more diversified versions of the same principle. But others are subject to development, elucidation and modification, either in their behaviour or in the way they are presented. Linnea, whom we learn to identify with humane impulses, is briefly seen at Hamilton's party describing the results of various traffic injuries with apparent relish; Hamilton's son, bashful and courteous at the same party, becomes a drunken lout at the fund-raising campaign smoker where Sueleen (Gwen Welles) does a striptease, while Sueleen herself shifts during this scene from a comic character to a tragic one. And after driving Sueleen home, Linnea's cuckolded husband (Ned Beatty) suddenly launches a clumsy seduction attempt of his own.

Alongside these uncertainties about characters are ambiguities involving events. The film offers evidence but no proof about which of Tom's four ladies he dedicates his new song to; and we may wonder whether Barbara Jean's behaviour at her concert actually constitutes a breakdown—or if it does, whether this is partially provoked by her husband (Allen Garfield) forcing her off the stage. We don't know if she dies after being shot at the political rally or why, indeed, she is shot at all.

Does Opal work for the BBC? She repeatedly claims she does, and most reviewers have followed her lead, often going on to criticise the part in those terms. But if Opal's scene with Triplette had included more of the original footage, in which she admits that she *doesn't* work for the BBC, her character would have been assigned another label, and in each subsequent scene would have registered differently. Multiplying this detail by twenty-four, one easily sees why the film should have been much longer, and how extensively our chancy and partial experience of it is a response to *work in progress*, the unfolding of a narrative complex rather than its ultimate destination. Thus to stop the movie at a precise meaning—and worse yet, a socio-political one—is to rob it of its complexity and consign it to the same dustbin of platitudes that Opal and Hal Phillips Walker both specialise in accumulating.

Not that Altman is entirely blameless in eliciting such a misplaced impulse. *Nashville* begins with a crowd of actors-as-extras—inviting us to ramble like tourists over the busy landscape, picking our own points of entry, our mixtures and degrees of interest—and ends with a crowd of extras-as-documentary-subjects, obliging us to accept them as emblems of some higher order, with the Nashville Parthenon and three screen-filling shots of the American flag to point the way. The camera zooms back to take in the entire spectacle of crowd, edifice and flag, yet the effect is constricting rather than expansive—a world of diverse possibilities shrunk to the dimensions of a Statement. Then another, recorded version of 'It Don't Worry Me', the emblematic theme song with which Barbara Harris' aspiring singer has lulled the crowd and forged her own unexpected ascendancy, is heard over the final credits, neatly balancing the film's hard-sell introduction, which also suggested the abstracting of a complex into a commodity. Acknowledging itself as a piece of merchandise, complete with packaging, price tag and succinct catalogue description, *Nashville* leaps from its exciting and individual state of grace—the open process of its initial making, and the better part of its unravelling—into the limited vocabulary and closed circuits of a public forum.

1975

Cannes '76

PENELOPE HOUSTON

In a shop window next door to the Festival Palais there's a poster from the 1930s on display. Wistfully elegant, it advertises the first Cannes Festival—the one that never happened. The advertised opening date: September 1st, 1939. But Cannes' actual thirtieth birthday celebrations (it started up very promptly indeed, in 1946) were conducted not with elegance but with some apprehension. 'Cannes suffocated by success,' said a *Figaro* headline, the article going on to claim, alarmingly enough, that the Festival now rates as 'the biggest international attraction after the Olympics'. 40,000 visitors; 1,700 journalists; nearly 500 films: the statistics of overkill.

The beginning of the mass overcrowding really dates from 1968, and the Festival's reasoned decision to accommodate potential 'counter-culture' rivals, and then to strengthen itself so as not to risk being overshadowed by them. But the big, indispensable jamboree has reached a point where the convergence of the world's film businessmen, the film press and much of the local tourist traffic is stretching facilities to the edge of tolerance. The embattled organisers asked for 'a minimum of discipline, you might say of courtesy, from festival participants'—don't, in other words, actually *try* to break down the doors getting into the cinema. But, as with the Olympics, it's easier to say that the scale should be reduced than practically to see how anyone can do it. The Mediterranean looks on, cynically blue; by 1980, at this rate, they'll have only the water left to walk on.

One director who didn't contribute to the crowding was Eric Rohmer. Courteously announcing that he really couldn't face it, Rohmer stayed away but sent his film, the perfect, cool antidote to the overheated pressures. *Die Marquise von O*, representing Germany, is his first period film and his first in a foreign language; but from the opening images there's no question that the director has returned in top form. Kleist's novel, published in 1808, concerns a virtuous young widow who finds herself mysteriously pregnant and finally takes the extreme course of advertising in the local press, asking the man responsible please to identify himself. To no one's surprise, he is finally discovered, after tearful imbroglios and parental tantrums, to be the Russian count who

67. *Die Marquise von O* (Bruno Ganz, Edith Clever)

rescued her from the ruder attentions of his soldiery during an assault on the citadel commanded by her father. The playing (Edith Clever and Bruno Ganz as the protagonists, Edda Seippel as the girl's mother) is beautifully shaded and coordinated, and the same unfaltering finesse extends to Nestor Almendros' camerawork and the re-creation not of 'period' but of settings to live in. At the opening, the count leaps on to the parapet, a hero bathed in blazing light; the masterly exaggeration is counterpoint to an objective irony which brings out all the comedy of the story without ever compromising or modernising its view of the sentiments of the period. Rohmer's control of tone, never more in evidence, is partly a matter of artistic discretion; his meticulously lucid and human film is a 'conte moral' in its own right, made in perfect sympathy with the original text.

After Rohmer, Rosi, whose *Cadaveri Eccellenti* is a genuinely heavyweight (not overweight) political thriller, moving implacably towards the discovery of conspiracy at the centres of power. Lino Ventura, a melancholy Maigret in a white raincoat, is the police inspector given the job of investigating a series of murders of judges in Southern Italy. Asking questions, scanning photographic evidence, visiting the scenes of crimes, he identifies the original assassin, then takes a step further, into the area of conspiracy which leads to his own death, shot

68. Rosi's *Cadaveri Eccellenti*

down under the austere gaze of statues from the classical past. The film is not 'realistic' (one reason, Rosi says, why he cast so many foreign actors, including Max von Sydow, Charles Vanel and Alain Cuny, all excellent); its many locations, brilliantly chosen and as brilliantly shot by Pasqualino De Santis, are selected to give a heightened atmospheric sense, a suggestion of the relation between the confidence of the past, when the institutions were fixed and seemed firm, and the apprehensions of the present. Continually moving forward, along the usual forceful Rosi trajectory, the film fills out its own scale, not as an expression of fashionable paranoia but as a more deeply pessimistic but also more bracingly enquiring study. 'The truth is not always revolutionary,' is the film's last line, spoken by a Communist.

For Bertolucci, the truth *is* revolutionary. As everyone knows, his *1900* lasts five and a half hours, and follows the fate of two boys, the sons of landowner and peasant, born on the same day in the new century. The scale is that of a 19th century novel (Bertolucci as Victor Hugo), and early scenes are drenched in feeling for the beauty and richness of the countryside near Parma where the director grew up; the main setting, a vast farm courtyard, is a thing of beauty. Gradually, however, a kind of implacable naiveté of political sentiment takes over. The propertied classes are inevitably decadent (Bertolucci is most at home here, including the portrayal of Dominique Sanda's progression from bright young thing of the 1920s to solitary toper of the 1940s); the local Fascisti are represented by Donald Sutherland and Laura Betti, both playing devilment to the hilt and beyond, including child-murder; the peasantry, often picturesquely wizened, emerge in 1945 into a vision of a revolutionary Utopia, cavorting under a vast red flag. It's ironic, certainly, that a film with such a conclusion should be financed by the full capitalist might of Hollywood; and rather more ironic that the Italian Communist Party is said to find Bertolucci's red flag waving something of an embarrassment. Artistically, such simple didactic schematism doesn't contain the family chronicle sprawl, the obesity of a film in which history becomes declamation.

The third of the big Italian films in the Palais, Visconti's *L'Innocente*, is a worthy grace note to a career of formidable distinction and courage, if not the posthumous masterpiece one might rather unreasonably have hoped for. Based on a novel by D'Annunzio, it concerns a man who expects his wife to tolerate his mistress, but gets a fierce shock when the wife acquires first a lover and then a child. While the household is at church at Christmas, he lets the baby die of cold, an act of willed ferocity on the route to self-destruction. Shot (again by the versatile De Santis) largely in ostentatiously handsome and heavy interiors of the turn of the century, the film has an enclosed, slow-paced, brooding distinction, and all Visconti's emphasis on the emotional décor of the past. Giancarlo Giannini, however, is not quite the actor to carry the central part; one watches with respectful detachment.

From Joseph Losey, temporarily established in France, comes *Mr Klein*, a story which must have appealed to him for its multiple ironies, but which he has turned into a film plumped out with overweight. An art dealer (Alain Delon) in the Paris of 1942 one day receives through the post a Jewish newsletter; it seems that there is another Mr Klein, a Jew, hovering dangerously on the periphery of his complacent life. Delon follows the elusive trail, in a kind of metaphysical detective story which can only lead towards the final takeover of his identity; at the end, caught in the Paris round-up of the Jews, he's gazing at us through the bars of a cattle-truck bound for Germany—a fate, the film suggests, which is also in some sense a punishment for the indifference and sharp detachment of his temperament. Enigmatic encounters, including a splendid one with Jeanne Moreau, and a careful shading of settings, from the bleakly realistic to the almost dreamlike, give the film a distinction of surface. But Losey talks of aiming for 'the unrelenting fascination of a Borges labyrinth'; and if he has failed to achieve this, it's perhaps because he is also too careful, too evidently constructing scaffolding for the maze and pointing the spectator in the significant direction rather than letting him loose in it.

Jacques Rivette's *Duelle* (formerly *Viva*) is more genuinely labyrinthine: a tale of a great jewel of mysterious powers, goddesses of night (Julie Berto) and day (Bulle Ogier), mortals who damagingly involve themselves with these fates, and a movie landscape in which the references—Cocteau, *film noir*, a Wellesian aquarium—ricochet off each other. I'm at a disadvantage in not having yet caught up with *Céline et Julie*: with a director like Rivette, who is following a line of very conscious development through a hermetic kind of submarine world, it's vital not to lose a link in the chain. *Duelle* is a riveting exercise in *mise en scène*, the versatile power of the tracking camera, the force of personality of players meeting mostly at tangents. Tentatively (since the film certainly demands a second look), one also suggests that the script is not quite up to its job.

The Rivette team are out in force again in *Sérail*, the first film directed by *Duelle*'s co-writer Eduardo de Gregorio, who also scripted *The Spider's Strategy*. A haunted house story, about an English writer (Corin Redgrave) who acquires a rambling, derelict chateau inhabited by two masquerading girls (Bulle Ogier, Marie-France Pisier) and a forceful housekeeper (Leslie Caron), the film is stuffed with predictable allusions—Rivette, Cocteau, Resnais, Borges, Wilkie Collins, etc. But it's done with a style which manages to absorb the references, and that particular impish irony which is evidently part of de Gregorio's Argentinian inheritance. The novelist's reflections on the spider's web of feminine hocus-pocus laid out to trap him are amused; but he still falls into the seraglio. And along with its elaborate apparatus of deception and illusion, *Sérail* has a reassuring practicality—Leslie Caron's cooking and gardening, of which agreeably much is made.

De Gregorio gets his ideas, familiar though they may be, into focus. Peter Weir, whose *Picnic at Hanging Rock* also deals in the landscape of supernatural mystery, finally lets his film wander disjointedly. The first half is concentrated evocation: a staid girls' school in the Australia of 1900, a projected picnic outing, and the transition to the hot, hazy, dangerously beautiful setting of Hanging Rock, where Pan pipes tootle, watches stop and four of the picnickers mysteriously vanish. There's no answer to the puzzle, though the film is prodigal with hints and evasions; and in the second half, Weir involves himself with too many characters—a lonely girl, a young Englishman, Rachel Roberts' hard-drinking headmistress—all variously haunted, all left haltingly undeveloped. After this film and the earlier *The Cars That Ate Paris*, it's evident that Weir has a real sense of odd atmospheric pressures, though in both films pieces are left lying, not yet locked into place by narrative.

Colin Westerbeck writes elsewhere about *Taxi Driver*, Martin Scorsese's picture of the New York night streets and the solitary, irrational and finally hideously murderous pursuits of the man who drives a cab around them. *Taxi Driver* is an unsettling film, certainly, with its fatalistic view of

69. *Taxi Driver* (Robert De Niro)

a mind slipping out of gear (we have the feeling that we are watching De Niro and that he is also watching us), its exceptionally blood-stained denouement, and its odd final scene, which amounts to a kind of acceptance of the violence. But the film actually comes across as rather less of a portent than advance reports had suggested; I'm not sure that there isn't too much natural exuberance in Scorsese for him quite to come to terms with sustained, introverted mania, however Bressonian his intentions—and those of his scriptwriter, Paul Schrader—may have been. There's a slight suggestion of thesis about the film, as though events were being willed in the scriptwriter's mind, antitheses thought out in terms of what might shockingly be made of them.

The lonely man in the Swedish *Giliap*, Roy Andersson's film in the Directors' Fortnight, is even more self-contained, though far less threatening. This is an odd film, very slow, full of silences that are evidently never going to be broken by speech but only by the camera's eventual decision to turn away. The central character (Thommy Berggren) takes a job as a waiter in a dour city hotel—his first period on duty coincides with a funeral lunch, of which one imagines the establishment may have many. Eventually, he becomes involved in hapless crime and violence. But part of the appeal of an ungainly, wryly comic, genuinely original work is its sense of the hotel as a setting, imposing its routine on staff who all think of themselves as transients, little islands of non-communication. Tables are carefully laid but the expected important guests never turn up; in the morning, a lone survivor from the funeral party surfaces from his lair behind a sofa, a sorry old man, twittering his reluctance to go home.

The Fassbinder team's latest, *Schatten der Engel*, is written by Fassbinder and Daniel Schmid, directed by the latter, and based on Fassbinder's play *The Garbage, the City and Death*, which caused some furore because its property speculator is a Jew, and because it contains such lines as 'If they'd gassed him, I could sleep better today.' All talk and tableaux, and featuring, as well as the rich Jew, a very melancholy prostitute who hangs about complaining of the cold, the film breaks the German post-war taboo on anti-Semitic reference with a dull thud. Fassbinder is said to have written it 'almost in a state of trance', during a flight from Frankfurt to Los Angeles. However the speeches sound in German, as translated into the French subtitles they read like daily mottoes for a rather *outré* tear-off calendar; or in-flight bulletins.

Two American documentaries of some reputation, *The California Reich* (directors: Walter Parkes and Keith Critchlow) and *Hollywood on Trial* (director: David Helpern Jr.), were both disappointing. Tristram Powell's BBC film on the Hollywood blacklist did a better job with much the same material, while the film about present-day Nazis in California relies on the *frisson* of the swastika and is notably short on historical perspective. On the whole, one suspects that European standards for the compilation/interview film are currently rather higher than America's. But *cinéma vérité* pulled off one of its most bizarre achievements with *Grey Gardens*, the Maysles' film about Jackie Onassis' aunt, Edith Bouvier Beale, her daughter (also Edith) and their somewhat crazed seclusion in an over-grown, cat-haunted mansion in East Hampton. The film has been attacked as 'exploitation'; and of course it's voyeuristic to watch mother and daughter reviving past triumphs (the aged Mrs Beale singing 'Tea for Two') and nagging over past miseries (the daughter's multiple resentments). But the film would seem if anything to have been a therapeutic experience for the Beales, who evidently feel they have found their biographers, and its mixture of performance and self-exposure is undeniably riveting. Alarmingly, the junior Edith suggests one of those snappy Hepburn debutantes from the 1940s, Tracy Lord herself perhaps, more than thirty years older, tremulous about life and herself, but still somehow frozen in time. Art and life, as usual, inextricably intertwined.

1976

All Along the River

DAVID THOMSON

'That's the second sentence you started with "I".'
Leland in *Citizen Kane*

Red River was the first film I saw twice, and I have made a habit of seeing it. It was an early indication that I loved the movie experience more than specific films, for it showed me that a film was not just a photographed story but a phenomenon. Long before I conceived of authors, I had felt character and force in cinema and wanted to draw both into myself. When it was reissued, in 1963, it struck me that films might be like places and the cinema a medium of location and activity in which the subject of *Red River* was simply 'seeing *Red River*'.

Ten years later, I tried 'teaching' the film to students and at the same time introduced it to my son. A teacher is expected to instruct objective study of films. But I realised how proud I was of *Red River*, and how awkward and embarrassed a defender of it that made me. Awareness of its part in my development left me vulnerable to students' condescension towards any John Wayne movie. In expounding it as a Hawksian picture, I only began to notice how far I was the author of my *Red River*. More recently, in August 1976, during an English drought, the full *Red River* passed by again, twenty minutes of its original flow restored—perhaps in the early 60s those cuts had been led away to irrigate arid TV Westerns. I am impressed now that it has always been a confluence of films, as many as there were Rouen Cathedrals for Monet, and as many as there are fleeting shells of appearance on a river whether it unwinds in sun or gloom, all alike but all unique. If films were truly singular, they would no longer be made. The medium exists through people in the audience seeing their own film, and feeling so sure of their vision that they enter into it.

Critics write about films decisively and in the spirit of explanation. It is the only way—one cannot wait twenty-eight years for a review, and readers expect clarity and guidance. But film's inescapable movement, and its mimicry of time, make it an intriguing model of the change that comprises our lives. Not much writing about film has dealt with the way films alter as we grow older, and I would like to consider thirty years beside *Red River* to suggest the importance of this property.

Red River was filmed in 1947 and released in 1948, and I saw it in suburban London in the winter of 1948–9, when I was nearly or just eight. That London was the only place I knew, but social history today might point to its pinched austerity, the scattering of bombed houses where kids could play and the natural delight of such a child in the cinematic expansiveness of *Red River*. I was intensely moved by the film, and I may have revisited it to calm myself, to repeat the pleasure or even to fashion myself further.

At that age, I must have had to be taken, and my father then was my usual companion at the movies. But I recall *Red River* as if I were alone with it, immersion obscuring all associations. In hindsight, though, I feel sure that my attention was drawn to the rivalry between a father and a son-figure and to the underlying wish for warmth between them. Thus, now, I see my identification with the film as predicting an actual tension with my own father. I will not invite embarrassment with an unduly personal revelation, yet it should be said that the Hollywood movie's playing upon fantasy involvement did regularly strike into our sentimental depths with an intimacy that we seldom admit. As a child, I fastened on the boy Matthew Garth who becomes Montgomery Clift as a taciturn young adult. Only now do I appreciate the lasting hold of that response.

Red River is one of those Hawks movies that begins, as it were, a moment too late, with the action already under way. A wagon train is passing through a picturesque valley and, simultaneously, one wagon pulls out of line and, in an epiphany of time and place, a cloud hurries across the sun and its shadow surges along the floor of the valley. I was pricked by that at eight and felt, as I hadn't done before, the precise actuality of film. Perhaps that moment helped me think *Red River* was preciously real and worthy of my participation.

The couple in the wagon quitting the train are Tom Dunson (John Wayne) and Groot (Walter Brennan). The wagonmaster claims it is Wayne's duty to stay, but he replies that he gave no guarantee and is free to go his own way, with the valuable bull trailing along behind his wagon. Obligation, independence and withdrawal from the group are lasting themes struck up in this first sequence. Wayne's girl (Coleen Gray) begs to be taken along too, but Wayne denies her because it will be dangerous. He is vague but firm, as if disconcerted by the prospect of a woman's constant company. She must stay with the others, and he will come for her later when he is established on his own land. As a surety he gives her a bangle that was his mother's. Even at eight I knew the parting was final; years later, it looks like escape for the man. How would he ever find her again in all the breadth of virgin America invoked in this valley? (Will Jack Nicholson be there months after *Missouri Breaks* when the girl comes looking for him, or off and away playing his clarinet in another state?)

70. *Red River*: before the drive

Wayne and Brennan depart, and the film goes with them. It is not long
before black smoke and ominous drums in Dmitri Tiomkin's score tell us
that the wagon train has been attacked. The two men prepare for a raiding
party sent after their obvious trail. It comes at night, with birdcalls from
the brush and a lovely flurry of painless action. The stars survive, but in a
hand-to-hand encounter Wayne finds that the Indian he is stabbing—in a
stream, or an infant river—is wearing the bangle he gave Coleen. It is a
memento passed through the film: a sentimental keepsake, but
something like a handcuff.

They move on and meet a boy—ten or twelve, I think—wandering in a
movie delirium, leading a cow. There is an immediate conflict between
Wayne and the boy: Wayne slaps his face to halt his hysteria and the boy
draws a gun. Wayne pretends to be impressed, relaxes the boy and then
simply but roughly disarms him. This signalled how far the lost child had
found a commanding father. Reconciled, they team up—bull and
cow—and Wayne hands back the child's gun with the advice to watch a
man carefully; young Matthew devours that homily with an eagerness
that promises eventual confrontation. Their pistol-play, I suppose, could
be as Freudian as that in *Bonnie and Clyde*, but I doubt if Hawks ever

suspected Penn's deliberate comparison in his own film. Still, the gun will be used again. Clift and John Ireland compare guns in a wary test of virility, and Clift's becoming a thoughtful critic of Wayne will be acted out in his marginally beating his 'father' to the draw, and thus preventing him killing, burying and reading over another man.

It is impossible to write now as I felt then. I have to reinvent myself, and must admit the tricky ground between reliable memory and the creative urge to be autobiographical. At eight I saw a bull and a cow, and not any personal implications of their coming together, much less a man who has lost his woman picking up a boy. My feelings were fixed on that quick clash of wills between the grown man and the orphan he was on the point of adopting. The slap that brought Matthew into action I felt as much as I have since felt the passionate vanity and resentment when Kane slaps Susan in their tent and someone far away—in the audience?—cries hysterically. In *Red River*, the meeting scene was compelling because I identified with man and boy: I felt heartened and safer that they would be together. But the scene also uncovered the rivalry possible between two males determined to make up their own minds and live by the decision. *Red River* deals with judgment, and the way kindness and flexibility must temper correctness. Wayne's dark solitariness—so impressive as the years and miles accumulate—is the effect of his righteous solitariness.

A great part of the mythic vitality in *Red River* has to do with activity. Hawks is not often a poetic film-maker, but the passage in which the three go farther south and come finally to 'their' land is deliberately beautiful. I measured the wagon's trek and then the fulfilment of coming to ideal spaciousness. Wayne grabs up a handful of dirt and strolls away from the camera: it is the very stance and image that Ford framed in a doorway at the end of *The Searchers* eight years later.

As a child I felt myself growing up when Clift returned from the Civil War, lean, dark and a gunslinger, but watchful of the way his father's back hurt as he hauled himself into his saddle. Before we detect it, Clift remarks on the hard crust of anxiety that has grown around Wayne's strength. The adult Clift combines sensitivity and ability, and this sympathetic watching of his father—like Wayne with Dean Martin in *Rio Bravo*—is followed by the duel by target shooting with Cherry. The latter is an uncouth but assertive gunman, played by John Ireland, who instantly throws in with Wayne when his cautious employer won't let him repossess the cattle Wayne has just stamped his own brand on. Cherry is shaggy and untidy. He seemed to the child distasteful and threatening, and he is an oddity in a Hawks movie who shows what a very conservative, dapper cowboy Clift is. Ireland's Cherry might have lasted long enough for a Wild Bunch; he is a mongrel who reveals the tight-lipped pedigree in Hawks heroes.

By now, there are more cows than people in the film. In the fifteen or so years covered by a fade out and fade in, the bull and the cow have produced a great herd that must be taken to Missouri to be sold. The larger part of the action concerns that drive, and I relished every detail of trail-life: riding point or drag, the fatigue of the day and the quiet company of the camp at evening, the stampede that results from a soft cowboy's craving for sugar, and the triumphal crossing of the Red River itself, when the herd comes to a river milky in the sun—a Renoir river, I saw later—and, within ten minutes, negotiates it. Men on horses chart a safe way across and then the hot cows spill into the water and Tiomkin's music takes up the line of advance and achievement while the images illustrate the genre subject: a Great Herd Crossing a Great River. The script refers to a few head lost, but we see none. It is a river made to display man's prowess, and not like the river in *Deliverance* that is as cold, swift and dangerous as nature treated too lightly.

Wayne has aged in the 15-year elapse. When I first saw the film I was impressed by the authenticity of this process: film can show the young what ageing means before they appreciate it in life. Growing older, Wayne withdrew into the domineering strictness in Dunson's character. He became tyrannical, driving the men remorselessly, never attempting the Hollywood officer-skipper who jollies and encourages his men, and makes for such a blissful harmony in *Air Force* that war itself is subdued.

It is a mark of Wayne's intransigence and isolation that only he fails to see the strain this extremism puts upon Clift. The other cowboys have noticed the son becoming a more silent, less convinced support, and the audience are waiting for him to rebel. Like feeling a body in the dark, so in a film you know where dramatic alteration will come. If men and cows were not merely to reach Missouri, a crisis was as necessary as the psychological antagonism between father and son.

Clift takes the cows by another, speculative route to Abilene, leaving Wayne wounded but balefully vengeful. The herd reaches its destination, and Clift's gamble is justified—every decision in the film is tested. But along the way they rescue a wagon train besieged by Indians: fifteen years later, it is the train Wayne abandoned, and there is another dark girl in it, Tess Millay, or Joanne Dru. She slaps Clift's face too, after he has sucked venom from an arrow wound in what the child thought must be the top of her fine breast, but the adult discovered was only a cold shoulder. The slap again promises love, just as the repression of any complaint when the arrow pinned her to a wagon showed that Dru was a girl fit for a Hawks hero, laconic, manly, yet performing bravery to show that no one takes it too seriously.

The rescuers stay awhile, and Dru talks to Brennan about Clift. Lyricism in Hawks consists of men recounting stories about comrades, and inspired she goes out into the mist to find a nervy Clift on guard. Ostensibly he is watching over the herd, but we know he is waiting for

Wayne and calculating how many days behind the limping father must be. Dru gathers enough of the story to arrest Wayne when he comes through days later in pursuit. She advertises the bangle Wayne gave to Coleen Gray, and the father sees that his son has a lover such as he was too proud or fearful to stay with. Their scene together is shifting and enigmatic: Dru hints at giving herself to Wayne to save Clift, while he longs for a true son. Times and characters merge in Hawks' favourite issue between the sexes: the ability or not to admit need and mistake.

But Wayne goes on to Abilene, apparently unable to soften. He crosses the railway tracks that proved him wrong and strides through the cattle milling in the street. He guns down Cherry without breaking stride and advances on the slender Clift. He challenges his son to draw, but Matthew is meek and allows himself to be shot at and then beaten with fists before he retaliates. The full fist battle is interrupted by Dru firing a gun and telling them to grow up. She scolds them for pretending to be unrelenting enemies when everyone else knows how much they love one another. The two battered men are transfixed by such understanding. Wayne tells Clift to marry the girl, and Clift tells him to stop telling other people what to do. Wayne grins and, in the dust they were kicking up, he redesigns the 'family' brand: a river with a D, and now with the addition of an earned M.

It is a very happy ending—such as Hawks has always attempted, without strain or loaded optimism. But I have imagined them all going back to Texas, and I suspect that Clift went on to become the querulous Braxton in *Missouri Breaks*, as dogmatic as Wayne, deserted one day by Dru and left with a daughter worthy of Hawks and with *Tristram Shandy* as a consolation.

In my life there followed something like the interval in the first part of *Red River*. I did not see the film again except for a glimpse in Visconti's forgettable *Bellissima*, when an open-air movie in the background was showing *Red River*. I could not hope to resemble the Montgomery Clift back from the war, and by 1963 anyway Clift was a shaken, damaged man, no longer sufficiently at ease for Hawks' world. By then I knew who Hawks was, and knew that he was to be admired. *Rio Bravo* had appeared in 1958, and though in all its length and delight there was no river, there was the same preoccupation with idealised action and friendship, the same impetuous, attractive girl, Wayne and Brennan an odd couple still together but perversely reluctant to declare their dependence on one another. Wayne in that film wore a belt with its buckle in the form of a river and a D—there are photographs of Hawks, too, wearing such a belt—but apparently the planned amendment at the end of *Red River* was never made. I wonder if Clift ever had such a souvenir?

Memories of *Red River* and the general availability of the river-like leisureliness of *Rio Bravo* in my late teens allowed me to follow the appreciation of Hawks in *Cahiers du Cinéma*, brought me to the National Film Theatre's 1962 Hawks season and made me feel part of a family when I read Peter Bogdanovich's long, easy-going and tolerant interview with Hawks in *Movie*'s December 1962 celebration of the director. A few months later, *Red River* was itself revived, initially at the Plaza, accompanied by a grotesque disaster, *The Cool Mikado*, which augured Michael Winner. Hawks' film was cut by twenty minutes, apparently for no other reason than to make room for the English silliness.[1] By then, *Red River* was one of the few Hawks movies that several of his adherents had not seen, and I am sure I claimed and revealed the film to those with whom I pursued picture shows. The auteur theory now seems to me a device whereby critics and enthusiasts appropriate films—no one else has felt the duty to explain them with such confessional diligence.

Hawks was so suited to the auteur theory that I cannot escape the suspicion that a band of ardent young men, wanting to make films but protected from industrial realities by the dark of the cinema and a high faith in art, invented him. (A boy lost in the prairie might hope for such an older man coming to rescue him.) Hawks is a character from his own world; and if that world now appears to rely on pretence, it does reflect on its author. Auteurism applied to the cinema is as romantic as hero-worship, but Hawks was a hero who disguised the greatest dangers of distant devotion. There has never been effort, pretension or artiness in his work. He has seemed comfortable in more Hollywood genres than any other director, yet able to draw his honourable and accomplished men to every surface, there to be perplexed by garrulous and emotional women. Never a complainer against the system, always entertaining and in character, Hawks appealed to young critics tired of European hostility to Hollywood and its disparagement of fluent and enjoyable movies. It was then and remains part of Hawks' depth that he is serious but never grave—his comedies exemplify this above all.

This warm approach praised him in ways that were curiously personal and tendentious. In France, England and America, there were those who seemed to be looking for a sensible, alert and wry father in Hawks, a man who made graceful movies under pressure. By 1963 I saw not the least reason to quarrel with *Movie*'s estimate of him: 'He makes the very best adventure films because he is at one with his heroes . . . For Hawks, who drove racing cars for a living and built aeroplanes before he was twenty, men prove themselves through mastery of their own actions . . . Hawks heroes are professionals doing jobs—scientists, sheriffs, cattlemen, big game hunters: real professionals who know their capabilities. Their

---

[1] I have since heard a story to this effect: the cuts mostly involve John Ireland (including the target-shooting with Clift) and were allegedly the result of some pique in Hawks when his newest discovery, Joanne Dru, fell in love with Ireland while the film was being made. That may shock those most devoted to the old man, but it is worthy of Grant in *Girl Friday*.

courage is the product of their self-knowledge . . . When one talks about the heroes of *Red River*, or *Rio Bravo*, or *Hatari!* one is talking about Hawks himself. The professionalism of his heroes is shared by the director. They get on with the job without any unnecessary nonsense. So does Hawks. He can say what he wants to through actions, because his is a cinema of action.'

In fact, that is remarkably close to the literary or ideological criticism *Movie* disapproved of in other quarters. It asks one to accept the virtues and integrity of a man, rather than scrutinise the text of his films. Indeed, it is very like the general critical estimate of Hemingway and apparently swallows the artist's own insinuation that there is a no-nonsense bond between himself and his work—that one can actually cross the river and go into the books. The very satisfying simplicity of Hawks' style and his unhurried structures easily persuaded young viewers of a maturity, a levelness and an uncluttered wisdom in the man himself. It was possible to come away from Hawks with a comfortable view of a manageable world, for his 'professionalism' made it subservient and responsive; it came when you whistled, like a Hollywood horse, or Lauren Bacall. Hemingway tried to reassure himself in this very way with his own portraits of conscientious, intelligent men caught up in decisive action. But he shot himself nonetheless, maddened by anxieties and old age and perhaps by his own inability to walk on the water across the river.

It is delicate to have to suggest that some of us grew up through Hawks' view of manliness, so I had better say that I think I sometimes modelled myself on, say, Grant in *Only Angels Have Wings*, Bogart in *To Have and Have Not*—so many worlds removed from Hemingway's Harry Morgan—as well as Clift in *Red River*. Hawks therefore became a test of character, and I fell in beside him, just as Clift obediently followed the unflawed authority of Wayne.

That state of mind held for a decade, during which I re-saw every Hawks movie that came my way and enjoyed Robin Wood's study of the director, even if I was a little disconcerted by the picture it conjured of Hawks and F. R. Leavis rolling cigarettes for one another. I nodded understandingly when *The Last Picture Show* proved to be *Red River* with the silent, circling pan at dawn before the great drive begins.

My happy attitude towards *Red River* was not jolted until 1972, when I included the film in a course on American cinema for American students in England. Their friendly approach could not accept the film on my terms, and I had to see how far my proprietorship isolated me from their reactions. They heartily disapproved of John Wayne and could only see one more instance of his capacity for bullying. The film entertained them, but they were amused by its steady allegiance to the romantic clichés of the Western. When I tried to argue the merits of practical realism

71. *Red River*: Dunson and the boy

embodied in the film, their eyebrows went up: they found it predictable, thoroughly artificial and impossible to take seriously.

The challenge was as demanding as Clift's mixed emotions before he commandeers Wayne's herd and re-directs the drive. I had to concede that *Red River* belonged to a tradition as much as to Hawks, and that the heroic postures available in the tradition might invalidate my sense of an elegant, curt realism in Hawks. To retaliate, I went deeper into *Red River*'s study of fatal stubbornness. I hold to that still—stubbornly—and believe it is worked out with unusual sensitivity, especially in the bitterness that overtakes Wayne's initial decisiveness. As his back stiffens, the face retracts and his hair goes ashen: it is an unsentimental picture of ageing, and I respect it more now that my own back gives me trouble. I insist still that the film is taut with the unowned affection between the two male characters, both of whom are essentially solitary, and that our identification with both characters ensures an unusually complex response to the pursuit and the final confrontation.

I hope I made some students consider that human subtlety, and demonstrated the self-effacing narrative felicity. But I could no longer abide by the notion of Hawks the professional, the describer of doing. *Red*

72. *Red River*: after the battle

River's tone is that of meditative legend, of campfire yarns[1] told by men actually less than easy with horses, guns and cows but yearning for the flourish of expertise and finding it in fiction. That is the West outlined in another film with a river, *The Missouri Breaks*, and its delicious trial scene in which a convicted prisoner is asked for a 'colourful' final address—'life on the frontier being what it is'—to which he willingly complies with the earnest hope that he might thereafter be known as 'the Lonesome Kid', harbinger of Warhol's melancholy and moody cowboys.

Perhaps *Red River* is made by one lonesome kid for others; most fiction is produced to meet such needs. The only practical skill it illustrates is how to make a compelling movie. The crossing of the Red—almost certainly filmed by assistant director Arthur Rosson—is an exercise in heroic generalisation. I doubt if the combined editorial boards of *Movie* and *Cahiers du Cinéma* could get a bull and a cow across the road on the strength of it. When Wayne fights the Indian wearing his mother's bangle, Brennan throws him a knife and, as if by magic and terse cutting, the useful weapon clings to his upthrust hand. That is how action occurs in *Red River*: with the sweet timing of daydream. The target-shooting is a reverie. No shot in the film goes anywhere other than where

[1] *Red River* is told by Walter Brennan's Groot. In the complete version seen in 1976, the film uses—rather laboriously—pages from a journal he has written. Yet I believe there are versions where Brennan narrates the story—if there are not, there should be.

ntended—no shot in any film ever misses—no remark fails to be both
aconic and revealing. Rummies in Hawks' movies sober up whenever
ut-throat music is played. Life's leaking inaccuracy and failed eloquence
re redeemed.

The drive itself is a glorious illusion. When the complete version of *Red
River* reappeared in the summer of 1976 in the National Film Theatre's
econd Hawks season, I realised that nearly every landscape is from the
alley where the cloud moves across the sun. The sensation of journey is
n artful trick. In reality, the cows must have trampled that one valley flat
or a fortnight as the camera covered them from a compass of angles. Only
hen would Hawks have gone into the studio, to dwell upon the
onversations he prefers, to construct an Abilene on the back-lot and to
ilm the several day exteriors in which there is crucial, close action,
ccomplished on screen with the deftness that persuaded some of us of
Hawks' own mastery of action.

All I see now is that there is no need or reason to be pleased with Hawks
s anything other than a compiler of fictions. Real men of action
resumably lead active, adventurous lives—and die young; real artists
pend much of their time alone ruminating on things that will never be,
xcept in a work of fiction. Man's favourite sport is to describe feats he has
ot managed in life. Such tranquillity may make one linger on past eighty.
n *Rio Bravo*, Walter Brennan is not just an amusing old man with a bad
eg, but someone hurt that those defects keep him out of things yet still
live. 'Kid' in *Only Angels* wipes himself out when he can no longer deny
hat his sight is going.

Hawks is not a forder of rivers; his dryness could never risk a real
oaking. He is a man who has filled his life contemplating the river and
urning away periodically to make a beguiling model of it, another
tream, dark and shiny as celluloid. He is not showing us men, but men
on film, where their words and actions are protected. But he is shrewd
nough to see how unreal and playful that makes the product, and I think
hat his films need to be approached as performances of a game—a game
alled man as contented hero.

With that approach, one can echo Joanne Dru's irritation when she
reaks up the family fight: who ever thought either one of that pair would
ill the other? Who ever thought there was the least element of reality in
he phantom shapes forming and reforming on the screen? One might as
asily suggest that there is a single appearance on the surface of a river.
Hawks offers us a world of straight-faced make-believe, and as soon as
ne looks past real ranchers and real cows in *Red River* it becomes easier to
discern the mythic quality of love between men.

One should not ignore the droll continuity of allusions to homosexual-
ty in Hawks' outposts. Of all American directors, he most teases us with
he implications of men feeling more comfortable and faithful with one

another than with women. All those sharp girls are outsiders, admired and able to help in moments of crisis but generally excluded from the most intimate associations—most of which are realised dreams of lonesome kids in which buddies achieve that rapt and effortless communion that is the one paradise glimpsed in American cinema.

Hawks is not a misogynist, but he is awed by women, fearful of the disruption they bring, perhaps as harassed as Wayne with Angie Dickinson or, like Bogart after Bacall has left the room in *To Have and Have Not*, grinning and whistling to himself. Notice how quickly Hawks despatches final embraces. His understatement turns to real reserve with love, and he is like Grant at the end of *Only Angels*, preferring a joke or an oblique admission that Jean Arthur only appreciates when he is up and away, in the air with a pal. I cannot think of a man in a Hawks movie who professes love naturally and willingly. That is always assumed but unadmitted in the turbulent sexual banter he pursues; whereas men live together in a harmony like the jailhouse sing-song in *Rio Bravo*, one of the supreme domestic tableaux in American cinema.

This is not meant as a rejection of Hawks. He remains my favourite director, and I would prefer his films on a desert island to any other director's—even if his films can make life like a desert island. But not because the movies apply themselves to the world, not for their practicality or actuality, not because he is any less 'frivolous' than Ophuls or Busby Berkeley. Like the rest of cinema, Hawks' river is an alternative to life's stream, sometimes able to water us better than the reality.

Hemingway, I think, was a fantasist, ashamed of playing with words and driven to pretend a feeling for flamboyant, masculine pastimes. His nature lay in imagining things, and the same applies to Hawks. Anyone truly interested in racing cars and flying planes would have got on with that, like the pre-eminent lonesome kid, Howard Hughes, who contrived to die while flying, and who fired Hawks from *The Outlaw*, so blatant a joke about Jane Russell's breasts that its tremulous closeness between males escaped censors and audiences alike. Hawks spent his adult life in film studios, on films about racing cars and aeroplanes, including the stunning 360° track from *Only Angels* when the plane lands on the plateau—flying made accessible for the armchair pilot. All of Hawks' pictures are versions of one work: like Renoir, and nearly as often, he made one film or kept wandering back to the river, like Slim Pickens in *Pat Garrett and Billy the Kid* who drags himself to the water to die.

Renoir has as many real rivers as Hawks, and his photography is more impressionistic and less polished. But for both men, the river is an ideal. *Rio Bravo* admits that the film is the river, and which of Renoir's films could not conceivably be called *The River*, with that picture's last lines as a motto:

The river runs, the round world spins
Dawn and lamplight, midnight, noon.
Sun follows day, night stars and moon.
The day ends, the end begins.

That endless mobility allows 'a girl' to be inhabited in passing by a dozen actresses from Louise Brooks to Paula Prentiss, just as it is the impulse of change that prompts restless cupid to fly away again.

In India, Renoir found the mystical expression of a reverence for life that had always informed his work, and armed us against the change, loss and passing time in his films. The same optimism possesses Hawks, and together the two look down on so much pessimism in the rest of cinema. That is why neither Clift nor Wayne dies: because it is only play, and it is in life that people die, whereas in films they are already phantoms or figments. The river is dappled light and motion, and so is film. The shapes we see in both—Boudu rolling away from tedious society or Wayne's cattle crossing the Red—are as fictional as the two boats that pass by at the end of *Céline and Julie*. And Hawks is like those two girls, just as either would have landed happily in one of his films. He has made the sweet last longer than most and it has conjured delectable and consistent pictures—a blithe, happy idyll of companionship.

But sweets dissolve and rivers exhaust the stamina of human lives. *Red River* is a fiction, and my writing about it now will not stop it changing. When I see it next it will be different and I will discover myself mistaken. The cinema is a river of no return.

1977

The Middle American Sky

JOHN PYM

Steven Spielberg has told an anecdote (*Sight and Sound*, Spring 197
which bears repetition since it so neatly encapsulates the simp
principles which lie behind the marketing of his new film, *Close Encounte
of the Third Kind*. The film's concluding forty minutes were shot in
hangar on a disused Air Force base in Mobile, Alabama; this was seale
off so thoroughly—as thoroughly, indeed, as Spielberg claims the L
Government has shrouded its attitude to unidentified flying objects
that a reporter from the *Washington Post*, having failed to inveigle his wa
in, resorted to late-night conversations in bars with some of the extra
Spielberg dismisses the account that was later printed as 'the mo
erroneous, far-fetched encounter of the fifth kind that I have ever read
But, he added, the reporter 'made it sound even more intriguing to tl
general reader, because, by not knowing what he was talking about, l
wrote a very interesting story'.

The artful secrecy which surrounded the making and content of *Clo
Encounters* caught the attention of other newspaper and magazir
writers: almost all of them, for instance, underlined the fact that tl
hangar set was 'six times larger' than any Hollywood sound sta§
(Spielberg himself modestly admits it was four times the size of anythir
at MGM or Cinecittà). The fact that cast and technicians were 'sworn'
secrecy about all aspects of the film fuelled speculation. Add to this th
the director was the 'boy wonder' Spielberg (an epithet that persis
although he is now thirty), who had made—need readers l
reminded—that seamless money-maker *Jaws*, and already, before hor
trading had begun between the US circuit managers and Columb
Pictures, largest shareholders in a production that is estimated to hacost some $19m, one could sense a ground swell of intrigued interest in
movie about which virtually nothing was known.

In April last year, Columbia, in what was announced as 'the mo
ambitious advertising campaign in the history of the company', laid tl
ground-work of the film's marketing by placing two-page 'introductor
advertisements in twenty-seven newspapers in cities across the Unite
States. The campaign steadily increased during the following six montl
before the start of the film's staggered release. Shortly before an openir

in a new city there were daily count-down notices in the papers, and movie theatres were blanketed with a long, sophisticated and wholly unrevealing trailer. Unlike *Jaws*, which had been a calculated hit movie from the time the novel was in galleys, the policy towards *Close Encounters* seems to have been to *restrict* its release until intrigued interest had developed into an urge to see the picture. (The same principles, it may be noted, were behind the delayed release of *Star Wars* in Britain.)

Close Encounters of the Third Kind—its title is sky-watchers' jargon for physical contact between a human and an extra-terrestrial being—turns out in the event to be an exercise in pseudo-scientific hocus-pocus. The film, rather in keeping with its pre-history, spends most of its 135 minutes coaxing the audience into a state of anticipatory excitement by swift cross-cutting between three loosely realised narrative strands each of which promises, though never finally delivers, an adequate explanation for all the flurry. The plot, briefly, concerns an amorphous group of scientists led by Claude Lacombe (François Truffaut) on a secret, world-wide mission tracking unidentified flying objects: having received and decoded a map reference from an unknown spacecraft, the group sets up a makeshift landing strip at the foot of a table-topped mountain in Wyoming. Meanwhile, a blue-collar power worker, Roy Neary (Richard Dreyfuss), and, separately, a four-year-old boy, Barry Guiler, are inexplicably affected by a night visit from three spacecraft—a close encounter of the second kind—with the result that the latter, despite the best efforts of his mother Gillian (Melinda Dillon), is subsequently subsumed into space, while the former drives his three children and his wife (Teri Garr) out of their home by his mysterious need to build models of ever-increasing size and detail of what later transpires to be the table-topped mountain.

The film opens in a sand storm in the Sonora Desert, Mexico, where Lacombe and his confederates come across six aeroplanes missing since 1945: they are in working order and, while the storm rages, the scientists learn from a dazed old man, witness to some inexplicable phenomenon, that the sun came out and 'sang'. Bemused and intrigued, the spectator himself then witnesses the appearance of a UFO on a radar screen: this by way of introduction to the principal sequence in the first half of the movie, the appearance of a trio of spacecraft over Muncie, Indiana. The craft black out the neighbourhood and have a strange effect on metal objects (toys wind themselves up, screws unscrew, cookers switch themselves on and judder up and down). Blinding lights appear; the police give chase to the craft; stolid Midwesterners gaze into the night sky; and then, as suddenly as they came, the craft—all flashing lights and fancy formation-flying—disappear over the horizon. What, one wonders, will happen now? Spielberg's answer is to initiate an elaborate game of hide-and-seek with the viewer, at one point whisking him off to India for

73. *Close Encounters of the Third Kind*

a baffling minute or two in which a crowd of saffron-robed men suddenly point their fingers to heaven, at another engaging in rudimentary domestic fun-and-games at the expense of the Neary household (given an immense bowl of mashed potatoes, the possessed Roy ladles its contents on to his dinner-plate and under the tearful gaze of his family begins fashioning a potato mountain).

A workmanlike professionalism has characterised Spielberg's earlier feature films, but *Close Encounters* is throughout an indulgent *folie de grandeur*. Neglecting firm characterisation or believable human drama in favour of decorative curlicues (the rattling machinery of the special effects department, the lackadaisical *hommage* to Hitchcock in a final crop-dusting/mountain climbing sequence, a gurglingly precious little boy who exits through the cat-flap in his mother's home to disappear who knows where), the film is marked by a hurrying pace and a tone compounded of awe and breathy excitement. Originally titled *Watch the Skies* (the last line of Howard Hawks' *The Thing*), the script of *Close Encounters* was written and extensively rewritten by Spielberg himself. Its esoteric title was drawn from the book *The UFO Experience, a Scientific Enquiry*, by the film's adviser Dr J. Allen Hynek. Julia Phillips, co-producer with her husband Michael, explained her enthusiasm for the film: 'As Spielberg outlined it, it was even more than a story about UFOs and a government cover-up of the whole UFO matter. I know it is Steven's feeling, and we share it, that there is something up there.'

One feels throughout a little like an unwilling guest at an evangelical meeting: being thumped about the ears (for the film is excessively noisy) with bits and pieces of received 'truth' to which the only response is acceptance or baffled disbelief. Thus, Spielberg would have us believe with the certainty of a von Daniken (another man who has made millions trafficking in 'evidence') that humans are indeed spirited into the heavens, that spaceships do indeed shoot across the middle American sky and that the United States Government has hushed up the matter for fear of the panic which might break out should this intelligence be made public. Judging by *Close Encounters*, however, the evidence is strictly side-show pyrotechnics: the judicious promise to bring the audience 'as close as possible to an event that could be the most momentous of our time'.

So, what finally do we have after the months of anticipation, the elusive press reports, the brochure costing $1.50 ('for additional copies of this book send $2.00 to Encounter Enterprises Inc. . . .'), the preliminary ninety minutes of running time? The poster shows a highway disappearing into the distance: on the horizon of the night sky is a bright white light. What lies over the horizon? At one point, early on in the film, Spielberg hints that he may not in fact take his subject altogether seriously. Neary's sons are seated before the television watching the DeMille *Ten Commandments*. Mrs Neary protests 'That picture is four hours long', at which Neary mumbles to himself 'I told them they could watch only five of the Commandments.' It is as if Spielberg was signalling that he did have some sense of critical perspective when it came to dealing with uplifting movies.

The end, however, proves us wrong. Neary and Gillian feel impelled to go to the table-topped mountain; they are taken prisoner by Lacombe's men—why exactly is far from clear—only to escape and then avoid his attempt to have them crop-dusted into anaesthetic sleep. They scale the mountain in time to see the trio of flashing spacecraft materialise once again and fly back and forth, hovering just above the ground winking at the scientists. At last, having determined that the benevolent Lacombe (and in this sense Truffaut is well cast) wishes them no harm, the trio depart to summon the mother ship.

Nothing that has gone before quite prepares one for the size or magnificence of this flying castle: its crenellated shape, its plethora of antennae, knobs and protrusions, above all its multitude of lights. It is a creation of great beauty. The film was, in one sense, made so that it could be put on display. Having communicated ('It's teaching us its alphabet') by playing a fortissimo tune, the mother ship lowers its undercarriage. There emerges a matchstick creature—only dimly glimpsed but with an unmistakably human form—who spreads his arms and then moves them slowly up and down. Before the appearance of this saviour, however, the little boy toddles out of the craft and is reunited with Gillian; a number of other individuals, including the pilots of the planes we encountered in the first reel, also emerge dazed but apparently unharmed. Matters are brought to a head when a line of faceless red-suited, crew-cut astronauts march towards the craft; prudently held in reserve for just such a contingency, their hour has now arrived. They march out to chance their luck aboard the mother ship, and the last of their number, hastily added to the back of the line, is the euphoric Neary. Finally, his long search for a meaning behind his possession has been revealed; he goes to meet the future.

Spielberg's method in creating a sense of awe-struck rather than ominous tension is based on the premise that his audience should be told nothing about what is going on. The screen is filled with activity—the worst offenders in this respect are the scientists, who spend a great deal of time physically running about—but Spielberg elects to cut away from the unfinished episodes of which the film is mostly composed just before we seem to be getting hold of what he's driving at. In *Jaws*, tension was partly created by an expectation (periodically fulfilled) that something horrible was indeed going to happen; in *Close Encounters*, we have been kept waiting so long to find out what is behind the horizon, what the scientists are up to, why Neary feels compelled to build model mountains, that by the time these questions finally become irrelevant we have had time to ask—as we never did in *Jaws*—why they were so fruitlessly posed in the first place. An argument can be made that Spielberg aimed at creating an entertainment (the jokey tone suggests more than simply a tipped cap to Hitchcock), but on the whole that pruned down narrative craftsmanship displayed in all his other features is absent. He does, it is true, make a nominal effort to link the elements of his non-narrative (in the first scene we see the lost planes, in the last it is revealed what became of their pilots), but in terms of embellishing the action he does little to develop motive or characterisation (we are, by the end of the movie, no wiser about what ordinary Roy Neary feels about his life and what has happened to him than we were at the beginning). *Close Encounters* is a little like a circus show: we are asked to marvel at its parts; we live in hope that the ring-master's hyperbole will be fulfilled; we know that the trapeze artists will come to no harm since we can see the safety net.

In recent years, we have witnessed the spectacular resurgence of the American popular entertainment movie: the three examples which stand out, primarily because they have demonstrated how out-dated are the figures by which we normally measure (or anticipate) movie profits, are—of course—*Jaws*, *Star Wars* and now *Close Encounters*. It is worth, I think, considering what these at base very simple films have in common: they all conjure before us the image of the unknown and in each of them it is represented by something immense and in an important respect unknowable. We shall, it is suggested, never understand the primeval shark, the nature of 'The Force', the metaphysical power that Luke Skywalker finally acquires in order to defeat his enemies, nor how the mother ship of *Close Encounters* works nor where it came from. In *Jaws*, we are presented with the terror of the unknown: it could happen; the model shark stands in for the real thing; an extremely remote possibility is artfully transformed into a present probability. In *Star Wars*, an unknown past, before the dawn of mankind, is transformed into a comic-strip reality: it couldn't happen, we are comfortingly reassured, but wouldn't it be fun to imagine . . . In *Close Encounters* the unknown becomes a visible fairy castle, the inhabitants of which are endowed, it seems, with an immense benevolent power. Spielberg posits that the evidence suggests this could happen; sit back and marvel.

The success of these films can be attributed in the main to the way in which the unknown has been packaged. The proof now exists that there are more than nickel-and-dime profits to be had from these products: they have been sold less as movies than as events and they have brought in their wake spin-off goods—rubber sharks, posters, books, robots, food, not to mention that tried, but recently revitalised gimmick, duplicating and imitating success.

There is nothing intrinsically wrong with purely escapist entertainment; indeed, in the case of the first two of these three films it signals a return to a masterly style of audience manipulation for the sake of 'horror' and amazement. However, the absence of any subtext (discounting the rather barren game of reference-hunting that can be played with *Star Wars*), leads one to ponder whether this form of movie-making—each new blockbuster attempting to out-gross the last—can lead to a regeneration of the criteria of popular entertainment movies. At present the appeal of these big three is that they offer if not a unique experience then at least something—because of their scale, and because part of the fun to be had from them depends on that old-fashioned sensation of sitting in a *crowded* movie theatre—that television cannot equal. To a generation of children and teenagers who have spent Saturday glued to the cartoons in the front room instead of watching a serial in the front stalls, these movies are a novelty: but to survive and prosper, a novelty requires, among other things, the combined, equally old-fashioned qualities of design, narrative and human as well as humane believability.

Jaws, Star Wars and *Close Encounters* require only that their audiences react; they demand no commitment—no strong feeling one way or the other; they are passive films; the first two ask no questions and expect none to be asked, the last puts a proposition but will bridge no argument. They are films largely unaffected by the sterner qualities of irony; they reassure us partly because they are themselves so effortlessly self-assured, and because they can, when they wish, make us sit up so smartly.

1978

The Eyes of Texas:
Terrence Malick's *Days of Heaven*

RICHARD COMBS

To the extent that a director's second film often proves a greater stumbling block than his first (especially if the latter has been any kind of critical or commercial success), then *Days of Heaven* must be accounted a particularly audacious gamble. It is now some six years since Terrence Malick made *Badlands*, one of the most remarkable directorial debuts in American cinema, loosely based on the real-life killing spree of two teenagers across the Dakota badlands in the late 50s, but turned by Malick into a complex reappraisal of the social and mythical terms of the cinema's many romantic odysseys since then. In *Days of Heaven*, only his second film, he has risked the charge of repetition by reshuffling many of the elements of *Badlands*: hapless youngsters on the run; a picaresque narrative wrapped in a blandly distanced commentary; an 'ecstatic' flow of imagery which begs our sense of wonder. Even more dangerously, he has increased the distance between the levels of enchantment and the levels of meaning. Visually, *Days of Heaven* seems to have set out to be more seductive than *Badlands*, while in terms of theme, character and even plot, it is more diffuse, dispersed and secretive.

In a collage of highly coloured and almost wordless scenes, Malick (and cameramen Nestor Almendros and Haskell Wexler) have conjured, pointillist-fashion, a beguiling landscape, both harsh and magical: the huge wheat-growing area of the Texas Panhandle, to which, in 1916, a pair of young lovers, Abby (Brooke Adams) and Bill (Richard Gere), and the latter's young sister Linda (Linda Manz), are driven from the urban squalor of the North. But Malick is as dramatically spare as he is visually ornate. *Days of Heaven* develops as a relatively simple tale of triangular passions—Abby becomes involved with a wealthy young farmer (playwright Sam Shepard), in an initially mercenary scheme which turns into a romantic complication. But the human content of the story seems to be buried somewhere beneath its telling, while its manifestations (the wheat harvest, a flying circus, a locust plague, a fire) are spectacularly more than satisfying.

Despite teasing hints that what we are watching might be a Greek tragedy, an allegory of primal passion, or a Tom Sawyerish adventure

Malick remains insistent that the inner life of his people is unknowable, that they will only be partially understood in any of these modes. Somewhere in the gap between character and action, in the silence that surrounds motive and feeling, Malick finds the tension that drives and 'explains' his characters. In describing the relation between the off-screen commentator of *Badlands* and what we see of herself and her teen lover on screen, he has commented on '. . . Holly's mis-estimation of her audience, of what they will be interested in or ready to believe . . . When they're crossing the badlands, instead of telling us what's going on between Kit and herself . . . she describes what they ate and what it tasted like, as though we might be planning a similar trip . . .' (*Sight and Sound*, Spring 1975).

Such a lack functions ironically in *Badlands*, but similar absences—or rather silences, such as Malick imposes at crucial dramatic points—work more mysteriously in *Days of Heaven*. The narration here is even more tangential to what one might take as the main events, and the fact that it is provided not by one of the central lovers but by a child emphasises that we are to be allowed little privileged information. What Malick has done, however, is much more radical than supplying a child's-eye-view of some strange adult drama. His film is split between the much that we see and the little that we know, and what we share is not so much the perspective of Linda, our informant, as her piecemeal acquisition of knowledge and experience.

Malick's narrative method, in fact, has more to do with this selective accretion of detail than with telling a story or developing a set of characters. It is a method which has a peculiarly literary flavour, not surprising perhaps given his invocation of *What Maisie Knew* as a model for Linda's commentary, but certainly a unique way of containing the visual superabundance of the film. In another sense, Malick may not be so far from the cinema: the significant 'silences' of *Days of Heaven* suggest a relation, in terms of subject and structure, to the movies of (roughly) its own era as strong as the interplay of 50s teen-movie mythology in *Badlands*.[1] In making what he has referred to as almost a silent film, Malick has found an apt context for his own dramatic processes and a strikingly original way of incorporating his sense of cinema—although in the category of more conventional *hommage*, one must include a lonely Victorian farmhouse out of *Giant*, stranded in the midst of the Texas plain.

The gamble Malick has taken is that audiences will be safely transported over the silences and lacunae by the fairy-tale atmosphere— which, to judge by the reviews that have willingly succumbed to the visual enchantment, seems to have paid off. That the film also sets up

---

[1] See the article by Terry Curtis Fox in *Film Comment*, September–October 1978, in which he compares *Days of Heaven* to Murnau's *City Girl*.

74. *Days of Heaven* (Brooke Adams)

other obstacles to audience involvement can be seen from even a cursory comparison with *Badlands*. Where the latter started from a powerful dramatic situation, and then took off into eccentric digressions, *Days of Heaven* begins with the digressions, and only after a while bothers to bind them into a kind of story. The opening scene, in fact, is the first instance of the quasi-silent, 'suppressed' narrative. In a Chicago steel foundry, Bill has an argument with the foreman, unheard above the roar of the furnaces, then knocks him down and flees. He leaves the city with Abby and Linda, sharing precarious passage atop some boxcars with other migrant labourers, to work for the summer on a Texas wheat farm. The next complication is audible but somewhat inexplicable: Linda tells how, presumably for reasons of propriety, Bill and Abby pretended to be brother and sister.

From the inexplicable, the plot proceeds to connections that are ineffable. During the summer that the three spend toiling in the fields around that incongruous Gothic citadel, Abby attracts the attention of the young proprietor of the farm. The source of the attraction, as Linda muses, was hard to determine: 'Maybe it was the way the wind blew through her hair.' But Bill, vaguely ambitious and increasingly discontented with the state of grinding poverty, encourages Abby to lead the farmer on, after he learns by accident that the latter is ill and not expected to live beyond a year. Abby and the farmer are married; Bill and Linda stay on after the other labourers have left, and move into the big house. Thus begin, for Linda at least, the days of heaven: 'We were all living like kings, just nothing to do all day but lie around cracking jokes ... I'm telling you, the rich got it all figured out.' But Abby begins to fall in love with her husband, while his awed announcement—'You've made me come back to life'—turns out to be literally true, as a year passes and the frustrated Bill finds himself no nearer his goal of appropriation. The farmer, in turn, begins to suspect, to his horror, that the supposed brother and sister are romantically involved.

'Just when things were about to blow,' in Linda's phrase, Malick drops in an outrageous *deus ex machina*, a troupe of flying clowns, who proceed to entertain the household with all manner of theatrical skits—including a Charlie Chaplin film sequence. At the height of the revels, Malick stages a climactic revelation in explicit re-creation of silent cinema: captured in silhouette behind the billowing drapery of a gazebo, Bill and Abby are seen kissing by the farmer. Bill later leaves with the fliers, but returns—out of regret, remorse, a desire to see Abby once more or a last hope of retrieving her—with the next influx of harvest workers. The farmer sees them together and believes his worst fears confirmed—ironically, at the moment when he is least in danger of losing Abby.

The sequence of events that follows seems to spring from passions way beyond the laconic spectrum of the film's characters, and from an artistic design parodically greater than the contours of its plot. First a plague of locusts descends—a sequence which Malick builds, with quiet ferocity, to proper biblical proportions—until a fire, accidentally started, sweeps across the wheat fields, destroying crop and parasite alike. In the aftermath, Bill is confronted by the farmer, whom he kills in self-defence. He, Abby and Linda then flee once more, enjoying a brief idyll as they travel downriver until the film, rather surprisingly but quite consistently, allows them to dwindle away to their separate ends.

Consistently, that is, because if anything explains the spaciousness and inconclusiveness of Malick's plotting it is his desire to have several narratives coexist. By comparison with the tight-fitting irony with which Holly's voice-over relates to the action of *Badlands*, *Days of Heaven* seems to be made up of a number of discrete worlds, with its narrator simply one small voice who scarcely impinges on the adults around her. But as in the earlier film, the function of her comments is to measure distance: her matter-of-factness prevents audiences from identifying too readily with the characters; her sense of wonder prevents the latter from being swept away too easily by events. Her third voice, that of an interpreter—as when she describes Abby's feelings during their flight from the farm: 'She blamed it on herself. She didn't care if she was happy or not. She just wanted to make up for what she had done'—testifies to things we know or see nothing of at all, and so emphasises the partiality, the incompleteness of the plot as such.

In other instances, Linda's awareness is itself clearly incomplete. Her expression of sympathy for the romantically doomed farmer—'I felt sorry for him, because he had nobody to stand up for him, to be by his side'—doesn't take into account the latter's close attachment to his grizzled foreman (Robert Wilke). It is this relationship, the most briefly indicated in the film, which finally impels events toward tragedy. Out of his fierce, fatherly protectiveness, the old man prompts the farmer's suspicions about what Abby and Bill are up to; after the farmer's death, it is his aggrieved foreman who whips up the posse that tracks the runaways.

But where *Badlands* preserved a narrative line, and some thematic continuities—the interplay of guilt and innocence in its recklessly self-deluded 'thrill' killers—through all its digressions and competing 'voices', *Days of Heaven* seems intent only on filling out its ever-expanding, coolly elegiac mood. The phenomena it collects and frames, with loving attention to the particularities of light and colour, seem to be related only in terms of the learning process delightedly invoked by Linda when she talks about her relationship with the farmer—'He taught me about parts of the globe'—or in terms of more mysterious and faintly foreboding associations (the huge tractors which work the farm recall the steel furnaces of the opening; the sparks that fly during a fireside celebration anticipate the devouring locusts).

That Malick manages to hold this eccentric, alchemical solution together is a testament to a sense of control and design that is clearly obeying its own laws even when it is defying those of conventional narrative. One suspects also that, in place of the local ironies of *Badlands*, he has arrived at a more overreaching perspective, as ambivalently compassionate and detached, in which the silences and absences of meaning in his characters' lives stand for all those things which are above and beneath their gaze. In one small scene, as Bill and Abby slip away from the farmhouse one night to lie together in the fields, the film moves with a strange grace from abstract contemplation of the cloudscapes and heavens above them to a brief shot in which we see a glass they have carelessly discarded sinking through water to come to rest amid the flora and fauna of the riverbed.

1979

A Television Election?

DAVID WILSON

In the entrance hall of Broadcasting House in London there is a Latin inscription. After invoking the banishment of all things inimical to peace and purity, it ends with a prayer 'that the people, inclining their ears to whatever things are beautiful and honest and of good report, may tread the paths of wisdom and righteousness'. The sentiment enshrines the Reithian tradition of public service broadcasting. And if it has been slightly tarnished in the five decades since its principles were first enunciated, it survives more or less intact in the one area of broadcasting where the broadcasters' own, much rehearsed idea of their function is tempered by circumstances beyond their control. The relationship between broadcasting and the state is complex and controversial. Its ambiguities are endlessly debated, not least by the broadcasters themselves. And nowhere are those ambiguities more sharply focused than in the way television covers a general election.

For most people in Britain, voting in a general election is their only form of direct political action. And since television is, as the BBC's chairman Sir Michael Swann (from whom I take my opening text[1]) has described it, 'the massest of the mass media', which is to say the medium from which most people derive most of their political information, how television reports a general election is in a parliamentary democracy of inestimable importance. It is only fairly recently that this has been obvious. Until 1959 television participation in elections was monopolised by the political parties, under the terms of an agreement between the three main parties and the broadcasting organisations. The 1949 Representation of the People Act had placed statutory constraints on the broadcast appearance of political candidates, and television news bulletins expressly excluded reference to election campaigns. When the *Daily Mirror* carried a front-page polling day appeal in 1959, 'To Hell With the Telly Until We've All Voted', what they meant was television in general, not the television coverage of the election. Twenty years later such a headline might be taken specifically to refer to the election on television.

What has happened in those twenty years is that the broadcasters have

---

[1] Sir Michael quoted this inscription in his MacDougall-Brisbane lecture to the Royal Society of Edinburgh shortly after the February 1974 election. Of television's coverage of this election he went on to say, revealingly: 'I suspect it is broadcasting that has forced things into a lower key'.

usurped the parties' monopoly. The relationship between the political parties and television has progressed from contempt to love-hate to a bond of political necessity. The parties still reserve to themselves the making of party political broadcasts; but as far as television and elections is concerned, they have accepted a shot-gun marriage and would not contemplate divorce. If 1959 was 'the first television election', it was so at the discretion of the parties. In 1979 it seemed at times that the election was being held at the discretion of television.

But does that mean that what we have now is a television election? It has been suggested, notably by Trevor Pateman in his monograph on television and the February 1974 election, that since the election campaign no longer has an existence independent of television, in the sense that the political parties organise their campaign in ways dictated by the presence of the mass media in general and television in particular, we should not talk of television coverage of an election but of a television election. If the television audience—the voters—experience an election campaign mostly through television (in the EEC direct elections in June, many voters in Britain experienced the campaign *only* through television), it follows, according to this thesis, that an election as a political event and an election as a television event are, by and large, one and the same thing.

This view of television and the election is implicitly supported by many of the public pronouncements of the broadcasters themselves. Sir Michael Swann again, talking of the February 1974 election: 'But if the election has done nothing else, it has shown that a lot of people do not want to be confronted with potentially divisive decisions between left and right wing solutions. Broadcasting brought home (quite literally) to them two very different and distinctive patterns for the solution of our troubles, and enough people rejected both to make the full implementation of either impossible.' Television, in other words, was a powerful agent in swaying many voters away from the main currents of the two major political parties and towards the safe haven of some (undefined) middle ground.

The argument is seductive (and disturbing). It has been much used in recent years to account in part for the supposed political volatility of British voters; and its implications were the foundation of the Liberal party's main appeal to voters during the 1979 campaign. But it seems to me an over-simplified view of the relationship between television and elections. Not least because, if it were valid, the Liberal party might have expected not to lose so many votes in the 1979 election to a Conservative party some considerable distance to the right of even a broadly interpreted middle ground. I want to argue here, by looking at television's coverage of the 1979 election, that the relations between television and elections—and therefore between television and the state—are more subtle than is allowed by the view that what happened in Britain in the spring of this year can be described as 'a television election'.

First, briefly, the political context—important because to a large extent, and in accordance with television's view of itself as 'a window on the world', it preshapes television coverage of an election. (Both the 1974 elections were seen as a debate about 'national unity'.) The Labour government, elected in October 1974 with a bare majority, and surviving for the last sixteen months of its life by a pact with the Liberals, was defeated on 28 March on a vote of confidence arising out of the inconclusive result of the recent devolution referendum in Scotland. On 29 March, Prime Minister James Callaghan fixed the general election date for 3 May, and that same evening appeared on television in a 'Ministerial broadcast'. The following day Airey Neave, Tory spokesman on Northern Ireland, was assassinated by a car bomb in the precincts of the House of Commons, an event which produced immediate speculation that the election campaign would be fought against a background of political ('terrorist') violence. Wrong, as it happened: the campaign began in an atmosphere of public rancour after a winter of discontent. Widespread strikes, particularly among public service workers, had followed the government's attempt to hold down wage increases to a general level somewhat below the inflation rate.

The most graphic effects of these strikes (piles of rotting garbage, empty shelves in supermarkets) had been shown on television news bulletins, subsequently cannibalised by the Conservatives for use in a party political broadcast. Political control of the trade unions seemed likely to be the dominant issue of the election, with the Conservatives promising (unspecified) reform of industrial relations law and the Labour party insisting that tighter legal controls were dangerously impracticable and seeking support instead for its recently concluded 'concordat' with the unions. It was identified as a dominant issue early in the campaign by Brian Walden, presenter of London Weekend Television's highly regarded current affairs programme *Weekend World* (and himself a former Labour MP). Walden introduced a programme on the trade unions with the statement that there was a 'fairly general feeling that the unions have a lot to do with what's wrong with Britain', and the programme proceeded on the *assumption* that more legal controls on unions were desirable. It was a theme echoed on television throughout the campaign. Yet on the same day as this *Weekend World* programme, Independent Television News reported on a specially commissioned poll which revealed that, in the public's mind at least, inflation and taxation were the major issues of the election. This was later confirmed by the BBC's *Campaign 79*, which identified the dominant issues as inflation and wages. If this *was* a television election, television did not get off to a very good start in setting the agenda for the campaign.

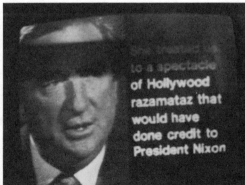

she wanted us
to a spectacle
of Hollywood
razamataz that
would have
done credit to
President Nixon

SEATS COUNTED 1 0 0

RESULT   FORECAST

5 4 LAB 2 6 0

4 5 CON 3 4 7

FORECAST

CON MAJORITY

5 9

SWING

SRP

OU

PC   3

MISC   2

LAB   CON

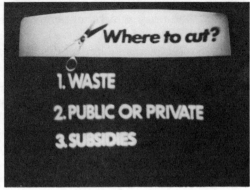

Where to cut?

1. WASTE

2. PUBLIC OR PRIVATE

3. SUBSIDIES

ELECTION
79

75. Television coverage of the 1979
    British general election

In fact, the political parties exercise a much greater influence on the television coverage of an election than is sometimes supposed. To give just one example: to the astonishment of the foreign press, and in spite of a provocative intervention in the middle of the campaign by a prominent Irish American politician, Northern Ireland was not an issue in the election. James Callaghan was repeatedly heckled at his public meetings by members of the Troops Out Movement (and was seen on television rebuking them), who wanted to make it an issue; but in deference to what amounts to a tri-partite policy on Northern Ireland, the main parties did not want it to be an issue, and television followed their wishes. The same is true, more or less, of the EEC (despite recent revelations of the cost of Britain's membership and the soon to be held elections for the European parliament) and of southern Africa (despite the election in Zimbabwe-Rhodesia, which happened in the middle of Britain's own election and and whose results have enormous implications for the future of British foreign policy). Both subjects were mentioned on television, but almost in passing. News bulletins, indeed, treated the Zimbabwe-Rhodesia elections as an event entirely separate from the British election.

Television avoided these issues during the campaign because the parties avoided them. However the broadcasters themselves may define their role, an overall view of television coverage of the election forces the conclusion that what we are seeing is a precarious balancing act between television and the political parties; between television's highly developed notion of itself as an independent political commentator (and promoter of political understanding) and the constraints, whether of statute or convention, under which it is obliged to operate. The balance may tip one way or the other, and its movement can be variously interpreted. So let us consider the evidence. I want to look at the various types of election programme, their format and their content; and also to suggest what they reveal about the relations between television and the political parties.

The party political broadcasts are the only election programmes which the parties control on their own terms. (In Britain there is of course no other form of direct political advertising on television of the kind which punctuates American election campaigns.) Allocations are fixed by a joint committee of the parties and the broadcasting organisations (which is self-nominating and has no statutory authority), the central criterion being that a party must put up fifty candidates to guarantee broadcasting time. In 1979 the Labour and Conservative parties each broadcast five programmes of ten minutes; the Liberals three of ten minutes; the Workers' Revolutionary Party, the National Front and the Ecology Party one programme each of five minutes; the Scottish National Party three programmes of ten minutes, transmitted in Scotland only, and Plaid Cymru (the Welsh National Party) one programme of ten minutes, transmitted only in Wales. The conventions covering these allocations, which are based on an *aide mémoire* described by a senior BBC official as 'prehistoric', have been much criticised, and both the BBC and the IBA want them reviewed. The minor parties, on their own admission, use the broadcasts less to win votes than to recruit members; the Ecology Party fielded 53 candidates with this in view, ending their five minute anti-pollution message with a membership address.

Despite evidence that party politicals are the least favoured by viewers of election programmes, the parties did not reduce their length and frequency since the 1974 elections. The broadcasts were revealing of how the parties construed their captive audience. The Conservatives, under the tutelage of their advertising agency, Saatchi and Saatchi, went for the hard sell. Their early broadcasts were characterised by a battery of live action and graphics. One featured a track race in which the British runners, Brown and Wood, lost ground to their foreign competitors as they were handicapped with weights labelled 'Inflation' and so on by their Labour managers. The race, commentated in television style, was punctuated by caption interludes in which various 'Facts' were spelt out ('Since Labour came to power we've had the worst peace-time inflation since the Great Plague . . .') and the phrase 'The Germans, the French and the Japanese', as Britain's economic competitors, was intoned like some incantatory spell. Disheartened, the stadium crowd—read the British people—called for a change of management, the Labour managers were 'sent in for an early bath' (a catchphrase of a popular television sports commentator, calculatedly used here to strike a chord in the minds of the television audience), and Brown and Wood raced home to victory after 'the dead weight of Labour government interference' had been lifted. Cut to Margaret Thatcher: 'We've always had a sense of humour' (though she seemed a bit sheepish about the example preceding) 'and heaven knows we've needed it lately . . . Give our people incentives and once again Britain will be back in the race.'

Subsequent Tory broadcasts played the same tune, though less stridently. Graphics and gimmickry were still used (a cash register filled with Labour's 'good intentions', a frozen pay packet, a globe sneezing with a slight chill but Mr Britain in bed with double pneumonia), but they were gradually replaced by party spokesmen talking direct to camera. The final broadcast had Mrs Thatcher, in hushed tones, addressing the nation in a speech which was a mélange of biblical/Churchillian rhetoric ('Let me give you my vision . . . Somewhere ahead lies greatness for our country. This I know in my heart . . . A land where all may grow but none may grow oppressive'), delivered as though from the throne and needing only a rendering of 'Land of Hope and Glory' to round it off.

Labour, as the party of recent government, wanted a quiet campaign, and this was reflected in their broadcasts. There was a modicum of graphic gimmickry—Tory 'promises' crumbling , a candle to conjure memories of the lights off winter of 1974, captions and 'facts' aplenty—but the emphasis was on 'experience', the appeal to voters to trust the party with the knowledge of government. Ministers were wheeled on to speak with the voice of authority (David Owen appeared with immense, learned-looking tomes in front of him); and the avuncular, Baldwinian, essentially conservative approach was climaxed in the final broadcast, two days before polling, which opened with a shot of 10 Downing Street at night, the single policeman at the door and the warm glow of the lights inside suggesting that the work of government was calmly in progress, and continued with Callaghan ruminating on the loneliness of a Prime Minister but emphasising the broad experience of his long political career.

The three Liberal broadcasts, in contrast to their excited approach in 1974 (when they imitated the format of a television news programme), were models of propriety. The central plank of the Liberal party's platform was an appeal to the middle ground—a plague on both your houses and a prayer for a hung parliament—and this was mirrored in the common sense, no nonsense style of their broadcasts, their trump card being the patent sincerity of party leader David Steel, everyman's idea of the model, moderate citizen. The minor parties all suffered from having to compress their messages: they were boxed out by the three main parties, and in terms of television time might legitimately complain that they were under-represented.

Interestingly, and a significant gloss on the notion of a 'television election', what evidence there is suggests that these party political broadcasts were popular with viewers in inverse proportion to the number of attention-holding devices they used. It is argued that since party political broadcasts (and indeed most election programmes) happen in the evening, when the viewing context is one of relaxation and of expecting to be entertained, those most likely to succeed are those which most meet audience expectations. Punchy graphics, frequent changes of image and voice and so on are supposed to keep the audience awake and interested. If this were true, on party political broadcasts the Tories should have won hands down. As it happens, a London *Evening Standard* readers' jury consistently marked down the Conservative broadcasts and thought the Liberals made much more impression—a view shared by everyone I have talked to about these broadcasts, whatever their political allegiance (with the exception, it should be said, of a man from an advertising agency). This is a verdict on presentation rather than political content, which in all the broadcasts never reached above the level of empty generalisations and emotive particulars. But it does seem to indicate that the television audience is less susceptible to coded messages, or more aware of how they are coded, than is often supposed.

Apart from agreeing their timing and providing technical facilities, the broadcasting organisations have no control over party political broadcasts. They observe other constraints on programming, such as cancelling any non-election programme which might be thought to have a bearing on the election. The BBC, for instance, postponed an edition of the arts magazine *Omnibus* in which a West Indian poet made what were coyly described as 'highly personal political judgments'; and a repeat of a Mike Yarwood show, which included an impersonation of Mrs Thatcher among others, was held up until election night—when, it might be thought, it probably did more damage to political 'credibility' than if it had been shown as scheduled. This apart, the broadcasters have a relatively free hand in their election coverage. I stress 'relatively'.

Election programmes can be conveniently divided into two categories. There are the regular news and current affairs programmes adapted for the election campaign; and special election programmes, culminating in the marathon coverage of the election results.

News programmes are, on the face of it, those over which the parties have least direct influence, though of course their daily doings form a large part of the programme content.

It is in the news broadcasts that British television's traditional separation of news and current affairs, 'fact' and comment, is most evident. The newscasters present the news items as they are structured by the programme editors: the sanctity of 'facts' ensures that they do not directly gloss what is shown (as happens on French television news, for instance). This may partly account for the curious division in the news programmes between the election and other news items, which were generally treated as events extraneous to the election and what it was about. The separation was even manifested physically. Both the BBC and ITV main evening news programmes were extended to accommodate the campaign, and the BBC newscasters, after reading the headlines, regularly handed over to the political editor, David Holmes, 'in our election studio'.

A complication here is the broadcasters' need to avoid interpolating into their election news any 'other' news item which could be interpreted as reflecting directly on one party or another. Thus although there were a number of industrial relations stories during the election, and industrial relations was a theme in the campaign, the news programmes could not link any such items to any of the parties' policies on industrial relations. On television news, and particularly during an election, facts are sacred and events autonomous. Here again constraints are operating: in this case, the (political) requirement of British broadcasting that it should give an unbiased, balanced view of the news.

Whether that balance is possible or desirable or in fact achieved is another question. But some examples of the way news was treated during the election will serve to illustrate the profound implications of this required practice. Balance is no longer as strictly interpreted as it was during the 1959 election, when it was calculated that BBC news bulletins gave 1,875 lines to the Conservatives, 1,850 to Labour and 507 to the Liberals. But it still makes of election news coverage a transparently ritualised event. The standard formula contains an extract from a speech by each of the three main party leaders, followed by items about the issue of the day, the latest opinion poll results, clips from the parties' morning news conferences (one news camera solemnly but uncertainly focused on a close-up of a telephone over which David Steel was talking from Scotland to journalists assembled in London), all preferably rounded off by a bit of light-hearted relief calculated to give offence to no party.

Thus ITV's main news on 16 April had extracts from speeches by Thatcher and Callaghan, a statement that Steel had attacked both Labour and Conservative administrations, and (presumably because the Liberals were felt to need a little more) a reporter watching the Liberal MP Cyril Smith shoehorn his considerable girth into a dodgem car in Morecambe. 'Head-on collision,' Mr Smith was heard to say, 'That's what politics are all about.' Back in the studio, it was concluded that 'the slightly phoney war of last week is over.' BBC-1's main news on 18 April led on the threat of a teachers' strike and statistics about average earnings. The election news had Callaghan on a walk-about in Hitchin balanced by Thatcher clutching a new-born calf in East Anglia; a clip from a Thatcher speech in which she answered a challenge made in the previous evening's Labour party political broadcast by saying that the Tories had no plans to increase health charges (which they did as soon as they were elected), balanced by an extract from a speech by Shirley Williams attacking the Tories for their 'abrasive' politics; a brief clip of Thatcher at a news conference; photographs of Steel (news conference) and Edward Heath (attacking Callaghan on the Common Market), which led into a film report on the Common Agricultural Policy, with Labour and Tory views briefly aired by respective spokesmen; the latest opinion poll; and brief items on the Scottish National Party, Northern Ireland, and the Plaid Cymru and National Front election manifestos.

I have chosen these news programmes at random, not for their particularities but for the general points they raise. First, the requirement of balanced coverage distorts the reality of the election campaign, creating the impression of a series of isolated events which relate to one another—and to the political issue at stake—only in so far as they follow one another in the oppositional structure of the news programme. Secondly, these events, or most of them, are essentially stage-managed, created out of a complicity between politicians and the media. The main public speeches are timed and structured partly with a view to ensuring that a suitable extract will fit the pattern of television programme scheduling. That practised television performer Harold Wilson used to repeat hecklers' comments, not so much for the benefit of his own audience but so that his repartee would not be lost on the television audience. In 1979 there *appeared* to be less heckling; but one of the most interesting incidentals of the television coverage was an interview with a sound engineer who explained how he amplified the speaker's microphone to drown out hecklers. Again, the constraints of balance ensure that news coverage gives a disproportionate emphasis to the party leaders, even if what they are saying or doing does not meet the usual criteria for a newsworthy event: if you follow one leader, you must follow them all (all three, at least).

The preponderance of campaign coverage on the main evening news programmes demonstrates the *convenience* of television to the main parties. Coverage is not guaranteed (election news was by no means always the first item), but it is guaranteed that in time and treatment one party's coverage will be balanced with that of the others. News programmes earlier in the day, with the parties' morning conferences as their main source of material, were conspicuous for the amount of non-election news they carried. There was frequently an air of desperation: on ITV's lunchtime news one day the newscaster interviewed a Busy Lizzie plant wired for sound. Several times during the campaign television commentators openly remarked on the low-key atmosphere of this election. 'There's a feeling of waiting for the action still,' commented the BBC's political editor on 20 April, explaining that one reason for the relative calm might be that the Tory and Labour parties had inconsiderately arranged to hold their morning news conferences simultaneously. This decision, it was implied, had considerably reduced the opportunities to indulge the television spectator sport of 'confrontation'.

It was left to the current affairs programmes, ostensibly less constricted than the news bulletins, to beef up the action. Here confrontation is of the essence. Two editions of *Panorama*, flagship of the BBC's current affairs fleet, were given over to what presenter Robin Day called 'a new form of campaign television'. Under the shade of an outsize orange rosette, a Tory spokesman was invited to present the main points of his party's manifesto; he was then cross-examined by two Labour MPs. A week later, in accordance with the convention that the government party has the last say before polling day, Labour had their turn. (The Liberals had already appeared, their relative political standing relegating them to the late evening *Campaign 79*, which has a smaller audience than *Panorama*.)

These *Panorama* programmes were extraordinarily revealing of the codes and practices of political, and especially election, television. They were addressed not just to an audience but to an audience of voters, and were structured and presented so as to create the impression that these fireside voters were privileged participants in a political drama of which those in the television studio were merely the stage managers. The party spokesman talked straight to camera, not to the people in the studio but to the People out there. Robin Day asked them 'to help if possible to bring the issues into sharper focus for the benefit of those who may feel that the arguments so far have been dull, stale or confusing'.

The choice of Robin Day to umpire these proceedings is itself revealing. Doyen of television's political interviewers, he is associated in the public mind as a 'tough' questioner who smokes out wily politicians and acts for the viewers as, in Day's own words, one of 'their inquiring representatives in strange places, their persistent fact-finders in confused situations'. Day firmly set the rules for these programmes, stamping on any deviation from the agreed formula. His style is a kind of interrogatory bonhomie, enabling him both to attract and deflect politicians' attempts to deploy his (often) personal acquaintance with them. (When Labour's Eric Varley called him 'Dear Robin' on the BBC's *Nationwide* programme, Day quipped 'That won't get you anywhere', then turned to a Liberal politician with 'Mr Penhaligon—or may I call you David?') His expertise as a questioner was graphically illustrated in the *Panorama* programmes by the politicians' lack of it. Day was clearly itching to get into the fray, and sometimes did.

Interviewers like Robin Day are concerned to project an image of themselves as champions of the public's 'right to know'. On ITV's *Weekend World*, Brian Walden fired some searching questions at a panel of party spokesmen following the programme's 'expert' analysis of the subject (taxation, economic policy) under discussion. Much the same format was adopted by BBC-2's distinctly up-market *Money Programme*. But the combative, probing stance adopted by these 'middlemen' (and how loaded is that word) is illusory: the internal rules governing these television debates ensure that the kind of question you and I might like to ask our elected representatives is seldom asked. James Callaghan walked off an ITV programme when his interviewer strayed outside the agreed area of discussion, and the Labour party elicited an apology from the company concerned when it was subsequently discovered that the offending question had been shown on American television. Margaret Thatcher reportedly refused to be interviewed by Llew Gardner on Thames Television's nationally networked *TV Eye*, and was soft-pedalled by his stand-in Denis Tuohy; though in fact Llew Gardner showed a kid glove deference to both Callaghan and Steel.

It is in the magazine format programme that one might expect to see some chipping away at the façade of complicity between television and the politicians. The BBC's weekday current affairs magazine *Tonight* was rechristened *Campaign 79* for the election and fronted by David Dimbleby, the BBC's election anchorman. It ranged far and wide, constructing a nightly montage of interview, studio discussion, film report, opinion poll survey, and rounded off with a light-hearted 'Election Diary' which ranged from a theatre critic discoursing on Shakespeare's view of politicians ('He hated all forms of extremism, so I don't think he'd be out canvassing for the Workers' Revolutionary Party or the National Front') to a clip of Callaghan laughing at a Japanese journalist's accent. The characteristic approach was to identify the issue of the day. On 20 April, for instance, it was law and order (this was a few days before a National Front meeting in Southall, London provoked a violent clash between the police and Anti-Nazi League demonstrators). Dimbleby chaired a studio discussion on the subject between the Labour Home Secretary Merlyn Rees (on the stump in his own constituency, and so interviewed via a monitor) and the Conservative spokesman David Howell.

The discussion was introduced by brief clips from speeches by Thatcher (on law) and Callaghan (on the police) and quotations from the party manifestos. It was, like most such staged confrontations, unrevealing and inconclusive. The next item was race and the election. It opened by quoting from the National Front manifesto, and continued with a film report on the 'Asian vote' in the constituency of Leicester South. Film reports like this are a carefully structured blend of local colour, vox pop and the local candidates. The reporter contrives, in accordance with television's notion of what the audience expects, to strike a balance between serious comment and colourful diversion: in this case the voters interviewed (it is naturally assumed that all those interviewed actually intend to vote) were Indian girl dancers, asked about their voting intentions after we had been treated to a snatch of traditional Indian culture in contemporary Leicester. The report concluded that within the Asian community there was 'a certain bemusement about the significance attached to their voting intentions', thus explicitly separating the Asian voters from the rest of the electorate.

Robin Day then interviewed two Northern Ireland MPs (Ian Paisley and Gerry Fitt) about the propriety of an American politician's comments on the Irish question. And the programme concluded with brief diary items on fringe parties (Screaming Lord Sutch, the Wessex Nationalists, Auberon Waugh's one-man Dog Lovers' Party); on the problems of the party news conferences being simultaneous; and on the Tory campaign song 'Maggie's March', which played out *Campaign 79* over a montage of Thatcher electioneering pictures.

Programmes like *Campaign 79* provide paradigmatic illustrations of political television's obsession with form at the expense of content. During an election campaign, television does not even have the luxury of spreading its 'balance' over a series of programmes: each programme must be non-partisan, and must be seen to be so. This is not simply a television convention. The constituency report which forms a standard item of magazine programmes (and of some news programmes) is governed by statutory regulations concerning the appearance of candidates. The only way to avoid having all candidates appearing (unless a candidate agrees to his/her non-appearance) is to have none appear; a device used by reporter Bernard Falk in his constituency reports on Derby North for *Campaign 79*, which concentrated on the voting intentions of a musical society who were performing Gilbert and Sullivan's *Utopia Ltd.* (much heavy irony was extracted from the contemporary relevance of the opera's libretto). Tory MP Norman St. John Stevas imposed conditions for his appearance in a *Nationwide* constituency report: 'You've got one game and I've got another,' he told the interviewer.

The only election programme which interpreted these balancing constraints with some latitude was BBC-2's *Hustings*, shown very late and presumably watched by a distinctly minority audience. Extracts from electioneering speeches were presented at some length and with little or no editorial interpolation. Except, significantly, when the National Front leader was filmed at a street meeting accusing the media of being 'a tightly controlled Mafia' biased against his party; in irritation, perhaps, the programme editor conspicuously 'editorialised' this speech, cutting to a shot of a black policewoman when the candidate was outlining the Front's anti-immigrant policies. This editorial gloss illustrates another aspect of television's balancing act: it instinctively veers away from what it identifies as the 'extremist' fringes of politics. At the other end of the spectrum was David Dimbleby's hostility towards the secretary of the Anti-Nazi League (identified as a member of the Socialist Workers' party) when he appeared on *Campaign 79* following the Southall clash.

With the possible exception of *Hustings*, the keynote of television's coverage of the election was its preference for personalities over policies, format over content. The cast of characters is small; and the gap between broadcaster and politician narrows as the party spokesmen learn the art of television performance. A BBC Audience Research survey after the February 1974 election revealed a widespread impression of 'overkill' in the television coverage of that election. Which perhaps explains why in 1979 the more popular magazine programmes regularly included non-political items in their self-consciously miscellaneous approach. The BBC's *Nationwide* on 17 April, for instance, went from a heavily orchestrated constituency report to items on (among other things) real tennis, Hell's Angels and model railways. With the audience suitably lulled by this patchwork of comment and entertainment, it then switched to Robin Day and the 'election forum'.

A relatively recent innovation, the election forum perhaps represents a recognition by the broadcasters of audience dissatisfaction with the standard studio interview. Here—and there were several variations on the basic format—party spokesmen answer questions put by a random but politically balanced sample of voters, either in the studio or on the telephone. These programmes are calculated to produce a livelier debate than normal; though the presence of a television 'moderator' effectively rules out of court any but the very occasional divergence from the norm of question and answer sessions on political television. Their very popularity has now effectively institutionalised them, turned them into television events. Nowhere was this more apparent in 1979 than in the king of election forum programmes, the 'Granada 500'. 500 electors from Bolton, Lancashire (Granada Television's broadcasting area) were transported to London to put questions to the three main party leaders. They had prepared themselves for 'the big day', we were told, in a series of local programmes in which they had questioned non-party experts on 'the key issues'. Now, in London and on nationwide television, they were marshalled by a compère into giving 'a really warm Boltonian welcome' as, one by one, Steel, Thatcher and Callaghan were ceremoniously ushered in from the wings and led down a flight of stairs to face interrogation from these no nonsense voters.

The showbiz staging of this event was so contrived that it was impossible not to be reminded of *This is Your Life*. And a few days later, on election night itself, the panoply of the television election spectacular, newly oiled and polished, was wheeled out on both main channels to entertain us into the small hours with the race for the results. Rival computers, the 'swingometer', a plethora of predictions and pundits, graphics and town hall declarations—all the machinery of the television marathon swung into action. The gloves are off and it's time at last for the countdown. Robin Day celebrates the occasion by smoking large cigars. The BBC warms up with a self-congratulatory montage of previous election night programmes. There is, throughout, the sense of television as master of the political process.

'Mrs Thatcher is convinced that television is crucial in this election,' concluded a BBC report on the Conservative party's polishing of its image. But was it, after all, a television election? Television has certainly changed the style of electioneering, in the sense that many of the campaign doings of the party leaders are specifically geared to television. The rituals of television, its obsession with personalities, the legitimacy it tends to confer on such dubious manifestations of modern politics as public opinion polls, all can be seen as helping to deprive an election of its independence as a political event; particularly when television construes its own role not merely as a passive provider of information but as an active mobilising influence on the electorate. If the professional ideology of television practitioners determines the structuring of a political event as 'news', and if that news is then incorporated into television's process of ironing out real political division, can television be said to have altered significantly the very nature of an event such as an election?

I suspect that this assumption is at worst tautological, at best only partially true. For one thing, it ignores the fact that the election *does* have an existence independent of television, as anyone who worked in it at a constituency level in 1979 would confirm. For another, it excludes the press coverage of the campaign. The constraints on political comment on television are not shared by the press. Most newspapers urged a Tory vote, and backed it with vitriolic attacks on the Labour party. 'Labour's Dirty Dozen,' screamed the *Daily Mail* on 25 April, listing '12 big lies' perpetrated by the Labour party (at least four of which have since proved to be nothing but the truth). 'Vote Tory This Time,' said the *Sun* on 3 May in a 'message to Labour supporters'. 'Don't Forget Last Winter,' pleaded the *Daily Express*, adding that 'A Liberal Vote is a Wasted Vote'. Smears and hysteria were the order of the day (the *Mail* identified a 'Screaming Mob of Left-Wing Extremists', and you had to read on to discover that they weren't even in Britain). In comparison, the *Daily Mirror*, the only popular national daily to back Labour, looked tamely reticent with its polling day message of 'Forward With the People'. Press and television fed on each other throughout the campaign; but the idea that British newspapers in recent years have become more pro or anti government than pro or anti party was stood on its head in this election.

Again, if television does 'homogenise' an election campaign, making it a nationally similar rather than a regionally distinctive event, one might have expected rather less regional variation in the voting than was in fact the case. And if television actually does mobilise the electorate, why historically is turn-out falling? One answer, it seems to me, is that the television audience is in its way as suspicious of the role of the medium in an election as those professional commentators who have 'identified' the tendencies outlined above. It may be that there is something about the nature of television, residing somewhere around its very rituals and repetitions and the very visibility of the constraints placed on it as a medium of political debate, which has implanted in the television audience, however unconsciously, a distrust of television as simply one more apparatus of the state. And that, paradoxically, at a time when television itself has been a significant (but by no means the only) influence on the growth of public hostility towards those institutions—political parties in particular—which are the basis of democratic society.

If that is true, the real question about television and elections is not whether we now have a 'television election', but whether by its tendency—particularly during election campaigns—to reinforce and promote consensus politics, based on a conflict of 'issues' rather than of opposed ideologies, television is contributing to a decline in political partisanship and therefore to a diminution in public awareness of what politics is about. That is a subject for further discussion. Meanwhile, my most enduring memory of the 1979 election on television is of a BBC reporter standing in the early hours of the morning at the end of a richly carpeted municipal corridor as he waited for James Callaghan to appear in his moment of defeat. Callaghan inconsiderately took another route, and the reporter was obliged to improvise on the town hall statuary around him. It was, in its way, the last word on the television election.

1979

Rohmer's Siege Perilous

TOM MILNE

Although a sense of poetry—the inimitable gesture, say, of one of John Ford's women shading her eyes against the sun—has long been acknowledged as a specifically cinematic property, no literary quality is necessarily implied. Indeed, with Abel Gance sounding the clarion call through his cry of 'The time of the image has come,' the theorists of the first French avant-garde defined the distinction once and for all during the early 1920s: a film is not a novel or a play, and the cinema is not literature.

Literature, it was understood, must be transposed and reoriented so that literary conceptions of plot, character and setting would be conveyed in visual terms. Words became the bugbear, required to play only a supporting role, and the history of the cinema is littered with unhappy testimonials to various foredoomed attempts to graft on some measure of literature's verbal richness, from O'Neill's use of interior monologue (*Strange Interlude*) to Joyce's stream-of-consciousness (*Ulysses*) by way of Maxwell Anderson's high-flown theatrical verse (*Winterset*).

Other more satisfactory solutions have been achieved, of course, with the development of voice-over narration (from evocative description in *The Magnificent Ambersons* to subjective impression in *Hiroshima mon amour*), the essay film (Godard, Marker), and above all the matching of literary with visual preoccupations (Cocteau and Bresson in *Les Dames du Bois de Boulogne*). Eric Rohmer, however, seems to be virtually unique in unequivocally proposing literature as cinema.

His first feature, *Le Signe du Lion* (1959), obeyed the basic rules of cinema in telling its tale of a man disappointed in an inheritance and gradually reduced to penury because the friends he might borrow from are all away from Paris on holiday. Although it could easily be transcribed as a novel, a diary of the hero's thoughts (on non-awareness) as he slips into both physical and moral degradation, Rohmer in fact *shows* the process. We watch as he worries over a stain on his only pair of trousers, later casually notes the flapping sole of his shoe, and finally comes to the point of no return when, a true *clochard*, he can make a shameful spectacle of himself without even noticing. Meanwhile, commenting on Rohmer's behalf, the streets and stone walls of the city close in, immuring him within their indifference.

By the time he came to embark on his six 'Contes Moraux' (1962–72), however, Rohmer's perspective had changed. Essentially a series of variations on a theme—each film deals with 'a man meeting a woman at the very moment when he is about to commit himself to someone else'—the moral tales elaborate a scheme which might be described as a literary conceit in which the theoretical spectrum of moral (or immoral) imperatives attendant upon the human triangle is geometrically proven.

Proustian in their concerns, these moral tales deal, as Rohmer has pointed out, 'less with what people do than with what is going on in their minds while they are doing it'. His characters consequently talk a great deal, probing delicately and obsessively into motivations, hesitations and clarifications, most notably in the Pascalian philosophical discussions of *Ma nuit chez Maud*. The result is uncompromisingly literary, yet never in any sense pretentious or verbose because Rohmer has understood that words can weigh equally with images *provided* that in the initial conception a proper balance is struck between cinema and literature.

This balance Rohmer achieves in two ways. At a time when the prevailing impulse among his New Wave colleagues was towards improvisation and analogous methods of investing actors with a greater measure of spontaneity, and characters wth a greater element of independent life, he elected to assume the all-seeing, all-knowing stance of the 18th century novelist who not only tells a story but, simultaneously and more importantly, comments upon it from a standpoint of ironical social observation. Not exactly puppets (they are too vividly alive to be so described), his characters therefore became manifestly subject to the urbanely witty, impeccably literary mind using them to enact its Olympian *jeux d'esprit*.

In *La Collectionneuse*, for example, a charmingly immoral girl roams St Tropez, every inch the spirit of modernity in her determination to sleep with a different man every night. Instantly assuming that she is eager to add him to her collection but adopting a superior stance to her availability, a young antique dealer (the past) conceives it to be his duty not only to resist for his absent fiancée's sake, but to reform the girl. He therefore tries, with boomerang consequences, to pair her off with an avant-garde sculptor (the future).

Perfectly worked out in naturalistic terms as well as in its past-present-future symbolism, the theme is orchestrated chiefly by the head-on clash contrived between two antithetical literary references: the emotional sterility of the thinking man's dandyism (the Choderlos de Laclos of *Les Liaisons dangereuses*) when faced with the simplicity of instinct (the Jean-Jacques Rousseau of *Emile*).

At the same time—and here Rohmer's literature becomes cinema—the teasing paradoxes of *La Collectionneuse* are set within, one might even say conjured by, the airy, inconsequential sensuality of an almost tangibly evoked St Tropez summer. Like Murnau, on whose *Faust* he wrote a doctoral thesis and whom he once described as the greatest of all film-makers, Rohmer is intensely aware of the richly sensuous, almost magical properties possessed by natural landscapes. And if there is ever any danger of intellectual aridity in these moral tales, it is instantly dispelled by the way the settings are used to supply an emotional dimension of their own.

In *Ma nuit chez Maud*, for instance, the airy Catholic debate on choice, chance and the possibilities of purity in sexual relationships is undercut by a bleak commentary proposed by the snowy landscapes of Clermont-Ferrand. During the projected marital seven year itch of *L'Amour, l'après-midi*, domestic interiors tranquil with familiar happiness give the lie to the illusion of adventure offered by bustling Paris streets alive with fantasy. And in *Le Genou de Claire*, a rosy celebration of the middle-aged mind's capacity to dwell not only on what might have been but on what might yet be, the setting—a lush green lakeside drenched by summer sun but ringed by snowcapped mountains—is a frosty reminder that nostalgia for youth means that old age is not so very far away.

In these films, in other words, Rohmer invites the spectator to attend to the intricacies of moral debate while a visual texture meantime gently caresses his senses with its own subversive intimations. And although *Die Marquise von O* and *Perceval le Gallois* seemed to herald a new departure after the completion of the 'Moral Tales'—a departure which one might characterise as the actual rather than the simulated adaptation of a period text—Rohmer in fact continued the exploration of his chosen path.

With *Die Marquise von O* there was no problem. Not only did Kleist's novella exactly echo the teasing spirit of the moral tales with its analysis of the social maelstrom stirred up by the discovery of an apparently immaculate conception, but Rohmer added his customary element of paradox through his use of décor: a series of classically serene, Empire-style interiors against which the romantic, or indeed Gothic passions of the principals rattled their brittle bones. *Perceval*, however, based on the late 12th century text by Chrétien de Troyes, was almost universally greeted as a disappointment, at best a whimsical exercise in the *faux-naif* in its attempt to recapture the poetic simplicities of medieval faith, at worst an anti-cinematic blunder ranking with the silent cinema's Film d'Art and its *Assassinat du Duc de Guise*.

The most obvious difficulty lies in accepting Perceval himself (Fabrice Luchini) as a Rohmer hero, since his intellectual capacity amounts to zero. When we first meet him, a featureless rag doll wandering through a mini-Waste Land of metallic trees and toytown castles, he has been carefully schooled by his mother in ignorance of all but the splendours and miseries of Good and Evil, with knighthood condemned as the particular anathema responsible for the deaths of his father and brothers.

Happening upon a small band of questing knights, and unable to reconcile the magnificence of their panoply with any demonic calling, he therefore confidently hails their leader as a logical subject for adoration: 'Are you not God?'

Yet beneath the more customary veneer of sophistication, such bland innocence is precisely the mark of the Rohmer hero. Whether juggling philosophical concepts or toying with literary conceits in proud expectation of a world obediently refashioning itself in accordance with their whims, characters such as those played by Jean-Louis Trintignant in *Ma nuit chez Maud*, or Jean-Claude Brialy in *Le Genou de Claire*, are invariably left amazed and chastened when the world, going serenely on its way, hoists them with their own petards.

So too with the Perceval of Rohmer's film (and of Chrétien's poem), although he is a creature less of cerebral whim than of pure instinct. The naiveté with which Perceval at first approaches his chosen realm of knighthood—treated by Rohmer with a bland solemnity that is an enchanting equivalent to the homely humour of these medieval chansons as he wonders whether a knight is born in a skin of mail and whether he must therefore dismember an opponent in order to appropriate his armour—soon ripens into a more pragmatic appraisal. Kisses, he learns, are not to be snatched uninvited from blessed damozels, nor are defeated opponents to be summarily despatched, but rather spared if an oath of submission can be extracted.

Yet even as he approaches the ideal of a perfect gentle knight, well schooled in the rules of chivalry by the various mentors he encounters along his way, Perceval remains essentially unchanged. Like Trintignant bending Pascal's philosophical formulations to his own ends in *Ma nuit chez Maud*, or like Brialy borrowing a friend's literary creation in order to conjure a last sentimental adventure in *Le Genou de Claire*, Perceval simply weaves the precepts he is offered into the ever richer outlines of his original concept: that a knight is God.

In the simple theological terms within which Chrétien works, Perceval is therefore a body without a soul. And when vouchsafed a vision of the Grail at the height of his courtly fame, having casually forced a series of opponents to bow to his superiority while absently swearing devotion to a variety of damsels, it simply does not occur to him to ask the question which will unlock its mysteries, curing the Fisher King of his wound and restoring harmony to the Waste Land. At which point, laconically abandoning Perceval, Chrétien turns to Gawain (André Dussolier) for a sequence of adventures demonstrating the humility and humanity required, beyond combat and amorous skills, to make a true knight. Returning eventually to Perceval, Chrétien simply has the mysteries revealed to him first by a band of penitents, and then by a hermit, who explain that he must seek grace for his sins of omission (he has forgotten

God) and of commission (he has caused the death from grief of his mother). 'Thus Perceval,' Chrétien abruptly concludes his story, 'took knowledge of the Passion and the Death that God suffered this Friday, and most piously partook at Easter of Holy Communion.'

As though aware that this end in received knowledge would be wrong not only for the creature of instinct that is Perceval, but for the essential innocent that is any Rohmer hero, Rohmer departs from Chrétien for a magnificent coup in which his Perceval finds himself actually suffering the Passion of Christ as protagonist in a mystic re-enactment of the Crucifixion. It is the final evidence of the senses, reinforced here by close-ups of blood spurting as the nails pierce Perceval's feet and hands, that ultimately persuades all Rohmer's heroes to abandon the folly of their pretensions and accept the less glamorous but hard-earned truth of their daily lives.

As with *Die Marquise von O* and even his own 'Moral Tales', Rohmer's only claim here is to illustrate a text he has justly described as 'one of the most beautiful in all French literature'. Since the Old French in which this text was written is almost as incomprehensible (though not quite) to the modern ear as the Anglo-Saxon of *Beowulf*, his first obstacle was the task, seemingly insuperable given the dreary flatness of other currently available translations, of adaptation. In the event, rendered into rhyming couplets, Rohmer's version certainly captures the medieval poetic flavour better than any other translation since Joseph Bédier's splendid 'renewal' of *Le Roman de Tristan et Iseut*.

If a certain linguistic quaintness nevertheless threatens, it is promptly trumped by the sophistication of Rohmer's solution to the second major obstacle, this one posed by the setting. In theory, the circular stage with cyclorama sky which serves as an all-purpose wasteland, forest, sea and jousting-ground, studded here with trees shaped in a flourish of metallic curlicues, there with a dwarfish golden castle recurring in assorted guises as Perceval proceeds on his quest, looms as a nightmarish cross between Art Nouveau garden furnishings and Victorian practicable toys. In practice, however, this clash between archaic language and vaguely modernistic décor introduces a certain note of disorientation which Rohmer accentuates through the Brechtian device of having the actors simultaneously perform and comment upon the action.

The effect, with the chorus of musicians introducing a scene, then dispersing to become actors in that scene while the principals themselves take over the narrative even as they perform the actions (about to despatch a knight he has unhorsed, for instance, Perceval suddenly hesitates, turns to camera, and explains: 'He remembers how the man of care/Taught him a repentant knight to spare'), is curiously analogous to the technique of the medieval *romans* where the poet, only too well aware that his tale derives from a common fund of legend, would often describe events from a standpoint implying that of course everybody already knows what is to happen.

Carefully avoiding psychological interpretations, or the sort of metaphysical concerns which Bresson brought to *Lancelot du Lac*, Rohmer perfectly captures the fundamental naiveté of Chrétien's tale. Watching the film is in fact rather like watching the animation of a medieval manuscript, with the text gravely read aloud while the images—cramped and crowded, coloured with jewelled brilliance, delighting the eye with bizarre perspectives—magnificently play the role traditionally assigned to marginal illuminations.

Rohmer has explained in an interview with Gilbert Adair (*Sight and Sound*, Autumn 1978) how, deciding not to use photographic means to achieve a flattened representation of the one-dimensional space of medieval paintings, he instead set out to use his single, semi-circular set to suggest the way in which the painted figures crammed into the illuminated capitals of a manuscript often seem to curve away from the edge of the frame. Actually, the effect of medieval illumination is carried more substantially by the constant clash in perspective whereby, riding up to a castle gateway on his charger, Perceval will seem to dwarf it into a miniature model until a maiden, very much alive and full-sized, appears at an upper window to welcome him.

But this single, curving set has two entirely beneficial side effects. One is that, as Perceval and Gawain pursue their adventures, manifestly returning again and again to the same point, it evokes the endless circularity of the quest for the Grail, whose mysteries, though known to all, remain ever obscured. The other, a fortuitous extension of the symbolism, accompanies such images as Perceval's first sight of the Fisher King, adrift in a boat on a 'sea' as dry and landlocked as when it served as a desert or a jousting-ground. In Chrétien, the sea is unequivocally a sea; here, however, an ambivalence persists, carrying with it the implication that the King, become a fisherman (and a fisher of souls) because his wounds mean he can no longer hunt, is marooned in a realm become so entirely an arid wasteland that there is nothing left even to fish for.

And the poetry? Well, it springs unbidden from a variety of sources. From the exquisite simplicity of such tableaux as the procession conducting the cup and the bleeding lance through the Fisher King's chamber. From the fragile, Madonna-like beauty of the faces Rohmer chooses as marginal illuminations to the action, like the damsel of King Arthur's court who is brutally slapped by a knight jealous of her prediction of pre-eminence for Perceval. Above all, perhaps, from moments fleetingly signalling the irruption of everyday life into chivalric artifice, such as the camera's marvelling track past the busy, bustling stalls in a marketplace, accompanied by a grave enumeration of the

76. *Perceval le gallois*

infinite variety of skills and wares on display there. Rarely has the absolute order and simple faith of the medieval world, tranquilly poised between the flesh and the spirit, been so exactly portrayed as in *Perceval le Gallois*.

With *La Femme de l'aviateur*, Rohmer is safely back on familiar territory, in a deceptively lightweight comedy so delicious that it promptly joins *Ma nuit chez Maud*, *Le Genou de Claire* and *Die Marquise von O* among his best work. The first in a new series entitled 'Comédies et Proverbes', manifestly intended to delve into a less urbanely sophisticated stratum, it deals with characters preoccupied less with moral casuistries than with more homely concerns. And in fact Rohmer opens it on a note of archetypal populism—post office workers, among them the hero, busy at the Gare de l'Est sorting-office in Paris—which is faithfully echoed by a bitter-sweet song at the end, 'Paris m'a séduit, m'a trahi', celebrating the perpetual death and rebirth of illusions in the big city.

Although the plot is negligible enough to be almost non-existent, it is attended by such complications that some explanation is necessary. As the film begins, François (Philippe Marlaud), a law student who works nights at the post office, happens to see a man leave after pushing a note under the door of Anne (Marie Rivière), a woman five years older than himself with whom he is currently sleeping, their affair somewhat fraught by the fact that he works nights while she works days, and anyway insists that she prefers to live alone since she enjoys sole possession of her flat.

Suspecting correctly that the man (Mathieu Carrière) is the airline pilot with whom Anne enjoyed an affair three years earlier, but incorrectly surmising that his early morning presence at Anne's door means a renewal of the former liaison (in fact the pilot was announcing his decision to return to his wife), François impulsively begins to shadow the pilot. The trail leads to a park, where the pilot is accompanied by a mysterious woman and François inadvertently picks up a shadow himself in the form of a 15-year-old schoolgirl, Lucie (Anne-Laure Meury). Delightedly entering into the Holmesian spirit, Lucie constructs a red herring solution which nevertheless leads circuitously to the truth and—with her image still looming tantalisingly in the offing—to a precarious reconciliation between Anne and François.

Once again Rohmer is concerned 'less with what people do than with what is going on in their minds while they are doing it,' with the difference that his characters here, less dedicated to cerebral gymnastics than their predecessors, are less aware of what they are thinking, or even that they are thinking at all. But as the film's subtitle proverbially suggests, *on ne saurait penser à rien*: 'one can't think of nothing'. And it is this thought beyond thought, this feeling as yet unperceived, that Rohmer is concerned to elucidate.

This proverb is put into words (slightly different ones) during the climactic quarrel which leads to the reconciliation between Anne and François. Pressed for details as to how he spent his afternoon, but having just learned of the pilot's decision and the shattering blow this has dealt to the hopes Anne has forlornly nursed over the last three years, François realises that the one factor in his afternoon he simply cannot mention, though at the centre of his thoughts, is the pilot. For one thing, Anne is under the impression that the pilot has already left Paris: for another, confused as to the identity of the woman with the pilot in the park (actually his sister), François has been imagining an amorous intrigue which will further upset Anne.

François therefore insists that he isn't thinking about anything: 'Don't you ever think of nothing?' he plaintively pleads. 'No,' Anne replies, 'because that nothing is something.' She speaks truer than she thinks, because as she coerces François into speech and he casually mentions his encounter with Lucie, Anne begins to uncover the 'something' of which

77. *La Femme de l'aviateur*

he is still entirely unaware: the idea that he may, just possibly, be in the process of falling in love with the girl.

Probing areas that the characters themselves prefer to leave unknown and unexplored, *La Femme de.l'aviateur* is endlessly perceptive beneath its casual surface, unerringly exposing the romantic attitude to love (with marriage) that lies beneath Anne's professed pragmatism, the unsuspected maternalism that enables her to deal sympathetically with the calfish devotion suffered by François, the entirely likeable woman underlying one who behaves throughout with a shrill and irritable selfishness barely excused by her unhappiness. With almost algebraic precision, but arriving at its equations through devious routes unknown to any mathematical formulae, *La Femme de l'aviateur* charts the progress of human aspirations from the sweet insouciance of fifteen (Lucie) to the ripeness for eternal love at twenty (François), from the first intimations of despair at twenty-five (Anne) to the thirtyish yearning for comfort and security (the pilot).

But the delight of the film, the poetic *bonne-bouche* with which Rohmer sweetens the talkative pill for anyone likely to taste it as such, is the long central sequence in the Buttes-Chaumont park. In echo of *Le Genou de Claire*, there is first of all the sun, the greenery, the placid water. Then there is the teasing presence of a nymphet, around whom Rohmer builds an enchanted web of fantasy as his hero tries desperately to keep his original quarry in mind while the red herring persistently pulls in the opposite direction. Above all there is the faint adumbration of 'something', an infinitely precious something which Rohmer somehow manages to keep alive as less than a promise, more like a hope, over the drearily precarious compromise with which François and his sentimental life are confronted as the film ends. A letter, rounding off the populist motif that encloses the film, drops into a pillar-box. Sadly it puts an end—or does it?—to the adventure with Lucie that François has only just realised may have begun.

1980

Grierson on the Movies

PENELOPE HOUSTON

'In my time I have seen critics in the other media miss by a mile. I saw some highly respected gents miss by a mile on Joyce and even on Eliot, as others were mournfully struggling to get in the good word for Cézanne. For that matter, *Long Day's Journey into Night* was separating the men from the boys not so long ago. Maybe the cinema was easier; but we lived on "firsts" and I don't think missed any ...'

The tone of voice of John Grierson in full cry is unmistakable. This particular quotation is from a late (1968) essay, which Forsyth Hardy uses to lead off his collection of Grierson's pieces on movies, or films other than documentaries.[1] By then, Grierson had hardened into the role of seer, pundit, international eminence and professional Scot. In old age, he was forcing the tone. What was lost 'in the illusion that we were all boys together in the good old first division of dramatic criticism,' he says later in the same essay, 'was the original sense of pioneering a new medium, the original warm sense of having been one-and-all together on the ships at Mylae'. That sort of sentence needs to be read in a broad Scots accent. But the old romantic was also an old realist: 'When that night mail crossed the border it was on a sort of last journey.'

The Grierson of thirty or forty years earlier was sharper, but rather more relaxed. And, of course, extremely influential. Those of us who began writing about films in 1950 or thereabouts can hardly have failed to absorb, probably at second or third hand, a great deal of Griersonian doctrine—some of which, no doubt, still clings. Cinema, he of course argued, should be an art of social (or socialist) purpose, in pursuit of large ideas. Film-makers were goaded to expand their horizons. Flaherty, Chaplin and Eisenstein were among the heroes, though his writing on them stops well this side of idolatry. His preferred cinema was masculine, and an early objection to the talkies was that they would encourage a cinema of idle chit-chat for 'the women audiences who hang like a millstone round the aesthetic neck of democracy'. An opinion only possibly modified by 1968, in a double-edged tribute to women critics: 'Now that the fashion in story-lines goes for the various deviations in domestic and personal derangement, it may be best to leave women to deal with it.'

[1]*Grierson on the Movies*, Faber and Faber, 1981.

Grierson insisted on active, or activist criticism. 'We promoted the Western to the notion of epic; we got the cinema closer to the social democratic actuality of American life,' he proclaimed, though leaving the boast for criticism rather unargued. But away from the claims for 'firsts' and 'first divisions', he also made those devastating comments which everyone knows and which here can be placed in context. The verdict on Sternberg, that 'when a director dies he becomes a photographer' comes in his piece on *Shanghai Express*. Sternberg, he said even more witheringly, had become 'the sophisticated purveyor of the meretricious Dietrich' and had 'the little warm thankful hand of Adolph Zukor for his pains'. (Earlier, Grierson had managed the feat of reviewing *The Blue Angel* without mentioning the meretricious Dietrich at all.) He was severe about Lang, noting that 'it is remarkable that Fritz Lang's instinct runs to bigger ideas than any other director; it is just as remarkable how little he ever makes of them.' He suggested that Eisenstein, after meeting Sternberg and Stroheim in Hollywood, 'wished that he also had the nerve to assume a "von"'. And his view of Hitchcock, as early as *Murder* (1930), as 'no more than the world's best director of unimportant pictures', was received opinion for a generation.

In the same review, Grierson said of Hitchcock that he was 'the only English director who can put the English poor on the screen with any verisimilitude' (interesting, and possibly true), but that 'he finds it more a matter of regret that they have no dinner jackets than that they have no dinners.' His views on British films and film-makers of the 30s add up to the book's most interesting section: scorn for *Cavalcade*; dislike for *Tell England* ('I would as quickly put it on the tumbril as any film I ever saw'); uncertainty about the brilliance of Laughton ('the greatest saboteur a film could have'); optimism about the future of Michael Powell, as early as 1931 and on the strength of a forgotten second feature called *Rynox*. And here, in 1938, is Grierson making the perennial plea for modesty, indigenous virtue and a sense of scale in British films, and proclaiming that 'there is no great mystery about the future of British film, only the mystery of really wanting it, really working for it.'

There is also a fine anecdote about the first London screening of *Potemkin*. Grierson had laid on the show for an audience of dignitaries, who turned out to be more taken with the spectacle than he had bargained for. 'The first man to make a practical suggestion about it was Rudyard Kipling: "These Russians," he said, "are doing all over again what we do so splendidly in our own country. They are making tattoos, and what we ought to be doing ourselves is making tattoos in film form."' Only the conjunction of Eisenstein, Kipling and Grierson could have produced the view of *Potemkin* as a Soviet answer to the Royal Tournament.

1982

Appendix: The Top Ten

In 1952, following a Brussels Referendum in which some 100 film
directors were asked to vote for the ten best films of all time, *Sight and
Sound* asked critics from all over the world the same question. The exercise
was repeated in 1962 and 1972. The results speak volumes about changing
critical fashions. *Bicycle Thieves*, top of the poll in 1952, did not even make
the runners-up list in 1972. *Citizen Kane*, first choice in both 1962 and 1972,
was not on the list in 1952. And 1982?

1952

Bicycle Thieves (De Sica, 1949)
{ City Lights (Chaplin, 1930)
{ The Gold Rush (Chaplin, 1925)
Battleship Potemkin (Eisenstein, 1925)
{ Louisiana Story (Flaherty, 1947)
{ Intolerance (Griffith, 1916)
{ Greed (von Stroheim, 1924)
{ Le Jour se Lève (Carné, 1939)
{ The Passion of Joan of Arc (Dreyer, 1928)
{ Brief Encounter (Lean, 1945)
{ Le Million (Clair, 1930)
{ La Règle du Jeu (Renoir, 1939)

1962

Citizen Kane (Welles, 1941)
L'Avventura (Antonioni, 1960)
La Règle du Jeu (Renoir, 1939)
{ Greed (von Stroheim, 1924)
{ Ugetsu Monogatari (Mizoguchi, 1953)
{ Battleship Potemkin (Eisenstein, 1925)
{ Bicycle Thieves (De Sica, 1949)
{ Ivan the Terrible (Eisenstein, 1943–6)
La Terra Trema (Visconti, 1948)
L'Atalante (Vigo, 1933)

1972

Citizen Kane (Welles, 1941)
La Règle du Jeu (Renoir, 1939)
Battleship Potemkin (Eisenstein, 1925)
8½ (Fellini, 1963)
⎰L'Avventura (Antonioni, 1960)
⎱Persona (Bergman, 1967)
The Passion of Joan of Arc (Dreyer, 1928)
⎰The General (Keaton/Bruckman, 1926)
⎱The Magnificent Ambersons (Welles, 1942)
⎰Ugetsu Monogatari (Mizoguchi, 1953)
⎱Wild Strawberries (Bergman, 1957)